THE
CHANCY
WAR

THE CHANCY WAR

WINNING IN CHINA, BURMA, AND INDIA, IN WORLD WAR TWO

Edward Fischer

Orion Books / New York

For Paul Speckbaugh,
of wonderful memory

Published by Orion Books,
a division of Crown Publishers, Inc.,
201 East 50th Street, New York, New York 10022.
Member of the Crown Publishing Group.

ORION and colophon are trademarks of Crown Publishers, Inc.

Manufactured in the United States of America

Book design by Shari deMiskey

Photographs courtesy of U.S. Army.

Maps of Burma reproduced from *Walkout with Stilwell in Burma*, copyright ©
1971 by Frank Dorn. Reproduced by permission of HarperCollins Publishers,
Inc.

Library of Congress Cataloging-in-Publication Data

Fischer, Edward.
   The chancy war : winning China, Burma, India in World War Two /
Edward Fischer. — 1st ed.
       p.   cm.
   1. Fischer, Edward.   2. World War, 1939–1945—Campaigns—Burma.
3. World War, 1939–1945—Campaigns, India.   4. World War, 1939–1945—
Campaigns—China.   5. World   War,   1939–1945—Personal   narratives,
American.   6. Soldiers—United States—Biography.   7. United States.
Army—Biography.   I. Title.
D767.6F57   1991
940.54'25—dc20   91-8093
                                                                           CIP

ISBN 0-517-58424-7

10 9 8 7 6 5 4 3 2 1

First Edition

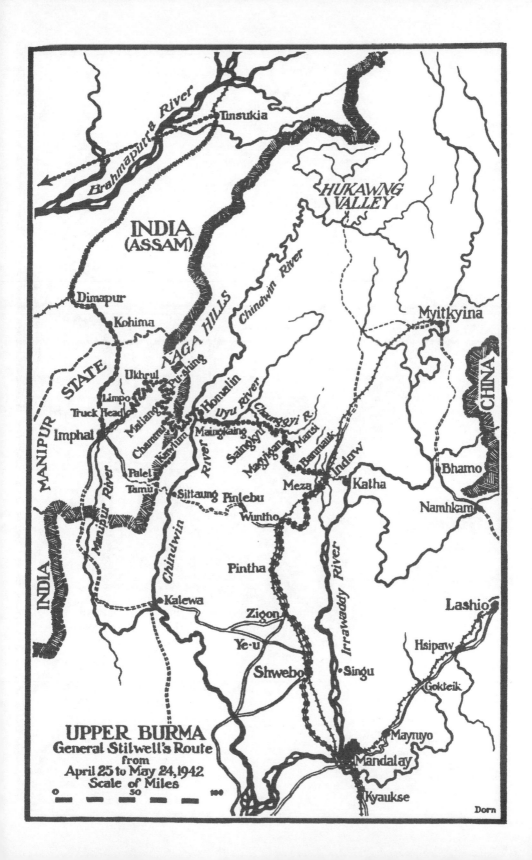

UPPER BURMA
General Stilwell's Route
from
April 25 to May 24, 1942
Scale of Miles

0   50   100

INDIA
(ASSAM)

HUKAWNG
VALLEY

Brahmaputra River

Tinsukia

Dimapur

Kohima

NAGA HILLS

Chindwin River

Myitkyina

CHINA

MANIPUR STATE

Ukhrul

Pu-shing

Limpo

Homalin

Uyu River

Changyi R.

Truck Head

Mailang

Maingkaing

Saingkyu

Magyigan

Mansi

Banmauk

Imphal

Chammu

Kawlum

Indaw

Bhamo

Palel

River

Meza

Katha

Tamu

Sittaung

Pinlebu

Namhkam

INDIA

Manipur River

Wuntho

Chindwin

Pintha

Lashio

Kalewa

Zigon

Irrawaddy River

Hsipaw

Ye-u

Singu

Gokteik

Shwebo

Maymyo

Mandalay

Kyaukse

Dorn

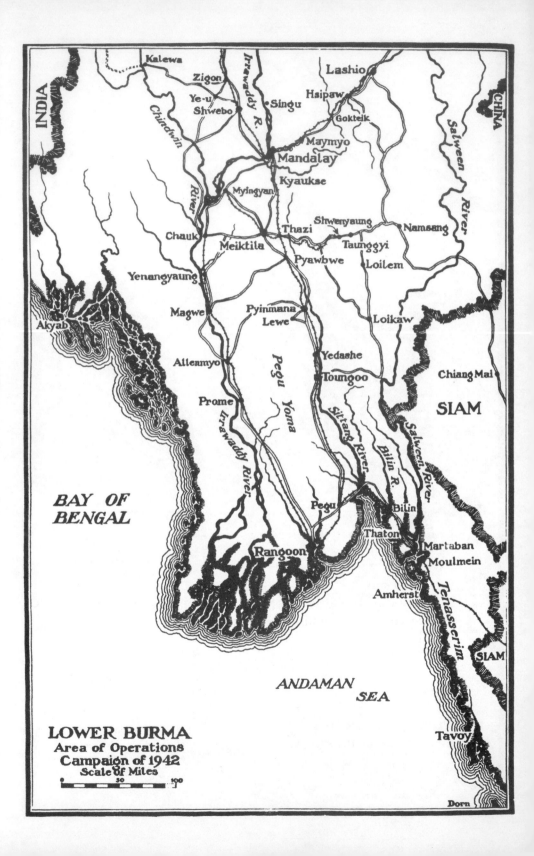

INDIA

CHINA

Kalewa

Zigon

Irrawaddy R.

Lashio

Hsipaw

Ye-u

Singu

Shwebo

Gokteik

Chindwin

Maymyo

Salween River

Mandalay

Kyaukse

River

Myingyan

Chauk

Thazi

Shwenyaung

Namsang

Meiktila

Taunggyi

Pyawbwe

Loilem

Yenangyaung

Magwe

Pyinmana

Lewe

Loikaw

Yedashe

Allenmyo

Pegu Yoma

Toungoo

Chiang Mai

Prome

Sittang River

SIAM

Irrawaddy River

Bilin R.

Salween River

BAY OF
BENGAL

Akyab

Pegu

Bilin

Thaton

Martaban

Rangoon

Moulmein

Amherst

Tenasserim

ANDAMAN
SEA

SIAM

LOWER BURMA
Area of Operations
Campaign of 1942
Scale of Miles

0   50   100

Tavoy

Dorn

ONE

Hundreds of letters and notes rested for forty years under our attic rafters. I had written them in India, Burma, China, and Ceylon during World War II.

Until deciding to write a magazine article about a colorful fellow in Burma, I had not been tempted to open the trunk. After the article had been published, letters came from old CBI hands urging me to tell the story about what may have been the most colorful theater of operations in the war.

The first note taken from the trunk in the attic quoted a frustrated supply sergeant in Burma: "Over here, we are fighting a chancy war. If you ask the States for something, there is a slim chance you'll get it and a greater chance you won't. A chancy war!"

To tell of the chancy war I began the story on Christmas Eve of 1944. A Chinese soldier and I had spent three days lurching in a Studebaker truck across the Ledo Road, a jagged scar hacked out of the jungles and across the mountains of Upper Burma. That remoteness—with its malaria, typhoid, and monsoons, to say nothing of tigers, rogue elephants, and cobras—was what American soldiers called Green Hell. As General Joseph Stilwell

1

wrote in his diary, "The jungle is everywhere and very nearly impenetrable."

Christmas Eve was our third day out of Assam province, in northeast India. The first night we had stopped at Shing-bwiyang, 103 miles into Burma. When Shing, as the Americans called it, was still a Kachin village, it was connected to other places by a few trails passable only during the dry season. The monsoon, lasting three or four months, brought about two hundred inches of rain, five times that which falls in twelve months on the Eastern Seaboard of the United States. The village had been the Japanese army's northernmost supply base, but now it was a depot for our Services of Supply.

As guests of an airdrop unit, we ate in a large bamboo dining room that had been decorated for Christmas with an abundance of what looked like wild poinsettias that grew along the edge of the Ledo Road. A kindly mess sergeant opened a bottle of bourbon, made a thick soup from vegetables bought in the bazaar, and roasted a jungle hen caught by a Kachin boy. There were even bamboo huts to sleep in.

Lest we enjoy ourselves too much, a cynical corporal told of how a tiger, with a swipe of his great paw, had ripped a wall from one of the huts and with another swipe scalped a soldier sleeping inside. The soldier had grabbed a carbine, crouched in a corner, and pumped round after round into the beast.

The corporal also spoke with zest about leeches, diseases, snakes, and headhunters. Leeches attached themselves to any exposed part of the body, he said, and ballooned out as they filled with human blood. They came in three sizes: one inch (common leech), three inches (buffalo leech), and five inches (elephant leech). "The best way to get shed of them," said the corporal, "is to hold a cigarette to them. If you pull them off, they leave a sore that festers."

He knew all about the anopheles mosquito, which carried malaria, sometimes a fatal strain of the disease; he told us of the spirochetes in water that caused a fatal, jaundice-like disease, and of a tick that carried scrub typhus, a deadly infection. The cobra was common in Upper Burma, the corporal said, but most deadly were Russell's viper and the krait. "The krait is the worst.

He's only a few inches long, but if he bites you, you'll meet your Maker in three minutes."

The corporal warned us that tribes of headhunters called Nagas lived in these hills. The Nagas believed that human heads, spiked atop poles, would keep evil spirits from the crops. The corporal seemed to regret not being able to describe at least one American head in a Naga display.

The next night we slept on the ground at Mogaung, soil on which many Chinese, Japanese, and British had died. On our minds, or at least on mine, were the stories the corporal had told. Since this was even deeper in Green Hell, a tiger was more apt to be on the prowl, and so I kept a rifle near the sleeping bag. I thought about leeches, snakes, and headhunters. And about home.

The next day, Christmas Eve, jouncing along the road in the Studebaker, I tried to tell the driver that I know well the town in which this truck was built. I had studied at Notre Dame and had worked for a newspaper in South Bend. This did not get through to him—he just grinned and grinned—but for me it helped pass the time.

At dusk the Chinese soldier swung the truck off the rutted road and we bounced into a jungle clearing near Myitkyina. With a broad gesture, and some giggling, he indicated that this was the end of the line.

The replacement depot for Northern Combat Area Command was unimpressive, comprising a bamboo *basha* surrounded by five pyramidal tents. In front of the *basha*, atop an ammo box, a phonograph played "Silent Night"; the cracked record's rhythmic *thomp-thomp-thomp* ruined Bing Crosby's rendition.

The smell of sour-mash bourbon hung heavy inside the *basha*. A disheveled major resented my interruption. I handed him a dimly mimeographed set of orders that he tried to focus on; the gloom forced him to light a candle. As he read with moving lips, his face went through contortions. For what seemed a long time he stared at me, maybe trying to figure out what to say and how to say it. Finally he decided.

"Lieutenant, we don't need you."

Christmas Eve, in Green Hell, on the other side of the world, and they don't need me!

"We don't use mules anymore. We airdrop everything now. Fly in low. Kick it out."

At Fort Riley, Kansas, on a Monday morning late in the preceding August, twenty men—jockeys, cowhands, polo players, horse trainers, and ranchers—had gathered in the riding hall at Fort Riley. Why a journalist had been accepted for the Officers' Animal Pack Transportation course I was never sure. In filling out a questionnaire, under "hobby" I had said horsemanship and under "place of birth," Kentucky; at Fort Benning I had ridden in wild pig hunts and had been in a horse show. Maybe those things had stood me in good stead. Then again, maybe the mule school was short on volunteers.

A sergeant strode into the dim shadows of the riding hall wearing a broad-brimmed campaign hat of the kind that had been popular in the First World War; his chino shirt and riding breeches were faded to near white, and his highly polished trooper's boots laced partway up the front and closed with three buckles on the side.

The sergeant told us to gather in the center of the riding hall as the mules made their entrance. The lithe, lean creatures switched their sassy tails, tossed their heads, and, stepping with the grace of professional dancers, lined up along one wall, rumps toward us. Looking over their shoulders, they danced around, kicking out to the side and straight back, warming up for the first round.

Sergeant Muleshoe (that is what everyone called him) was not a polished speaker, but he knew how to get attention: "These are green mules. Ain't been packed much. Reckon the ones you get overseas might not even be halter-broke."

He stressed that the safest place around a mule is close in. When he starts to kick, never jump back, but throw yourself against him. If you throw yourself against a kicking mule, all he can do is shove you, but if you step back he can really tee off on you. Every instinct in your body screams to jump back, but after you make the right move a few times the action becomes automatic.

4

We moved among the animals, sparring to learn their weaknesses while they felt us out for ours. The dusky riding hall came alive with the snorting of mules, the thudding of flesh against flesh, and frequent outbursts of profanity.

Muleshoe handed each of us a pair of leather cups, something like a bra, with a leather thong attached. These blinders covered the mule's eyes while we packed him, a handicap to make the contest more even.

The sergeant directed a corporal to lead a mule to the center of the riding hall and directed another to carry in a saddle pad, a packsaddle, and some breeching harness. The two enlisted men demonstrated how to adjust this equipment and fit it so as not to rub the mule the wrong way. I was highly motivated to learn how not to rub a mule the wrong way.

Animal management was our first class in the afternoon. The room, like most college classrooms, had a lectern atop a podium, blackboards across the front, an easel for charts, and chairs with a large writing arm attached. The only unusual thing was the exceptionally wide middle aisle.

A cavalry officer entered, flourishing a pointer like a swagger stick, slapping it against the side of his boot. He grasped the lectern and began with an accent from below the Mason-Dixon Line: "Gentlemen, that justly famous Southern cavalry officer, General Nathan Bedford Forrest, once said, 'I get there fustest with the mostest.' He might well have added, 'Because I keeps my hosses in the bestest condition.' For there is no doubt, gentlemen, that much of his mobility was due to the excellent condition of his hosses."

After that tribute to the Southern cavalry, a *clop, clop, clop* came from the back of the room. Down the broad middle aisle walked an elderly groom, copper-complexioned and wearing a white jacket and black trousers, leading a strawberry roan. So that the horse, whose name was Reno Hindoo, would be standing sideways to the class, the groom edged him around, and the anatomy lesson began.

With the cooperation of the live animal and the aid of several anatomical charts, we learned about the outside and the inside of a horse. The lecturer stressed such things as the shallowness of a horse's stomach, the lesson being that a horse should be watered before it is fed; if it's watered after feeding, the grain is washed from the shallow stomach and, as horsemen say, "He don't get the good of his feed."

The instructor described the bad habits of some horses. For instance, a "stargazer" was a horse that went along with its nose high in the air, looking all around and not paying attention to dangerous footing.

After a pause, the instructor asked, "Captain Hopper, what is a stargazer?"

The rancher answered, "That's a scenery-lovin' sonofabitch."

How anachronistic it was! Those lessons scarcely fit into a war that was fought with bombers, tanks, and jeeps. As the instructor's voice droned through heavy autumn afternoons, the years rolled back and we enjoyed gentler times.

Equitation was the class we most enjoyed. All of us knew how to ride before coming to Fort Riley, but now we had to learn to ride cavalry style, also called the "forward seat." The change was most radical for those accustomed to riding big Western saddles with long stirrup straps; now they had to ride a smaller military saddle with shorter straps. Elongating a new set of leg muscles hurt the pride of those who felt that every muscle in their bodies was as long and as tough as nature allowed. They were embarrassed to find themselves walking stiff-legged after the first day's ride.

Horseshoeing was the course I disliked. It was all right while we were using charts and models to study the structure of the horse's lower leg and hoof—coffin bone, cannon bone, deep flexor tendon, and all the rest—but in the blacksmith shop the hours seemed long.

I may have led the class in ineptness. First off, I am built all wrong for blacksmithing. A blacksmith ought to be short and stocky so that he fits under a horse with ease. By the time I got folded up enough to fit under him, my back was screaming, and for some reason horses and mules tended to lean on me.

Nor did I shine when it came to packing a mule. I cannot even wrap a Christmas gift well; so while lashing up clumsy cases of ammo and awkward cartons of rations in thick canvas mantas, I created some lumpy bundles.

My wife, Mary, and I rented a room in a home in Manhattan,

Kansas, a few miles from Fort Riley. Each night I took a rope home to practice tying knots on the bedpost—butterfly, square, bowline, and a half-dozen others. I could not long remember the intricacies of the squaw hitch, single diamond hitch, and double diamond; on Saturday I would learn to throw a Phillips cargo hitch, basket hitch, and Sweeten diamond hitch, but by Monday the ropes would get muddled.

What would I do if in the Far East I had to teach enlisted men how to pack mules? The cavalry had manuals with dozens of pictures showing mules packed with various hitches, but we would not be allowed to take the books with us because there was a shortage of them in the world. So I took a manual to Mary and she made drawings; few women in history have drawn as many pictures of mules as she did.

After packing mules in the corral, we mounted horses and took the lead mare through the gate. This pretty little chestnut, Misty Girl, fulfilled her destiny by going through life with a bell around her neck. At the beginning the green mules didn't know they were supposed to follow the bell, but as days went by they got the habit, and soon you could hardly get one away from the herd. The sergeant, instead of saying they were "herdbound," said, "They got a deep groove in 'em."

Muleshoe never spoke of herding mules, but of "hazing" them. We recognized the aptness of that verb while crossing the Kansas flatlands and seeing a haze of dust hanging over the pack train.

Herding mules across the flats and through the hills around Fort Riley should have been fun, but I could not relax. Sooner or later my mule's cargo would ride at a crazy angle and, a few steps later, slide into the dust. This meant cutting the mule out of the herd and repacking while the rest disappeared into the haze on the horizon. My herdbound mule disliked seeing his friends depart and sometimes took off like a snake on hot concrete, leaving me standing there with the cargo at my feet.

During one pack trip, Sergeant Muleshoe finally lost patience. On that hot afternoon in mid-September—as they said in the Army, "one hundred and forty in the shade, and no shade"—my pack was just one of many to hit the dust. Ammo boxes, bales of hay, and sacks of oats were scattered all over the landscape; mules kicked and shied off to one side and reared back on their haunches as the last flies of summer got in their hot licks. If the packers were doing one thing more than sweating, it was cussing.

Usually, when somebody had trouble with his load, Muleshoe dismounted and helped resling and relash it. With an expert slap here and a push and a pull there, he made the load taut and sure, and ended by saying, "There, Lieutenant, that'll make it look better from the road." You felt he was saying, "Don't be discouraged, Lieutenant, you'll catch on."

The day everything hit the ground at once, the sergeant didn't even bother to dismount. He just sat his horse in dark silence, a stony figure carved into the pediment of Purgatory. His better nature came surging back only when the last hitch was tied off and everybody was remounted; then he grinned and said, "I ain't seen so much trouble since the day the lead mare took sick and the rest of 'em caught it."

That night we bivouacked in a woods. Of course, the first thing we had to do was water and feed the mules and rub their ornery backs. You get to hate a mule when you're rubbing it down while your own hunger gnaws at you.

After tying haltershanks to a picket line, we sat down to open cans of C rations and talk. I recall a polo player from the East asking Muleshoe where he was from. The sergeant named an unheard-of town in Texas. The polo player said, "More people live on my block than live in your whole town."

"Yeah, Lieutenant," said Muleshoe, "but how many of them do you know?"

We would have stayed up later, had a campfire been allowed, but we were simulating combat conditions. It was just as well that we didn't stay up, because we were due to start at 0300 hours.

At 0200 I was doing guard duty on the picket line when a mule broke loose. He ran through a clearing where nineteen officers were huddled in their blankets on the ground. The mule danced, jumped, twisted, and dodged like a halfback who had taken ballet lessons. He didn't so much as clip an officer, didn't even awaken one. He was a black mule, and he blended into a woods as dark as evil.

By the time I found him and retied him to the line, the order came, "Pack out!" The word *out* is much used among mule-skinners. "Pack out!" "Move out!"

Without lights, we had to pack by feel. The only sounds were the grunting of mules as the cinch straps tightened, and the *slap, slap, slap* of ropes flying into place. Packing a black mule on a black night is uneasy business; even though you can't see him, you have a clear mental picture: ears flat back, eyes rolled white, teeth showing, hind legs cocked to kick.

It reminded me of that night in infantry training when we were crawling up a black hollow in a mock attack, and a rattle-snake rattled. From which direction did it come? The squeak of fear was almost audible.

The final exam, the day after the pack trip, was the most practical ever devised by the mind of man:

1. Go to the Animal Management Lab and judge the feed.
2. Go to the riding hall and judge the horses.
3. Go to the blacksmith shop and shoe a horse.

Judging feed was easy. In a room fragrant with the warm, sweet smell of a hayloft, we found numbered boxes filled with linseed meal, timothy, lespedeza, and a dozen other feeds. We had to note the safe and the unsafe. Most were safe, except the oats, which were so mildewed they would give a horse colic, and the alfalfa, which had so much dust in it that it might give him the heaves.

Judging horses was not difficult, either. We stooped and eyed the horses from the front and sighted them from the rear. We ran fingers up and down their legs and felt their withers. We waved our hands in front of their eyes to see if they would blink; a blind horse wouldn't blink.

Trail Blazer was roach-backed and spavined. Reno Kismit was sickle-hocked. Red Currant had a Roman nose and was blind in the left eye. Reno Jason toed in and had a bowed tendon. Blue Points was over at the knees and had a knocked-down left hip. Big Parade had a large spavin on the left hock, and a small umbilical hernia. French Girl, we noted with regret, was goose-rumped and cow-hocked.

Although the Jockey Club has rules for what you can call a

racehorse—the name may not be more than three words and may not contain more than fourteen letters—there are no rules for what you can call a mule. When berating a mule, the packers used to take such terms as "goose-rumped" and "cow-hocked" and combine them with more prosaic profanity to create colorful, rhythmic expressions that rivaled the picturesqueness of Oriental cussing.

Dot Kilty was in the riding hall as a "trick question." She was a well-turned mare, sweet and feminine. Nobody was supposed to find fault in her. But a polo player was the kind of fellow who could find fault with anything. Behind Dot Kilty's name he wrote a list of flaws as long as a mule's ear.

When the animal management instructor corrected that paper, he must have tasted the dark draught of bitterness. He believed Dot Kilty was a four-legged song. Surely he wanted to hold the stirrup to mount a movement to get the polo player expelled.

But it was impossible to flunk a course. I proved that during the third problem on the exam—shoeing a horse.

Big Chief was waiting for me. Right from the start it was evident that the massive black gelding, designed more for a dray than a saddle, had gotten up on the wrong side of the stall that morning. After folding myself like a road map, I grabbed the off-hind fetlock to lift the hoof. Big Chief threw his weight in that direction to show that he did not want it lifted. After a good deal of unprofessional tugging I cradled the hoof between my thighs, and the gelding started pumping his leg back and forth like the driving rod on a locomotive.

This brought the packers more merriment than anything they had known since the morning we were introduced to the mules. A sizable crowd gathered. I was a sorry farrier even when the hoof was still, and now everybody wanted to see the results of a horse shod in motion.

In the midst of unsought advice I got the shoes pulled off and Big Chief's hooves trimmed to a shape God never meant them to have. At the forge I pumped the bellows until sparks danced upward. When the shoe throbbed with a red glow, I held it on the anvil to beat the daylights out of it, but the shape of the shoe and the shape of the hoof never did jibe.

Smart remarks and the acrid smell of scorched hoof filled the air. Sweat ran into my eyes. I couldn't even drive a nail straight into a soft pine board, and now I had to drive nails into a moving target at an exact angle. The tip of the nail was bent slightly to make it curve as it went in so as to miss the quick, a very sensitive spot. The instructor had warned, "If you hit the quick, the hoss does kick." Big Chief started kicking. It was not a pretty sight.

At commencement exercise, our class of twenty, and a few proud relatives, gathered in the auditorium of the Cavalry School. Brass glistened and boots shone. We were well scrubbed, but the air around us was still enlivened with the aroma of saddle soap and horse liniment.

By now the muleskinners had developed a rabid esprit de corps, the kind that Marines, submariners, and paratroops wallow in. Some of the muleskinners were so gung-ho that they had replaced their branch-of-service insignia with a pair of crossed horseshoe nails. Brotherhood binds together human beings who do something a little different, a little difficult, and a little dangerous.

A general walked onto the stage to begin the commencement address. He said, "Gentlemen, great adventure awaits you!"—a sentence sometimes repeated in the jungle night months later. The general paused to beam at us, and his beam covered a vast expanse; he was big enough to budge a barn, more a landscape than a portrait. Each turn of his head, each movement of his body, revealed new vistas.

When he moved his arms, his suntan shirt gave off a swishing sound, it was so starched. His suntan breeches had a nice flare and dipped into riding boots that looked varnished. His spurs had a glint that would shame the stars of a winter's night.

The general described the muleskinners' rendezvous with destiny. He made it sound as though we held the future of civilization in the palms of our well-callused hands.

As the conflict wore on, the general said, the Army had found it needed mules to carry supplies through the mountains of Italy and the jungles of Burma. File clerks and typists, not busy at the moment, were assigned to operate mule trains, but they did not understand mules, and mules did not understand them. Before long, mules with sore backs and sore feet lay down on the job, refusing to recognize their rendezvous with destiny. K rations and ammunition were not getting through. So now our mission was to go forth to organize bigger and better mule trains, keep the animals on their feet, and make sure K rations and ammo moved forward.

The general's speech was somewhat ornate but, all in all, not bad. The instruction at Fort Riley had also been direct and to the point, with little or no military jargon. That was important to me, because I had volunteered for mule school to get shed of gobbledygook.

In the Infantry School at Fort Benning, I had spent a year writing Army field manuals. Dan Dowling, the political cartoonist for the New York *Herald Tribune* syndicate (he later won a Pulitzer Prize) was assigned to illustrate the manuals.

During basic training at Camp Croft, South Carolina, and while studying in the Officer Candidate School at Fort Benning, I had groped through enough field manuals to know how riddled they were with gobbledygook. If everyone was to understand the material in those manuals, so that we might hurry up and win the war, it seemed sensible that the prose be clear and concise.

My first manual came bouncing back from the review board in Washington. Nothing was omitted, the board said, and there were no errors in fact; it just didn't sound like a field manual. The colonel who headed the writing project lacked interest in simplicity and clarity; all he wanted was the approval of the Pentagon. He said just that as he tossed the manuscript to me and stomped into his office, where the grapes of wrath were stored.

The only way I could write military prose was to burlesque it. So I made some rules for myself:

Never write a simple sentence if you can stretch and torture it into a compound-complex sentence.

Never use a one-syllable word if you can entice a five-syllable word into doing the same job.

Never use the active voice, if you can back the idea around into a passive construction.

Always substitute *utilization* for *use*, *subsequent* for *after*, and *initial* for *first*.

Use frequently the words *supersede*, *implement*, and *impracticable*.

Ignore the advice Horace gave: "More ought to be scratched out than left." Instead, keep adding to what is there; federal prose is not written, it accumulates.

So put the idea into a simple declarative sentence and spend the morning building on it. Enlarge each word, nail on more phrases, synonyms, and redundancies; twist the sentence structure until scarcely a tag-end of the meaning sticks out.

As a final test, read aloud what has been translated from English to gobbledygook. If it sounds like an excited turkey going, "Gobbledy, gobbledy, gobbledy," the translation has been successful. (Perhaps Congressman Maury Maverick had the sound of an excited gobbler in mind when he coined the word *gobbledygook* to label government jargon.)

The rules that I compiled worked well. My manuscript was long and wordy and as dull as a butter knife. Reading it was like slogging through a swamp under full field pack.

But the Pentagon liked it! The book was printed in five languages. I often wondered how that gobbledygook sounded in Chinese. But there was no pride in my heart.

Through a hot summer I sat in Infantry School, hoping for an assignment that would not require a heavy hand. I pictured lovely trees being felled to make paper for my gobbledygook. One day a note appeared on the bulletin board, asking for volunteers to go to Cavalry School at Fort Riley, Kansas, to train in animal pack transportation.

Until then I'd thought that army mules had disappeared after Appomattox. And here they were, back in action! It all sounded so *right* to me. It was something I had to do, and so I volunteered.

At the close of his speech, the general at the Cavalry School commencement had us come to the stage one at a time. We advanced to within a step of him, paused, snapped to attention, and threw a hard salute which he returned. From his hands we received a handsome diploma with a gold seal affixing yellow ribbons.

Mine read: "This is to certify that 1st Lieutenant Edward A. Fischer, 01320030, Infantry, has successfully completed the Course of Instruction prescribed by the War Department for the Officers' Animal Pack Transportation Course." It was signed by the Commandant of the Cavalry School, the Assistant Commandant, and the Cavalry Secretary.

After the ceremony, Mary and I returned to our room in Manhattan, Kansas, and began an uneasy wait for my overseas orders. For most of the next two weeks we walked around town on lovely Indian summer days, and developed some affection for the campus at Kansas State University.

When my orders finally arrived, I boarded the night train for the West Coast, the first step in my journey to India, Burma, China, and Ceylon. Since I was traveling with overseas orders, I was assured a seat on the train, but whoever gave me that assurance was gifted at fiction. It was not unusual to stand for hundreds of miles on those wartime train trips. I remember a sailor asleep on the floor in that jiggling area where two passenger cars meet; through the night his head switched one way and his feet jibed the other.

Eventually I inherited a seat in the anteroom of the men's room. There I stayed for three days until we got to California.

At Ford Ord, near Monterey, we muleskinners waited until a troopship was ready to sail for India. For a couple of weeks we spent our days training with aquatic jeeps called "ducks." Each evening we got down and got under to lubricate the Zerk fittings; it was simpler than shoeing a horse, but more mundane.

One morning a major took me into a storeroom stocked with rifles, machine guns, and antitank mines. "These were captured from the Germans and from the Japanese," he told me. "Learn how to use them, and teach the other officers. Knowing how to use captured equipment can come in handy in combat."

Why he picked me to teach the use of enemy weapons, I never knew. Maybe because I had written field manuals about U.S. weapons. I remember that the Japanese weapons seemed rather cheap, and that the German weapons were beautifully crafted. I'm afraid I did an inept job of teaching the muleskinners how to use them.

On the crowded, month-long sea voyage to India, I was editor of the ship's newspaper. A mistake in the paper, on November 11, caused me embarrassment. Either the radio operator or the typist got things mixed up and said that Notre Dame had defeated Army 59–0. So bets were paid off all over the ship, and gamblers settled down with the money to begin playing poker. The next day the ship's paper announced that Army had won and Notre Dame had suffered its greatest defeat. I suffered from some unkind remarks. Both winners and losers thought that the mistake had happened because the editor was from Notre Dame.

TWO

I was standing at the rail, thrilling to the sight of Bombay, the gateway to India. At this port, on the southwest coast, thousands and thousands of English men and women, during the era of the Raj, had seen this startling land for the first time.

Three busy little tugs—*Ready*, *Willing*, and *Able*—nosed our troop transport up to the pier. As the gangplank creaked into position, an Army truck roared up and, stopping suddenly on the slippery pier, shied off to one side, like a nervous mare. Five GIs vaulted out over the tailgate. Somebody inside the truck threw out a bass fiddle, a saxophone, a clarinet, a trumpet, and a set of drums. Within seconds the combo bounced "Pennsylvania Polka" off the Bombay waterfront. To Captain Hopper, leaning next to me on the railing, I remarked that this seemed an inappropriate welcome. He responded, "What did you expect, 'The Road to Mandalay'?"

I answered that I had always thought of India as a romantic place. The captain said I would have a chance to check that against reality, for the rumor was that we would ride a troop train for at least eight days from Bombay diagonally across India

16

to Ledo, in the province of Assam, in the northeast, just at the edge of Burma.

For once a rumor was correct. A polo player, a rancher, a jockey, and I shared a compartment that had two wooden seats facing each other and two wooden baggage racks hanging above them. Two of us were to sleep on the seats, and two on the baggage racks.

We were hardly in the compartment when beggars appeared at the window. They begged for *baksheesh*, alms, in a whining chant: "*Baksheesh, sahib . . . sahib, baksheesh . . . baksheesh, sahib.*"

A woman thrust a baby toward me, and I drew back quickly. She had chosen an inopportune time; two hours earlier, aboard ship, a lecturer had told about an officer who was approached by a woman with a child in her arms. When the officer handed her sixteen annas (about thirty-two cents), she thrust the baby upon him and took off on a run. He had to find an agency to care for the child.

Along came an old woman with a face as furrowed as a field tilled by a drunken plowman. She led an emaciated old man with thighs no larger than my wrist. We would see such couples time and again in the next eight days.

Vendors jostled with the beggars. A fellow with a filthy turban and a shifty eye and the smell of a wet sheep dog wanted to sell me a mongoose that was draped like a furpiece around his neck. He said, "Where mongoose go, no snakes, no rats. Mongoose fight rat. Sahib, better buy." The long, lithe animal resembled a rat run over by a truck. In months to come I would wonder if perhaps I should have bought the mongoose.

A vendor tried to sell a baby monkey for ten rupees, about three dollars. A British officer standing on the station platform came to the window, leaned in, and said, "Better buy him, Lieutenant. If you run out of food in the jungle, just watch what he eats. Whatever fruits and berries he eats are safe for you." I lost interest when the monkey began scratching for fleas, revealing mangy patches.

The knife vendors struck just before the train pulled away from the pier of Bombay. Their timing was perfect; it was like a big production number at the climax of a musical. They jumped in through the windows and burst through the doors. With dark

17

eyes glittering and white teeth flashing, dozens shouted, "Buy knife, Joe. Damn good knife, Joe!" They pressed buttons, and long, lean blades leaped out beneath our noses. Shouting, cussing, and flashing blades filled the compartment.

Suddenly everything was quiet. The knife vendors dissolved as quickly as they had formed. The train was moving. The four of us agreed that it reminded us of a song then popular called "Pink Elephants," the refrain of which went, "Close the door! They're coming through the window. Close the window! They're coming through the door."

Captain Hopper stuck his head into the compartment and asked me, "Does this suit you? Is this the kind of welcome to India you wanted?" I said it was better than five GIs playing "Pennsylvania Polka."

As the train crawled through Bombay's slums, we saw living conditions such as we had never imagined: large families growing up in huts and lean-tos no larger than our pup tents. The hovels were of driftwood and reeds stacked against a crooked framework. Some Indians lived in holes with rotting hides stretched over the tops. Many had not even that much of a home; when night came, families huddled together on the ground to keep warm.

The train's schedule was written on a whim. We stopped long and often. At most stops we went sightseeing. When the engineer was ready to start, he tooted his peanut-vendor whistle and we hurried aboard. No one was ever left behind, because the strangeness of the country made us herdbound.

At our first stop we went tramping down a dusty road to a village. Children came running, shouting, "*Hubba, hubba, Umbriago!*" a meaningless expression taught to them by the GIs. Some chanted, "*Baksheesh, sahib, baksheesh*, no mama, no papa, no per diem, no flight pay, *baksheesh*, sahib!"

A few children worked for their baksheesh by singing "Pistol Packin' Mama" and "Oh, Johnny." Many spoke English fairly well. I asked a little boy how he had learned the language, and he said, "I meet all troop trains."

Some children wore orange cords around their stomachs, and nothing else. I asked an elderly Indian why the orange cords, and he said, "For fertility." Later I observed that if you asked ten

Indians such a question you might get ten different answers. The red spot, for instance, that some women wear in the middle of their foreheads: One Indian told me it meant she was married, another said it was just a beauty mark, and yet another answered, "These things vary from village to village." I am inclined to accept that last explanation. As Captain Hopper said, "Start askin' questions in India, and before long you are one confused sahib!"

Americans began exchanging observations the way small boys exchange baseball cards. One told of a village policeman who wore such a large badge that it was something of a breastplate. Another said he'd seen a man bossing some coolies; he wore a very official-looking badge, but it was something from a business convention in the United States. One of the legends making the rounds concerned an Indian who took the label off an American beer bottle, tacked it to the railing of a bridge, and collected a toll from everyone using the bridge.

Badges and academic titles were cherished in India. A bicycle shop had a sign above it that read, "Bola Ram, brother of Khrishen Lal, B.A." And a column in front of a private home featured a plaque reading, "Kirpa Ram, B.A., 1932; B.A. honors, 1933; M.A., failed, 1935."

Later I heard that when Stilwell had stepped from the train at Tinsukia, the stationmaster had handed the general his calling card. In the lower left-hand corner was inscribed, "Failed to matriculate for a Bachelor of Science Degree." Stilwell said, "That means he almost made the grade. Just missed it. But that is a hell of a lot farther than most of them ever get."

Once, while the engine was taking on water, we found near the end of a village street a camel with a great pink flower tied behind its ear. It was an amusing sight; camels were such snooty beasts. With their noses high in the air and turning their heads slowly from side to side, they seemed to have nothing but scorn for everybody. And despite their large feet, they walked with the precision and grace of a professional model.

A Muslim told me a legend that explained the beast's superiority: "There are one hundred names for Allah. Every good Muslim knows ninety-nine. Only the camel knows the hundredth. And he won't tell."

At village bazaars, we were never tempted to buy food. Flies covered mounds of sticky candy and slabs of raw meat. And what smells annoyed the air! It was like a neighborhood that had both a stockyard and a glue factory in it. Everything shimmered in heat, dust, stench, and flies.

Muleskinners could not resist buying such things as pith helmets, brass elephant bells, and ivory letter openers. Aboard ship we had been told that vendors in the Far East expected the buyer to haggle, that haggling was a part of the seller's social life; he would always ask much more than he expected to get. Muleskinners tried it, but were inept, and so they either paid the price or turned and walked away. If they turned away, the vendor came running, imploring them to come back and talk things over.

The window of our compartment was a proscenium arch that framed an ever-shifting scene. Sometimes the scene was a jungle filled with bottle-green light; sometimes it was desert country, with sand blowing before the wind.

Caravans of camels, herds of goats, and an occasional elephant passed the window. So did Muslim women in heavy, tentlike birkas, sloe-eyed Hindu women draped in graceful saris, and girls with soles and palms painted with henna designs. Green parakeets tumbled in a gold mohur tree, multitudes of monkeys chattered, and donkeys nodded away the miles under heavy pack loads.

During those first days in India, the Americans on the troop train treated Indians with kindness and were shocked to see the way some British colonials treated them. Late one night our train stopped, for reasons known only to the engineer, and the four of us in the compartment got off and headed for a restaurant. We could not get to the door because a dozen Indians were sleeping on the sidewalk in front of it to take advantage of some warmth on a chilly night. While we stood there wondering what to do, a British army officer came along and said, "Step on the bastards!" He did just that. When the white-sheeted figures scattered like a frightened covey of quail, the officer said, "It's all right to use your feet on them, but never your hands."

The concern that Americans showed in those early days did not last. In time, many rivaled the colonials in arrogance when dealing with bearers in Burma, rickshaw coolies in China, and

tonga-wallahs in India. It was easier to feel contempt than com-
passion.

From our compartment window we saw that the women of
India worked exceedingly hard. Groups of them often worked on
a building project while several men sat around as straw bosses.

"Look at that!" exclaimed the jockey. "Thirteen bricks on her
head. I counted them. Thirteen bricks!"

He suffered when he saw women balancing heavy water jugs
on their heads or sweeping manure from the streets. He made
sure we noticed women gathering cow dung and shaping it into
loaves, slapping it against a wall, and stacking the flat loaves to
dry for fuel.

While reading a newspaper one afternoon, the jockey suddenly exclaimed, "Damn!"

An editorial in the paper decried the sale of Indian women.
Such sales were illegal, the writer said, but were still held in
remote areas. The current prices ranged from three hundred to
four hundred rupees (a little more than a hundred dollars at the
time) for a mature woman, and from four hundred to five hundred rupees for a girl.

"A mule costs more than that," said the jockey.

"Are you complaining about the sale or the price?"

"Both."

"It's a good thing you weren't here in the days of *suttee*," I said,
and explained that *suttee* was a Hindu practice in which, when a
man died, his widow threw herself on his funeral pyre. The
British government had outlawed it.

The matrimonial ads in the newspapers fascinated the jockey.
No matter how many he read, he could not believe that parents
would advertise their daughters for marriage, or that a man
would run a classified describing the kind of wife he wanted.

> WANTED: a suitable match for an Arona Sikh,
> beautiful and well-educated girl of marriageable
> age, well-dressed, well-versed in domestic du-
> ties. Apply to agent, Northern Bank, Ltd., Be-
> nares.
>
> WANTED: A well-educated, beautiful girl, pref-
> erably hating gold and ornaments, for Goyal

Vaish boy, 22, settled in life and having independent views. Box 9757-CA, Hindustan Times, New Delhi.

WANTED: A suitable match for a Bisa Agorwal gentleman of 25, in Gov't service, monthly income Rs 200. Permanent separation with previous wife. Virgin widow will also be considered. Box No. 616 care "Leader," Allahabad.

The rancher specialized in the medical ads. He read aloud those of blatant quackery in which the words "panacea" and "radical cures" abounded. Some advertisers ran a list of practically every known ailment—from leprosy to falling hair—and guaranteed that one bottle of their medicine was a sure remedy for all. The more farfetched the ad, the more sure it was to contain the words BEWARE OF QUACKS in boldface letters.

MIRACLE WORKER loomed in large type above an advertiser's photograph. Under it was the statement, "He has received many gold medals from his high class patients. Truth needs no colouring. All that glitters is not gold. Beware of imitators copying our advt. and stating to have experience of many years when they themselves are of 24 years of age, and recently trained under our hands."

One ad featured the promise, "Be taller. Two to six inches guaranteed in fifteen days only." This miracle was wrought by "T.S.P. Tablets."

Wrecked trains at the foot of embankments were usual along that route. Sabotage, said the engineer. Saboteurs needed only a nudge to cause everything to go tumbling down along that grapevine track. The roadbed's vagaries were evident; while I slept high up on a baggage rack, the old wooden coach groaned and swayed beneath me.

During those eight days and nights, none of us griped about living conditions. Even C rations and K rations brought no complaints. Living conditions as seen from a slow train through India were such that everyone felt satisfied with his lot.

Whenever the train stopped longer than usual, we went into restaurants to dine on *puris*, *rocharis*, *lachha*, and *rosella gullas*. After such a meal, an American soldier stationed nearby told us, with feeling, that we should never have done it. Poor sanitation, he said. Even the Imperial and Maidens, two of the finest hotels in New Delhi, were off limits to military personnel. The soldier said that an inspecting officer had walked into a hotel kitchen to find toast stored in long lines on the floor, waiting to be scooped up by waiters and served in a glistening dining room. The inspecting officer, so the soldier reported, saw a cook put a slab of bacon on the floor and hold it with his foot while hacking off slices. The soldier so dramatized this that we filed back into our compartment feeling we had lived dangerously.

Our troop train stopped in the middle of the jungle one afternoon, and a corporal in the Transportation Corps came to our compartment window to start a conversation. He lived in a tent near the edge of the track; his job was to throw a switch now and again, and to make sure nobody tampered with the switch between trains.

"How do you keep your sanity?" I asked. "What's your defense against jungle madness?"

"You learn little tricks," said the corporal. "For instance, right now I'm going to walk the full length of this train and give them the word. That helps. Giving them the word helps."

"What do you mean?"

"I tell them there's a train up ahead filled with WACs. A trainload of WACs. And they're drinkin' White Horse scotch and havin' a great time."

"But how does that help you keep your sanity?" asked the rancher.

"The gullible ones believe it. Their eyes bug out. I get a kick out of that. It gives me a lift. So long."

"So long," said the rancher. "If we catch up with those WACs, we'll let you know."

No bridge spanned the Ganges, so we unloaded everything, loaded it on a ferry, and reloaded it on another train, on the opposite shore. In the process, everything was carried on the heads of Indian bearers, wiry little men capable of going along at a dogtrot under great burdens.

At the Brahmaputra we went through the same effort. With each reloading, fewer cars. By now there were six in our compartment, and so two of us slept on the floor.

The Dibrugarh-Sadiya railroad, on the final jaunt, ended in a fine mist near the Ledo bazaar. Before the war, Ledo was a last outpost of civilization; usually, only big game hunters went beyond, and they were told to travel at their own risk. With the building of the Ledo Road, the Americans had stretched a thin ribbon of civilization through the jungles and across the mountains of Upper Burma.

A captain with the silhouette of a buggy whip came up to the compartment window to tell us to shift our gear to tents in a clearing a few yards from where the railroad track ended. Avoid stepping outside of the clearing, he warned; if we did take that chance, we might end as a mangled mess in an elephant trap. A rogue elephant had been trumpeting in that area, and natives had set traps for him consisting of pits dug in the ground and covered with vines for camouflage.

"The pit is so well camouflaged," said the skinny captain, "you won't be able to spot it until too late. You'll be squirming on the pointed bamboo stakes at the bottom."

We stood in the clearing, watching the train back away. At the end of the track began the Ledo Road, stretching a thousand miles across Burma and on up into China. With top travel priority, it had taken us thirty days by water and eight by rail to reach this spot near the frayed end of the longest supply line in the world. Our supplies and mules would take twice that long. And everything we wanted had a low priority. An old Burma hand said, "The only thing that keeps us in the ballgame is that Vinegar Joe is a tough sonofabitch."

Right off, the skinny captain told us to throw all excess baggage onto a pile at the side of the railroad track. He made a special point of separating us from our gas masks.

This came as a surprise, because at camps in the States we had heard, again and again, how the masks might save our lives. To impress this on us, the instructors had put us in a chamber full of tear gas and ordered us to remove our masks inside. They often warned us, "Don't go using your gas mask as a pillow, and don't carry candy bars or oranges inside it. Take good care of it; it may save your life."

We had taken care of our gas masks, even in that wooden train

24

compartment where we were tempted to use them as pillows. Now there they were, stacked at the end of the railroad track at the beginning of the combat area. The reason given was, "We don't have enough for the Chinese soldiers. It won't look right if we have some equipment they don't."

Next the captain led us to a tent in which two medical corporals awaited us with needles. Yellow fever shots. By now our immunization cards were so fully stamped that hardly any white space remained. The yellow fever shots must have come from a bad batch; every muleskinner took sick, and there was much vomiting in the night.

At dawn on December 22, the skinny captain led seven of us to a Studebaker truck in which a sleepy Chinese soldier nodded at the wheel. The captain told me to get in the cab next to the driver and "take charge of this detail." The other six muleskinners climbed into the back.

Just before we took off, the captain said, "You're the first troops to go all the way from Ledo to Myitkyina by truck. You'll like this road; it doesn't bypass any swamps or rough mountain terrain."

The Ledo Road lunged headlong into the precipitous Patkai Mountains, that jungled tailbone of the Himalayas separating Assam from Burma. We found the road clinging to mountainsides, spanning rivers, and then lunging breathlessly down into Burma's vast Hukawng Valley.

After crossing the battleground of Jambu Bum Pass, where Merrill's Marauders and Chinese infantrymen had fought for the gateway to the Mogaung Valley, we dropped into marshlands thick with tall elephant grass. Beyond Warazup on the Mogaung River, the road skirted low, jungled hills, formerly known only to natives and big-game hunters in search of elephant or tiger.

Jungle country fascinated me. It was tall and dark and as silent as death, an ageless confusion of tangled, matted undergrowth that had confined progress for thousands of years to dim, narrow trails. And now here was the Ledo Road, making an audacious slash across the face of this breathtaking world!

That was the night we stayed at Shingbwiyang. The next

night we slept on the ground near Mogaung. The following night, Christmas Eve, we reached a jungle clearing near
Myitkyina, and that was where I heard the news:

"Lieutenant, we don't need you. We don't use mules anymore.
We airdrop everything now."

THREE

When I left the bamboo basha where the major had given me the bad news, the *thump-thump* of the broken record seemed louder, and Bing Crosby still filled the jungle darkness with "Silent Night." In front of one of the pyramidal tents I came upon the youngest muleskinner, a second lieutenant, tall and boyish, with a reputation for breaking wild horses. In those days a second lieutenant was called a "shavetail" because his GI shirts lacked shoulder straps until he was commissioned, and then a tailor cut the shirttails to make shoulder straps.

In the darkness I could not see Shavetail very well, but his dejection came through in every sentence:

"Why did they have to bring us this far if they don't need us?"

"You're in the Army."

"Why did they have to do it?" he repeated.

"That corporal back in Shing," I said. "He told us about tigers, leeches, snakes, headhunters. Even he didn't have the heart to tell us this."

"He must have known. With an airdrop outfit, he had to know we weren't needed."

Inside the tent, Shavetail and I came upon a captain from the Corps of Engineers, holding a lighted candle to let the wax drip onto a carton of rations so that he might mount the candle there. He had worked on the Ledo Road for a year or more before taking ill. Now, just out of the hospital, he feared reassignment, but hoped for a trip home. Dark shadows in his deepset eyes and sunken cheeks gave him the look of death.

The engineer started a nonstop lecture on the building of the Ledo Road. Back in Ledo the skinny captain had given us some of that information, but now we were getting it from a man who had watched it happen.

The road became a necessity, said the engineer, when the Japanese captured Rangoon on March 8, 1942, and raced northward to take the Burma Road. That strategic move cut China's last route of land supply. From then on, to send aid to China, the United States had to fly equipment from India across the Hump, the backbone of the Himalayas. Somebody needed to cut a new land route across northern Burma to link India with China. The British started the job early in 1942, but soon declared it impossible and quit.

When the British gave up the road project, General Joseph W. Stilwell continued fighting for it. At a meeting with Gen. Archibald Wavell (later viceroy of India), Stilwell agreed to make building the road an American responsibility. On December 19, 1942, it became a U.S. Army project.

A pipeline running alongside the road would be just as important as the road itself. General Patton had once said in Europe, "My men can eat their belts, but my tanks gotta have gas." So four-inch pipes started at Tinsukia in India and, in time, moved across Burma and on up into China.

Those early plans were so indefinite that just remembering them caused the engineer to shake his head. About the only thing everybody agreed on was that the road should follow roughly the refugee trail to Shingbwiyang, on the edge of the Hukawng Valley. That ancient Naga route across the Patkai Mountains was used by refugees fleeing from Burma to India in early 1942, with the Japanese just behind them.

The first detachment of American engineers to arrive in Ledo turned tea plantations and matted virgin jungle into bivouac areas. With a few bulldozers and a fleet of sorry British lorries, they set to work pushing the road into the Patkais. When the shortage of equipment slowed progress, the engineers sought Indian laborers.

At this point in the story, the engineer told us that even though he had been there himself, he could scarcely believe so many things had gone wrong. He seemed to have difficulty finding words to impress on us how tough it had been.

The laborers—Kachin and Travancore coolies, workers from the tea plantations of Assam and Bengal, and porters from the Garo and Darjeeling hill country—cleared the new trace by hand. Their labors accomplished something, but they were never really satisfactory. Most of the untrained workers had contracts that ran for only three months, and so, just as they were getting the knack of it, they left for home and new, untrained labor arrived. The placement problems were mind-boggling. For instance, some contracts stipulated that the men be stationed in the high altitudes to which they were accustomed, so as soon as the trace took a dip into a valley, they sat down on the job.

The language barrier was insurmountable. Since all of India's seventy-five languages and dialects were represented, sign language was the only solution for the Americans.

Ration supplies caused the Quartermaster Corps migraines. Since religion and custom decided the eating habits of various groups, the Army had to stock a dozen different kinds of rations.

The caste system and the variety of religious sects made strict segregation necessary. Self-feeders, for instance, refused to eat food prepared by another, lest the cook become a brother and claim all the possessions of the man who ate the food. As individual meals were prepared, thousands of tiny fires blinked in the jungle night, a dangerous custom with Japanese pilots looking for something to strafe.

The captain kept returning to "those sorry British lorries." He said that most were on the "dead line" much of the time. The cannibalization of parts from one vehicle to keep others running was of some help, but Chinese ponies and native porters did better than the lorries in getting supplies to engineers in the forward areas. When the monsoon turned that part of the world into a quagmire, however, even ponies bogged down in the mud, broke legs, and slid off the cliffs of Pangsau Pass, and only a few native porters still hoisted supplies onto their heads and stumbled along jungle trails.

"Damn!" Shavetail exclaimed. After every few sentences in the engineer's story, the second lieutenant added exclamation points.

By the end of March 1943, the lead bulldozer, using fuel carried to it by natives, was at mile forty-seven. Heavy rains impeded work still more. Engineers stopped clearing a new trace to fight landslides, doing their best to hold the roadway they had already cut.

When the rains slowed down even the most determined native porters, airdrop units began supplying forward troops by parachute. It was ironic that the most modern system of supply was perfected in a combat zone that also depended on ancient modes—bullock carts, elephants, native bearers, and mules.

The engineers endured untold hardships. Wet all the time, they slept in waterlogged tents, bamboo lean-tos, and jungle hammocks. The soggy jungle was infested with the long purple leeches inflicting bites that festered. Tractors tumbled over steep banks when rain-saturated shelves collapsed. Slides and bottomless mud buried bulldozers.

At this point in his story, the captain of engineers began speaking of Brig. Gen. Lewis A. Pick. He did so with admiration, and for the first time a note of optimism entered his voice. When Pick had assumed command of the project on October 13, 1943, the work seemed hopelessly stalled in the densely forested and precipitous mountains. Eighty percent of the engineers were hospitalized with malaria. Crews were working only one eight-hour shift a day.

On his first evening in Ledo, General Pick, robust, sanguine, and silver-haired, held a staff meeting in the officers' mess hall. He said that he had been called from his work on the Missouri Valley Flood Control Plan, and was here to make sure the Ledo Road got built.

The captain quoted Pick, "I've heard the same story all the way from the States. It's always the same—the Ledo Road can't be built. Too much mud, too much rain, too much malaria.

From now on we're forgetting this defeatist spirit. The Ledo Road is going to be built, mud and rain and malaria be damned!"

The general's first act was to move road headquarters right up to the point where the jungle was still untouched. Without delay he started a round-the-clock schedule; to light the jungle for night work, buckets of oil were burned.

General Stilwell came up to road headquarters and met with Pick in a rain-soaked tent. Stilwell asked about detailed maps and progress charts, but Pick said he had none.

"Where is the point of the road now?"

Pick took a dogeared map and marked an X in the Patkai Mountain sector. "Here at the fifty-mile mark."

"How soon can you build me a jeep road to Shingbwiyang?"

"How about a military road that will handle truck traffic?"

"By when?"

"When do you want it?"

"January first?"

"Okay."

The two generals hiked up to the point, laboring through a knee-deep quagmire. They passed bulldozers stalled in mud up to their stacks. Stilwell asked, "When did you say you'd get the road through to Shing?"

"By the first of the year."

That was November 3, 1943. On December 27 the lead bulldozer reached Shing. The engineers had conquered the Patkais four days ahead of schedule. They had cut fifty-four miles of road through the roughest terrain in the world in fifty-seven days.

The road moved ahead at about a mile a day, except when combat got in the way. Sometimes the lead bulldozer cleared the way for infantrymen, enemy bullets ricocheting from its great blade. The longest work delays were during the siege of Myitkyina, two and a half months, and the battle of Bhamo, one month.

While the Corps of Engineers captain was telling us his story, an elephant trumpeted across the Irrawaddy. The captain said that elephants and mahouts, working the great teak forests, offered skills the Army could use; they were especially helpful

31

in handling logs used for building bridges across mountain streams.

I said that an officer in Ledo had warned us against falling into elephant traps. The captain of engineers said that the guerrilla fighters of the OSS used something of an elephant-trap technique against the Japanese. The Kachin fighters who signed on with the OSS made *punjis*, bamboo spears, which they hardened over a fire until they were as strong as steel and as sharp as daggers. These they anchored on each side of a trail, slanting inward, hidden in the tangle. When the Japanese were going down the trail, the Kachins aimed a burst of machine-gun fire at them. In such circumstances, soldiers of every army were trained to dive into the underbrush. When the Japanese did so, they impaled themselves on the *punjis*.

When two other muleskinners came into our tent, the conversation shifted to Christmases past. It was impossible to hold back memories. My contribution was slight. I told of the night Santa Claus came to our farm in Kentucky. My cousin's boyfriend, a tall, lean fellow padded with pillows, made his entrance coughing and sneezing.

"How did you get such a cold, Santa?"

"Last night I slept in the lumberyard. Somebody left the gate open."

When the candle sputtered out and we stretched out on our cots, I kept thinking of how Christmas in childhood was especially transcendent, how a walk through the woods on Christmas morning brought a restrained joy that walking those same paths the next day would not bring.

Across the tent, the young lieutenant, the one with the reputation for breaking wild horses, must not have been able to sleep either. From his direction came the sound of sniffling.

Suddenly it was dawn. A chorus of monkeys awakened us to Christmas morning. We stood shivering in line with our mess kits, waiting for a tangerine, creamed chipped beef on toast, and strong coffee. Not a bad breakfast, considering we were dangling out at "the end of the thinnest supply line of all," as General Marshall had described it.

As we cleaned our mess kits in a drum of hot water, the major lurched from his tent in sad disarray. After a few disjointed announcements he said, "In an hour . . . Roman Catholic Christmas service . . . up that trail a piece."

Along the trail I came upon the scorched fuselage of a Japanese Zero partly hidden in the dense undergrowth. Then suddenly, at the edge of a stand of coarse elephant grass ten feet tall, with edges so sharp they would cut human flesh, I found Father James Stuart, a Columban missionary. With the compactness and agility of a gymnast he moved around arranging a portable altar in a clearing surrounded by the elephant grass. A dashing figure he was in paratrooper boots, GI suntans, a neckerchief of yellow parachute cloth, and an Aussie hat with the wide brim swept up rakishly at one side.

Through all of Upper Burma he was a legend. The captain in Ledo had told me an anecdote or two about the Irish priest from Derry, and the captain of engineers, in our tent on Christmas Eve, had mentioned Father Stuart in connection with the OSS.

One anecdote had to do with the time an American intelligence officer complained of not having any Japanese prisoners to interview. He told Father Stuart that prisoners were so rare the British had a standing offer of two weeks furlough to any Tommy who brought one in.

"I know where a Japanese is," the priest baited the high-strung American. "But he won't talk."

"He'll talk!" declared the American. "You just take me to him."

The missionary led the intelligence officer across three hills, through some tall elephant grass, and over a mountain stream before coming to a remote bamboo *basha*.

At the door the priest paused and said in a whisper, "Now promise me you won't make too much of a scene."

The American pushed past him into the hut, and there he found a sleeping Japanese baby.

"I told you he won't talk," said Father Stuart.

James Stuart had arrived in Burma late in 1936 as one of eight Columban Fathers from Ireland sent to serve as missionaries to the Kachins in the northern wilderness. He never expected to see anything of war until, on May 13, 1942, a runner arrived at his remote parish with a message from a British colonel. It said that thousands of refugees were straggling into Upper Burma just ahead of the Japanese. The colonel had hundreds of them on his hands, and wanted to know what to do.

Within an hour the missionary was hurrying by foot across forty miles of jungle trail between Kajihtu and Sumprabum, where the British colonel asked him to accept forty-nine refugees. Twenty-five were children from the Church of England orphanage in Rangoon and the rest were women. They had walked a thousand miles with the vague notion that this route across mountains and through jungles would take them to India.

The refugees greeted the priest in near hysteria. Then suddenly, without warning, into the middle of the confusion walked the Japanese.

Were it not for the refugees, Father Stuart would have fled with the Kachins and blended into the jungle. But now he had to stay and do some playacting.

So as not to be suspected of spying, he played the role of a simple fellow, hoping the Japanese would consider him harmless and lose interest. He did the most naïve thing he could think of: he walked into the middle of the trail and stood there waiting for the Japanese major to approach on horseback.

"You Chinese?" Father Stuart asked. The major spit and said, "Japanese!"

"You English?" asked the major. The man from Derry spit and said, "Irish!"

The major dismounted, took a sword in one hand and a pistol in the other, and began a deliberate inspection of the missionary. Slowly he circled him, making hissing sounds as though sucking air through his teeth.

"Where Irish?" he asked.

The priest took a tall stick he carried, something of a shepherd's staff, and drew a circle in the clay. "United States," he said, pointing. Six feet away he drew another circle. "England."

Not wanting Ireland to appear too near either country, he then drew his homeland in the mid-Atlantic between the circles representing the United States and England.

The major held a long conference with his staff. They decided they could not remember having declared war on any Ireland.

Besides, the simple soul had enough trouble with those hysterical women and screaming children. Let him go.

Later, General Stilwell said, "The biggest mistake the Japanese made was not taking Father Stuart prisoner."

Stuart and his compatriot, Father Denis McAlindon of County Armagh, both half-starved and filled with fever, worked themselves to exhaustion finding rice during the monsoon to keep the refugees alive. After five months they had collected enough coolies and elephants to take the women and children from Sumprabum to Fort Hertz, up near the Himalayas. From there they would be flown to India.

By then the missionaries looked so wraithlike that a British officer ordered them to go to India with the refugees for rest and medical care. Hardly had their plane landed when they began pulling strings to return to Burma.

The two Irish priests found their way back under the auspices of a group of Americans who called themselves Detachment 101. It was a unit of the OSS dedicated to espionage and sabotage.

Father Stuart, accustomed to pulling other people's legs, thought these bizarre Americans were pulling his, especially when they told him that some of their instructors in the States had been selected from among the nation's top criminals. Who could better teach someone how to crack a safe, pick a pocket, or forge a document than those who had spent their lives developing such talents?

So that the OSS could put agents behind enemy lines, some Kachins, Father Stuart's parishioners, built an airstrip of sorts—on a slant and somewhat curved. On it they placed portable bamboo huts. When a plane wanted to land, the natives carried off the huts like stage scenery and replaced them after the plane left.

The commanding officer of Detachment 101 saw right off that Father Stuart was his kind of fellow. Besides, the Kachins, who knew the wilderness and every trail in it, respected the priest and would do anything he asked. One of the OSS assignments, the commanding officer explained to the missionary, was to rescue American airmen who frequently crashed onto the Hump during the India-China flight, and he asked for the help of the missionary and his Kachins.

Back in Burma, Father Stuart soon encountered an American fighter pilot tangled on a tree limb fifty feet in the air. "Drop your parachute," the priest yelled. When the chute hit the ground, he unzipped the pocket containing emergency rations and calmly sat beneath the tree enjoying a rare treat—real chocolate. Up in the branches the American was fuming and shouting.

"Be patient, lad, be patient," admonished the priest. "The Kachins will be along to get you down. Unless the Japanese hear you first."

Then it dawned on the pilot. "Are you Father Stuart?"

"Who else would be stupid enough to be in this part of the world?"

Refugees once more became the missionary's burden. He was asked to lead 241 of them—mostly women and children and old men—on a twenty-one day trek in January of 1944. Rain fell almost incessantly during that march, starvation was an ever-present threat, and the Japanese were near.

Stuart described the events of one day: "It was a hard journey, and about five miles of it meant wading upstream in a knee-deep river. It was very difficult for the children and for the blind women. There were heavy thunderstorms and everybody felt very cold, being wet through and through. We came upon a village that had been abandoned for a year and wild elephants had knocked down all houses. We put up some temporary shelters. No rice was available. Our patrols went out to search for game, or even buffalo left behind by the villagers, but had no success. Some of the refugees were sick, and some had developed sore feet and swollen joints."

Those refugees were fortunate that Father Stuart was in charge. Thousands of others did not do nearly so well. As Dr. Gordon Seagrave, the Burma surgeon, wrote: "There were skeletons around every water hole, lying sprawled out where the refugees had collapsed. At the front of every ascent were the bones of those who had died rather than attempt one more climb, and up the hills were the bones of those who had died trying. Still standing along the road were some extremely crude shacks,

36

each with its ten or twenty skeletons of those who couldn't get up when the new day came. In one of the shallow streams we were horrified to find that the Chinese had placed a long row of skulls to be used as steppingstones."

Stuart used to say that he had never in his life felt a sense of relief as profound as he did on the day he and his refugees met up with Merrill's Marauders at Naw Bum. General Merrill saw right off that Father Stuart had great rapport with the Kachins, the best fighters in Burma. So the general tried to keep the ubiquitous missionary near his headquarters as much as possible. Shortly before his own death, General Merrill wrote, "Father Stuart was the bravest man I ever met."

At Mass on Christmas morning I did not know all of this about Father Stuart. I would come to learn still more in the months ahead.

His Christmas sermon was but a few sentences spoken in a voice too soft to understand. He was extremely shy.

What I remember best is that during the reading of the Gospel a shift in the breeze brought the sickly sweet smell of shallow graves. The incense after battle. Those men had died for a place they could neither spell nor pronounce. Myitkyina.

On the trail after Mass I tried to estimate what time it was back home: still Christmas Eve. About mid-evening. What was Mary doing?

Back in camp after putting a helmet of hot water on the seat of a jeep, I stood at the side, looking into the rearview mirror, lathering my face. The major floated up, surrounded by a miasma of sour mash, and said, "I'll have an assignment for you, Lieutenant." He floated away, bobbing like a toy balloon on a summer morning.

That was better than the word he had for me on Christmas Eve. Yet it would have been nice to know on Christmas morning that soon I would have some interesting assignments that required scant training as a muleskinner.

The major suddenly returned. "I forgot. Here's something for you. Merry Christmas!" He held out a packet.

Fourteen letters from Mary! They must have been flown in the Red Ball express from the States to Chabua, India, and then by a plane that flew supplies into Myitkyina.

My first impulse was to rip them open, to devour them. I forced myself to walk over to a banyan tree and sit down.

While gripping the packet in both hands I decided to hold a vigil. Be aware of the wonder of the day, minute by minute. Fourteen magnificent hours left! One letter for each hour.

The next morning the major was sober, but very hung over, when he said, "Lieutenant, just to keep you busy for the time being, I'm going to have you censor mail. Something will turn up soon."

A postal censor, I soon learned, was more sinned against than sinning. Uncomplimentary remarks about censorship appeared in most letters. I felt like scrawling on them, "If you think I enjoy reading this, you're crazy!" Most letters were so dull. The usual opening was, "How are you? I am fine. Hope you are too." The words, "Ha! Ha!" came at the end of every third or fourth sentence, except for black troops, who wrote "Smile-Smile," and whose letters, even to loved ones, were often highly formal, starting, "Dear Mrs. Jones," and closing, "Your husband, Pvt. John J. Jones."

Many soldiers had a secret fondness for the censor, for he gave them an excuse to be dull. Often letters ended, "I could write some interesting things, but the censor would cut them out."

Years later, in *The Stilwell Papers*, I found Stilwell writing his wife: "My letters must be dull as dishwater. I could pep them up but it would just be a field day for the censor."

The censor had authority to delete only military information. The correspondent was free to write about the dozens of human-interest happenings he came across each day, the material that Ernie Pyle used to become a famous correspondent.

Writers of barren letters adhered to a three-point formula: (1) Avoid anything that hints of human interest; (2) repeat everything in many ways; (3) beat around the mulberry bush avoiding the shortest distance in expressing an idea.

Sometimes a censor felt like a father confessor. He caught glimpses of heartaches caused by the eternal triangle, financial worries, petty family feuds, adulteries, mother-in-law versus daughter-in-law squabbles, new-bride-versus-old-flame jealousies. Letters with everything definite in them usually held more tears than laughs.

Some letters were disturbing. There was the man who used to write very intimate things to his wife, and the same things, word for word, to an old flame. Another GI wrote to a man he called his "best friend," a civilian who was having an affair with the soldier's wife. He told the best friend, "You're welcome to that woman and good riddance because she is no account." He enumerated her faults; if only half of what he said was true, the characterization "no account" was most charitable. Some wrote sordid stuff to members of their families, often to married sisters, yet in the many letters I read, nobody ever wrote anything even the slightest bit off-color to his mother.

Some GIs tried to impress someone. One soldier, who at that time had not seen the enemy, put a piece of Japanese currency in a letter. He told his girl friend, "The Jap did not want to give up the money, but a few well-placed bullets convinced him that he ought to."

Many letters closed with the phrase "sealed with a kiss." I wondered if any girlfriend kissed the envelope flap. She would be disillusioned to know that I had sealed the flaps with damp toilet tissue or a pair of soggy shorts that had been hung out in the rain.

The job as postal censor was not without moments of beauty. One letter put a lump in my throat. It was from a middle-aged Italian to his wife. She was ill from a miscarriage. From what he wrote, I judged that, because of her age, they would probably never have children. He tried to console her and express his love for her. His penmanship made reading a hardship. The grammar broke all rules; the spelling was original. But he wrote from the heart. The simplicity of his expressions gave them dignity.

I censored on and on while each day a few more officers went forward. We had dwindled to a small group by New Year's Eve.

Near dusk the major said to me, "You are officer of the guard tonight. The word going around is that the Japs think the Americans will be celebrating New Year's Eve. So some of them will drift down the Irrawaddy and come in behind us, and others will attack from the front. Post the guard with that in mind."

So I was especially careful in setting up guard posts along the Irrawaddy. Having put into practice things I had learned in the infantry school at Fort Benning, I felt pleased with myself. I went into a tent, lowered the flaps, lit a candle, and began writing a letter to Mary.

Bang!

I came out of the tent on the run, and headed for the Irrawaddy, to the guard post from which the shot had come. After stumbling over a few vines, I came upon a private first-class, a redneck from South Carolina, who stammered, "I saw him, Lieutenant, I saw him."

"Who?"

"I saw his eyes."

"Whose eyes?"

"The tiger's."

"The tiger's!"

"He came down for a drink."

I raised hell and slid a block under it.

"Why did you have to fire at a tiger? Now the Japs know where you are! Didn't you learn anything at Camp Croft?"

To jar out the old year, a supply sergeant planted several sticks of dynamite in the bivouac area. The concussion at midnight was terrific. Several sleeping soldiers awoke thinking that Jap bombers were overhead, and jumped into air-raid trenches.

Up the road a few miles, several GIs fired rifles to welcome in 1945. The Chinese guards, mistaking the racket for an attack, opened up with machine guns on anything that moved. The celebrants crawled back to their tents beneath a ribbon of tracer bullets.

Near dawn, when I was checking the guard for the last time, I came upon three black soldiers sitting on the ground, leaning against a jeep. We got around to trying to guess what the future held. One of the soldiers said, "Home alive in '45." Another, more of a pessimist, responded, "Still in the sticks in '46." The third soldier continued with downbeat predictions: "Maybe in heaven in '47," and "The Golden Gate in '48." We all felt great uncertainty.

Such uncertainty is the quiet horror of war. It is not portrayed in movies or on television and only rarely in books. It is simpler to dramatize bursting shells and stalking snipers, but those things are temporary, and there are some defenses against them; uncertainty gnaws at you twenty-four hours a day.

I first became aware of that persistent uncertainty at dusk on October 5, 1942, when the Monon train chugged up to the railroad station at Rensselaer, Indiana. Thirty of us stood on the platform, clasping an assortment of overnight bags. We represented Jasper County's semimonthly quota of draftees; that was before the War Department decided we should be called "selectees" because that sounded better than "draftees."

About a hundred people were there to see us off. No bands, no speeches. That sort of thing had died out after the first few months. We were thankful for it; we were embarrassed and anxious to get past the last-minute good-byes with as little show of emotion as possible. The one public expression of appreciation came from the Tri Kappa sorority—ditty bags filled with a comb, a notebook, a pencil, chewing gum, and other items donated by local merchants.

Not many tears were visible on the station platform. The few smiles were strained, pathetic, and unconvincing. Everyone was pale and tense.

As the train pulled away from the platform, thirty draftees made a great pretense of peering out of windows. They were not trying to get a last look at home; they were trying to hide tears.

That scene was repeated thousands of times each day, all over the United States.

When a porter came through the coach, he mentioned that he had served for eighteen months during the First War. It seemed that in the last weeks of civilian life, every middle-aged man we talked with had served for eighteen months in the First War. Eighteen months, we decided, wouldn't be too bad. Hank Hoover brought the conversation to a close when he said, "There was once a Hundred Years War."

In Burma, on the day after New Year's, Lt. Art Kaltenborn and I were the only officers left in the field replacement depot. Being stranded with Art in a jungle clearing was not boring; he was an intelligent and cultured man, a cousin of H. V. Kalten-

41

born, the radio newsman, and before the war had taught speech at Wooster College, in Wooster, Ohio. He liked to keep in practice. It was amusing to hear him read aloud, while standing beneath a banyan tree, selections from a pocket-size copy of Shakespeare's tragedies.

A sergeant stationed at the replacement depot kept a mare captured by the Marauders from a Japanese officer, who in his turn had captured her from the Chinese. I spent pleasant hours on the trails riding the trim, compact little animal, who had the conformation of a polo pony. Since her pasterns were especially long, she gave a springy ride, and as cavalrymen used to say, she had such a collected way of moving that "she could canter all day in the shade of an old apple tree."

The mare took me to villages at some distance from the Ledo Road. The houses tended to look alike—a wooden frame filled with bamboo walls, and a roof thatched with elephant grass. Each was mounted on posts about six feet tall, leaving an open space beneath to shelter pigs. Buffaloes, cows, and ponies lived in a separate extension attached to the back. Stairs from ground to veranda were not elaborate: sometimes a bamboo ladder, but often only six-inch boards notched in such a way that the toes of one's bare feet might grasp them.

The Kachins near Myitkyina kept up their property better, dressed better, and seemed more civilized than those we had come upon in the Hukawng Valley while riding the Studebaker truck along the Ledo Road. I did not know that many of the Kachins living in the Hukawng were former slaves. They had been born in a vast, mountainous tract north of Myitkyina, a triangular area formed by two rivers, the Mali and the N'mai, which start sixty miles apart near the Himalayas in Tibet, and tend toward each other over their 120-mile journey south. They converge to form the Irrawaddy, which continues down the center of Burma past Myitkyina, Bhamo, and Mandalay, to reach the sea at Rangoon.

Although England had controlled parts of Burma since 1826, it was not until 1927 that the government sent a detachment of military police up into the Triangle to free the slaves. After some killing on both sides, the Kachin chiefs agreed to release their slaves if the government would pay for them. The rate settled on was 10 rupees for children, 120 for maidens and young men, and 60 for older people. (One rupee in those days was worth about thirty cents.)

Freed slaves fled westward from the Triangle into the Hukawng Valley, a dreadful place destined for an invasion of strangers known as Merrill's Marauders.

My favorite ride on the little mare was across a tiny path, hardly a yard wide, that picked its tortuous way along a steep incline. On the right towered the jungle, and on the left a stream hurried through the valley. From all sides came incessant buzzing and occasional birdcalls—the voice of the jungle. (One of the soldiers wrote home, "What you see most in the jungle are the noises.")

A fever got me away from the field replacement depot. An attack of chills had me shaking like a riveter. When a sergeant in the field hospital slipped a thermometer between my chattering teeth, I feared I might bite it in two. I expected it to show a zero reading; instead, it recorded 104 degrees. The sergeant stuck my finger for a blood smear. No blood came. He pricked the lobes of my ears. Still no blood. It was embarrassing.

Stretched on a cot under the field hospital tent, I read *Our Town*. Each month a committee of book editors decided on twenty-five books to be printed in a long and narrow format, so that the volumes would slide easily into the pocket of a combat jacket. Thornton Wilder's play was a part of that series.

On the cot next to mine was an officer from the adjutant's office of the Northern Combat Area Command. When he learned that I was an ex-newspaperman, he encouraged me to go to NCAC headquarters in Myitkyina and introduce myself.

"They need somebody who understands the points of view of both the military and the press, somebody to take charge of all those war correspondents gathering there. They're coming in from all over to ride the first convoy across the Ledo Road and on up the Burma Road to Kunming."

After several days in the field hospital, my fever disappeared. No one knew what caused it. Such inexplicable fevers were common in the jungle.

Back in the replacement depot, I told the major about the correspondents gathering at NCAC headquarters. He told me to go over to see if I could be of any help.

On the Ledo Road, I flagged down the first jeep going toward Myitkyina. The driver, from Jersey City, was full of observations. He pointed out, for instance, that when Kachins walked along a trail or on the Ledo Road, the women always walked ahead of the men, and said he'd figured out why.

"Why?" I asked.

"In case there's a booby trap or a land mine."

FOUR

I reported to Col. Joseph Stilwell, Jr., son of the famous general, at the headquarters of Northern Combat Area Command, in Myitkyina, and was assigned as escort officer for fifty-five war correspondents. Journalists from five countries were waiting to cover the story of the first convoy across the Ledo and the Burma Roads, one that had started in India, would continue across Burma, and on up into China.

Among the Americans were Theodore White from *Time*; Fred Friendly from the paper *CBI Roundup*; Hal Isaacs from *Newsweek*; Al Ravenholt of the United Press; Ed Sauder from the NBC Blue Network; Jack Wilkes from *Life*; Tillman Durdin from the *New York Times*; Ralph Henderson from *Reader's Digest*; Frank Cancellare from Acme News Service; and Bert Parks and Finis Farr, a team recording radio documentaries for a weekly stateside program, "Yanks in the Orient."

The correspondents were getting squirmy—they wanted to get the show on the road. But the Army could not do that because the Japanese still held an area from Namhkam east to the China border. Some correspondents seemed to find that a lame excuse. They wanted action.

I set up a press room in a large, battered building known as the Pentagon, which housed the staffs of combat command. The original structure had served the colonial British as a clubhouse; for years they had lolled on the veranda at sundown, drinking gin and watching polo. A British officer said, "Life in Burma in those days was like a lovely Saturday afternoon." Of the old clubhouse, only the framework remained; our engineers covered the walls with burlap and the roof with corrugated tin.

In the crowded, hot press room, correspondents griped and pecked out lame stories based on unexciting reports from staff officers. They got on one another's nerves, and on the nerves of the military. I started out with some sympathy for each side, but soon realized that I was acting as a buffer between two of the most arrogant groups in the entire scheme of things.

Some of the old hands in the military took the attitude of the censor who said, "I wouldn't tell the people anything until the war was over, and then I'd tell them who won." On the other side, some journalists were interested in promoting themselves, grinding axes, and scoring points.

I finally became resigned to this, realizing that it would be forever so. The only solution would be to have both sides, military and press, blessed with an abundance of goodwill, prudence, generosity of spirit, and common sense. The day that happens, there will be no wars to report.

One afternoon during that uneasy time in Myitkyina, waiting for the convoy to start, Theodore White jumped up from his typewriter, rushed out the door, and began pacing back and forth in front of the building. I fell into step beside him and asked, "What's the matter, Teddy?"

"I can't work in that commotion! I'm no hack! I'm an artist."

Through the years I watched from afar as the artist inside Teddy White developed while his personality mellowed. Whenever he appeared on television to promote one of his books, it was evident he had changed. From a slim, surly *Time* reporter fresh out of Harvard, he grew into a rotund, somewhat benign elderly writer.

To ease tension among the press, I began conducting Cook's tours. These gave the correspondents something to write about. The first tour, a flight over the front, nearly had a grim ending.

I made a special point of asking for a C-47 transport, the
military version of the twin-engined DC-3, because at that time
everybody still felt uneasy about its less reliable predecessor, the
C-46. The problem with the C-46 started when Madame Chiang
Kai-shek appeared in Washington before an assembly of senators
and congressmen, asking for more war materials for China. To
give help in a hurry, the United States military put the new C-46
into service before it had been properly tested. It was full of
problems. Flight crews hated it. Many bailed out while crossing
the Himalayas. The OSS rescued about a third of those who
bailed out; the others died from the jump, or were captured by
the Japanese, or died of starvation while roaming in that remoteness. In a relatively short period the OSS rescued more than 125
crew members. In time, though, the bugs were worked out and
some pilots began preferring the C-46 because of its ruggedness.

When our C-47 arrived in Myitkyina from Chabua, I filled it
with American, British, Indian, Chinese, and Australian correspondents. The pilot asked, "Where to?" I told him to fly eastward over an area where Americans of the Mars Brigade, a
combat unit that started after the decline of Merrill's Marauders,
and some Chinese troops were trying to push the Japanese from
the Burma Road.

Some of the correspondents were interested in doing a story
about supply by airdrop, and so we began circling the combat
zone. Cargo plane after cargo plane came in over a sandbar at
about 140 miles an hour, at three hundred feet. Dozens of
colored parachutes flowering in their wake floated earthward,
bearing food and ammunition.

An Australian correspondent, sitting in the bucket seat next to
me, said that the small broadcloth chutes, procured from the
British via Lend-Lease, cost twelve dollars; the large U.S. rayon
chutes cost about seventy-five dollars.

I said, "All the natives in these valleys will soon be dressed in
brightness."

"Yes, they do like to dress up," he said. "Remember what I
told you yesterday?"

The day before, the Australian correspondent had told me
how Kachins rarely wore shoes, but liked to own them as
emblems of prestige. So the OSS had many shoes dropped to

guerrilla units behind enemy lines. A Kachin soldier would go along the trail barefooted, but would stop at the edge of a village and put on his shoes; at the other side of the village he would take them off, tie the laces together, and drape the shoes around his neck.

While we circled the sandbar, it began to look as though it had been struck by a snowstorm with flakes of myriad colors. Long lines of Chinese pack ponies converged to gather supplies. The correspondents seemed intent on that scene below, and I began to congratulate myself for having arranged this tour.

Suddenly the Japanese fired on us.

"We've been hit," said the pilot.

The copilot spotted an unidentified fighter zooming up the valley, and the pilot enacted a maneuver known as Getting the Hell Out of There. We ducked into an adjoining valley and flew low over a river with high mountains on each side. Flying low in those mountain passes was touchy business; the downdraft was sometimes fierce.

I started thinking about how wrong I'd been in planning this tour. An escort officer is supposed to keep correspondents from getting killed; of all his duties, that is number one. Three months later, when I heard that Ernie Pyle had been killed, my first feeling was one of sympathy for the escort officer.

Five minutes after we had left the area, a cargo plane came crashing down. Not from Japanese fire, but from Chinese mortars. American liaison officers had warned the Chinese to hold their fire when cargo planes came in low for a drop, but the Chinese had a way of disregarding instructions.

Back in Myitkyina, dinner parties helped pass the time for restive correspondents. Lt. Gen. Dan I. Sultan, who had recently succeeded General Stilwell as theater commander, gave a party for us. So did General Pick.

To respond to such hospitality, the correspondents went into the bazaars to buy food. Then they hired Chinese cooks. Just before the feast, several American soldiers complained to me that their dogs had disappeared. Like soldiers everywhere, they had the custom of adopting stray dogs when moving through villages destroyed by war. It was easy to guess what had happened to the dogs, since the cooks were Chinese. I said nothing, but that night I avoided the meat dish.

Finally, on January 22, the convoy began to move. There were vehicles of all sizes, 113 of them, some with artillery pieces hitched behind; many carried supplies along with Chinese soldiers and American engineers. We crossed the Irrawaddy at Myitkyina on a pontoon bridge said to be the longest in the world.

In jeep number thirteen, driven by Sgt. Bud Celella, Lt. Walter Kerns and I lurched along, wondering how many headaches awaited us. The fifty-five war correspondents occupied thirty-three jeeps for which we were responsible. Kerns represented Services of Supply; I represented the combat command.

After a hot and dusty first day, we stopped at night near battered Bhamo. I did not know that, in time, Bhamo would become a part of my life, that I would always remember it with affection and some uneasiness. When heating rations that night on small gasoline stoves, with the tension of waiting now dispelled, we felt effervescent. Later, stretched on the ground under blankets, we talked long into the night, until temple bells lulled us to sleep.

The stench of decaying bodies hung heavy in the air most of the next day. In midafternoon the convoy descended from the hills into the fertile open country of the Shweli River valley. The town of Namhkam, pride of the valley, still smoldered from a recent battle. Just as we passed the last heap of rubble, a captain stopped us.

"The Japs are on the road up ahead," he said. "And they are in the hills over there to the right. They can see every move you make. They got artillery. Their one-fifties forced our artillery out of position twice yesterday. Go on up the road a couple of miles. Somebody will show you a bivouac area. Don't know how long you'll have to stay here."

Enough things happened during our three-day stay in Namhkam to keep the correspondents from getting bored: snipers, skirmishes, and a couple of unusual parties.

Snipers fired just often enough to keep all of us alert. Japanese snipers often watched the forward troops pass, and then shot officers at close range. They seemed especially interested in shooting radio operators. A volley of shots rang through the bivouac one afternoon—bullets buzzed like bees. A Chinese patrol set out to find the enemy; no one expected that they would, and they did not.

At dusk, Lieutenant Kerns and I were eating rations behind a pile of rubble that protected us from a sniper working across the road. Sergeant Celella decided to bathe in a stream about ten yards away. Hardly had he stripped off his combat fatigues than a sniper's rifle cracked, and a bullet dug into the soft bank. Without collecting his clothes, Celella landed headfirst in our sheltered spot.

That night the Chinese and the Japanese put on a good show atop a hill just outside of Namhkam. Tracer bullets and bursting shells reminded us of a fireworks display.

Artillery thunder was rolling up the Shweli valley that evening when I came across a sergeant seated in a heap of rubble beneath the skeleton of a house. He hovered over a candle. Beneath his fingers were a pencil, a piece of crumpled paper, and a ruler, and at his elbow were two booklets for homemakers. Leafing through the booklets, he picked out a fireplace that struck his fancy, and an open stairway that pleased him. All of these dreams he worked into a floor plan. This attempt to create beauty in the midst of destruction was both amusing and saddening.

In making my rounds that night, I came upon five Americans who had seen much fighting. I was struck by how little credit they would give the Japanese soldier, a tough competitor. In the European Theater, Americans saw German soldiers as fellows they might well share a bottle of beer with, and Italian soldiers as fellows they could drink red wine with, but in Burma the Allies looked upon the Japanese as little more than animals. Stilwell called the Japanese "these bowlegged cockroaches" and "buck-toothed bastards." I think the setting led to these primitive feelings. In Europe the war was waged through cities and towns and across cultivated fields, and mainly with the enemy at some distance; in Burma the jungle was primitive and the fighting often close up, eye-to-eye.

Gen. Sun Li-jen, commander of the First Chinese Army, gave

a press party the next morning on the side of a little hill not far from the front. He served peanuts, fried cakes, and rum. The handsome, elegant general spoke English well; he had studied at the Virginia Military Institute.

I got into a conversation with a young Chinese major who also spoke English well; he had a Midwestern way of speaking, and knew Americana. When he used the expression, "There are no flies on you," I asked, "What American university did you attend?"

"I have never been to your country," he said. "I was never out of China until I came to Burma."

"Where did you learn to speak English so well?"

"At the University of Canton. What university did you attend?"

"Ever hear of Notre Dame?"

"The Chinese officer leaned back and sang, "Cheer, cheer for old Notre Dame . . ." never missing a word or a note.

That incident became a sequence in a film a decade later; it still appears on the television screen from time to time. More about that in due course.

A great feast followed General Sun's party. Natives within walking distance of Namhkam slipped through Japanese lines. Day and night they arrived to celebrate the return of Dr. Gordon Seagrave and his native nurses. Seagrave, then a lieutenant colonel in the United States Army, had been "family doctor" to the natives of Upper Burma for twenty-two years.

When the Japanese overran Burma in 1942, Seagrave and his nurses fled with Stilwell. That flight and the experience of building a hospital in Namhkam provided the material for his best-selling memoir, *Burma Surgeon*. He and his nurses cared for soldiers in India for two years, waiting for American, Chinese, and British brass to agree on an invasion of Burma. When the invasion came, Seagrave asked for "the dirtiest job you have." His unit was assigned to serve as a portable surgical unit, moving through the jungles with combat troops. He did not get the assignment without a fight, for American officers did not want women so near the front, even though they were Burmese nurses. But Seagrave won his point; he had made a habit of doing that all of his life.

51

Now he was back in his beloved Namhkam. He reached there just before the convoy to find his hospital bombed, but not beyond repair. The good news of his return ran through the hills. For a day and a night, tribesmen infiltrated enemy lines. Dressed in their brightest colors, they came bearing food, like American families bringing a potluck supper to a country church. Shan, Chinese, and Kachin cooks prepared jungle hen, wild boar, greens, garlic, onions, and rice. All day and all night the preparations unfolded, accompanied by squealing pigs, singing natives, and gurgling rice wine.

At the feast, Doc Seagrave proposed a series of toasts—to the Chinese Army, to the U.S. Army, to the British Army, to the first convoy, to the war correspondents—and closed with, "To the Tenth Air Force and their precision bombing of the Namhkam hospital." The massive stone buildings, raised by Seagrave's own hands, had taken a pounding when the Japanese used them as headquarters.

Entertainment followed the feast. The only place large enough to accommodate even a fraction of the crowd was the second-floor dormitory in the nurses' home. That building, although in better condition than the others, had felt its share of bombings. Perhaps we were foolhardy to pack so many people on a weakened floor.

When the room was well filled, Doc Seagrave asked that a guard be put on the stairway to prevent anyone else from crowding in. A GI took the post. I was seated at the head of the stairway when suddenly I heard the guard say, "Stop him! He's got a grenade!" A Chinese soldier, angered at not being permitted to come up the stairway, had threatened to lob a hand grenade into the crowded room. Several Americans hurried him, none too gently, from the building.

Americans, Chinese, British, Indians, Kachins, Shans, Karens, Burmese, Australians, and representatives of several other nationalities settled themselves to enjoy the entertainment. Doc Seagrave, as master of ceremonies, welcomed us. He said that he hoped he was the only American soldier to return home to find everything he owned destroyed by his own air force.

An ancient Shan opened the program with a sword dance. Tattoos, in various shades of purple, covered the old man from head to foot. He went through a most intricate and strenuous dance with a massive sword flashing in each hand. As the drum-beat increased in tempo and the swords flashed faster, occupants of the front row wished they had taken seats farther back. At the end of his dance, we applauded. The old man also applauded and went into an encore. At the end of the encore, we applauded; he again applauded and went into another encore. After a time we quit applauding for fear he might dance himself to death. Among the Shans, the men often dance until they urinate blood.

The second dance on the program was a great contrast to the first. It was presented by the charming Princess Louise, one of the Seagrave nurses of royal native blood. Her dance, like many in the Orient, emphasized graceful movement of the hands.

Karen girls, in lovely costumes, sang in close harmony the songs of their people. Next came a chorus of nurses, presenting their interpretation of Chinese dances. Their Chinese clothes had been fashioned from silk parachutes.

Some of the British and Americans on the Seagrave staff staged a couple of comedy skits that might better have been left out. They did not offend good taste, but there was a certain harshness about them that tended to break the magic of the evening.

The startling part of the celebration, a Kachin *manau* dance, came as a climax. The Kachins were still ranked just behind the headhunting Nagas and the vicious Was as the wildest tribespeople of Burma; they had not held a *manau* during Japanese occupation. So they were well primed for this one. Doc Seagrave defined the *manau* as a "religious, sexual, alcoholic trance."

For this dance we adjourned to a clearing a hundred yards from the hospital grounds. A bright moon lighted the strange ritual. In the center of the clearing stood two *nat* poles, similar to Eskimo totem poles.

Two hundred men and women formed a line, grasped each other at the waist, and started a movement similar to a college snake dance. The men, with rifles or muzzle-loading shotguns strapped to their backs, carried vicious swords. The women wore black Kachin robes heavily encrusted with silver ornaments. Two chiefs in massive feathered headdresses led the dance.

Between the *nat* poles, musicians performed with pipes, cymbals, gongs, and drums. The rhythm started soft and slow, but as the minutes wore by, it throbbed with greater vigor. The mongoloid features of the animists grew more sullen as they moved deeper into their trance.

I was standing on the sidelines with Ralph Henderson of *Reader's Digest*, an interesting companion because he had grown up in Burma, the son of missionary parents, and he could explain the *manau* and other customs of the Kachins.

Doc Seagrave joined us. He said he had felt encouraged during his early days in Burma because the natives seemed so anxious to get religious tracts. Later he was dismayed to find them using the paper to roll the "whackin' white cheroots" immortalized by Kipling. Seagrave called it "smoking the Gospel."

Suddenly three of our correspondents burst into the clearing. They had downed just enough rum to think it would be great sport to sway back and forth with the natives. They had hardly begun to enjoy themselves when Doc Seagrave grabbed my shoulder, breathing fire and brimstone. He said that a Kachin in a trance was apt to kill anyone who interfered with a *manau*. Seagrave ordered Lieutenant Kerns and me to haul the revelers from the dance. That brief orientation was enough to make us hesitant. As we tugged the correspondents from the swaying line, some of the natives tried to pull us, none too gently, into the dance. After clearing the *manau* of all war correspondents, we walked back to the hospital and left the Kachins to their trances.

Doc Seagrave suffered his second major annoyance of the evening when he had to rout out his weary nurses to record songs for a Chungking radio broadcaster. Early in the afternoon, when the girls had given a special performance for news cameramen and American recording teams, the Chinese commentator had not bothered to set up his equipment. Now he felt that he had to get every song in the girls' repertoire down on record.

Seagrave had my sympathy, because the same Chinese commentator had given Lieutenant Kerns and me trouble the previous day, when he'd wanted General Pick to make a recording. We adjourned to a secluded wooded spot for the ordeal. The general went along beautifully, speaking extemporaneously, until the closing sentence, when he stumbled over a few words. We suggested that he cut a new disc. During the closing seconds of that record, a jeep came roaring upon us. Pick thought that wouldn't sound good, so he decided to cut another. During the third attempt he stumbled and stuttered over quite a few words, and being a perfectionist at heart, tried again. Again he stumbled and stuttered. Then he asked Kerns to write out a quick speech. He muffed the first reading. The next reading was strictly professional. We sighed with relief. But in the playback we found that something had gone haywire with the recorder; the thing kept repeating "convoy, convoy, convoy." After that, every time Pick was on, the recorder was off, and when the recorder was on, Pick was off. It took us three hours to make a three-minute recording!

The morning after the Seagrave party, I took several jeeploads of correspondents forward to witness the final fight to link the Ledo Road with the Burma Road. The objective was to clear the enemy from the village of Pinghai, move on to the road junction, and throw a screen of troops along the route to hold off the enemy while the convoy slipped through.

Mist filled the Shweli valley when we started out, but a warm sun had dispelled it by the time we reached the observation post atop a hill about two hundred yards from Pinghai. Four tanks of the Chinese-American Composite Tank Group were waddling into the village as we settled ourselves for the show. All around the hill, Chinese infantrymen crouched, waiting for the signal to move in. Up near the top of the hill, Chinese machine gunners trained their weapons on the village to keep the enemy occupied while the infantrymen went forward by leaps and bounds.

Suddenly things began to happen. The Chinese troops, pointed for Pinghai, began to fire beyond it. They launched into some of the best fighting of their careers. They were men inspired. But they were fighting their own troops.

This is what had happened: The bedraggled Chinese Expeditionary Force, which had experienced a couple of years of the meanest campaigning in the history of warfare, had finally entered Burma from China. The American-trained Chinese, who had spent a couple of years fighting from India across northern Burma, always pointing toward China, were, at last, near the border. When both armies met, each mistook the other for the enemy. High brass on both sides realized the mistake almost instantly and sent messages down through channels to stop the battle. But it was hard to stop; the Chinese soldiers were taking an unexpected interest in their work.

While the Chinese fought each other, the tanks chased the Japanese out of Pinghai. I led the correspondents down the hill for the mop-up. They bunched together as though they were on parade. One burst from a machine gun would have cut down the lot of them. I asked them to scatter; they made a feeble effort, but were soon back together, in a tighter knot than ever. Correspondents seemed to think that since they did not carry weapons and were considered noncombatants, all bullets would respect their status. Jack Wilkes of *Life* was the only one to carry a weapon. Each time a picture was taken in which he appeared, he unstrapped his holster; it was against regulations for him to bear arms.

The Japanese fled from Pinghai to an adjoining hill. No sooner did they reach their new location than Chinese artillery shells began to pepper them. The jeep trail that we were going to use to get out of the area twisted through the valley that separated Japanese from Chinese artillery. Just as expected, as soon as we started down the trail the shells began to fall short. It is annoying to have the enemy fire on you, but twice as annoying when your own troops do it.

That night in bivouac, I sat listening to the veteran drivers of the Ledo Road. They had developed a lingo all their own. When they spoke of a "cowboy," they meant a driver who enjoyed speeding and taking chances on the mountains. A "cockpit driver" was one who out-cowboyed the cowboys. When a GI said he'd "tanked one," it meant he'd driven his truck into a bank when it got out of control in the mountains; when he said he'd "put her down," he meant he had abandoned his truck, leaving it to crash into the gorge below. If he said that he'd "waved his back wheels," it meant he'd passed a truck and left it far behind.

That night, Kerns and I went around and reassigned several drivers. Up to Namhkam our jeep had been cowboyed by Sgt. Bud Celella, from Brooklyn or the Bronx, I forget which. I am sure it was one of the two, because I remember his saying, "I hafta go back after earl."

I asked, "Earl who?"

He answered, "Earl, earl, the stuff you put in the crankcase."

Celella was a cousin of Jimmy Durante. Whenever Durante visited the family, Bud said, he brought a crate of live chickens.

Jitterbugging was Celella's abiding passion. He kept talking about the jitterbug contests he had won, and describing the zoot suit he would have tailored the day he shed his army ODs.

We reassigned Bud, not because we were tired of listening to him—although we were—but as the result of a complaint the correspondents had made while waiting for the convoy to move beyond Myitkyina.

Teddy White said to me, "There ought to be some Negro drivers on this convoy. They did a lot in building the Ledo Road. General Pick is from Mississippi; he probably has an 'ol' massa' attitude. Talk to him about it."

At the dinner party the correspondents gave for the military, I approached General Pick, who was sitting on the twisted trunk of a great banyan tree. When I spoke of bringing in some black drivers, he became annoyed. "These correspondents think that because I'm a Southerner, I'm against having Negro drivers on this convoy. They're wrong! I want those drivers. But Generalissimo Chiang Kai-shek has made it clear he does not want them coming into China. I'll take this up again with General Sultan."

It must have taken some inveigling on Pick's part, because General Sultan was new in the job of theater commander, and the memory was still fresh in his mind of what had happened to Stilwell for disregarding Chiang's wishes. Pick probably put some pressure on Sultan, because he was anxious for his Ledo Road and his first convoy to have a favorable press. The situation must have been embarrassing for Sultan; he could not easily refuse such a just request from a man who had accomplished what the British had called impossible. So seven black drivers were flown in.

All went well until we neared the China border. Pick learned that Chinese officials wanted him to take the seven drivers from the convoy. The general, with fifty-five war correspondents breathing down his neck, decided that the Chinese would be so happy to receive 113 vehicles, and the equipment loaded on them, that they would overlook the seven drivers. But, a man of caution, he told me to take one of the seven as my driver and to place the other six with correspondents who would look after them in case there was a problem.

My new driver, Sergeant Butler, was less talkative than Bud Celella. The silence was welcome as we moved toward China. Once we were across the border, Chinese peasants began taking an inordinate interest in us. Every time Sergeant Butler stopped, Chinese swarmed around us, pointing to him and saying, *"Bu hoa,"* which means "no good." When we went into a teahouse, the giggling peasants jostled against us in their eagerness to get a look at the soldier whose skin was black. After two days of such embarrassment, Sergeant Butler got jittery, and began dreading the sight of a village. He said, "They make me feel like I'm naked."

This is getting ahead of the story of the first convoy. Back in Namhkam, I lost one of the war correspondents. An inept Chinese driver had run into the weapons carrier in which Fred Friendly was riding, and Friendly's hand had been injured.

One of Dr. Seagrave's young surgeons repaired Friendly's battered hand under a tent one night near the bombed hospital. Fred wanted to continue on with the convoy, but Seagrave insisted that he fly back to India for further medical attention.

The convoy broke bivouac at Namhkam the morning after the tanks had sent the enemy scurrying from Pinghai. We were glad to have been delayed in the lovely Shweli valley. And yet, excited to be on the way, everyone moved with a springy step in the early morning chill. It was January 28, the day the blockade was officially broken.

We were anxious to run the gauntlet without delay that morning, and slip across the border into China. We knew that anywhere within a few miles of the junction of the Ledo and Burma roads we were apt to come under enemy artillery fire. There was probably not enough artillery left to be effective, but it seemed only natural that the enemy would bring down a token barrage upon us. The Japanese were aware we were going to make a break for it; Tokyo Rose had announced our starting time in her broadcast the night before, and wished us an ironic "Good luck."

We were eager to run the gauntlet, with its threat of snipers,

artillery fire, and Jap raiders, and get into China, where our only
concern would be bombers, bandits, and the fanatical Chinese
drivers on the Burma Road. But high Chinese brass had other
plans. They could not resist the opportunity to make speeches
and hold a military review. So we had to stop at Mu-se, just a
few miles from where the Ledo Road joined the Burma Road and
let the Chinese hold their celebration.

During the speeches, which no one paid much attention to, we
had a chance to observe the two groups of Chinese soldiers who
had mistaken each other for the enemy. Those trained by Americans in India looked well fed and natty in their suntan uniforms,
GI shoes, and steel helmets. They carried Enfield rifles and
tommy guns. Those who had fought their way in from China
looked gaunt in their torn, faded blue cotton uniforms, sagging
caps, and bare feet. They carried ancient German rifles and
Japanese Arisakas. The soldiers from China looked with amazement upon their brothers from India, and the latter seemed to
strut just a little.

From Mu-se the convoy highballed in to Mongyu, where a
sign had just been put up saying: JUNCTION—LEDO ROAD—
BURMA ROAD.

Ten miles above the junction, we halted, and the drivers
bedecked their trucks with American flags and red, white, and
blue ribbons. General Pick was a great believer in making a
colorful entrance.

The convoy rolled slowly down a hill into an open field, where
thousands of Chinese and American soldiers gathered around a
platform to hear speeches of welcome given by leathery General
Chennault, of Flying Tigers fame, and T. V. Soong, Chairman
of the Chinese National Executive and brother of Madame
Chiang Kai-shek.

The correspondents, in a nearby tent, punched out their first
stories since Myitkyina. The theater public-relations officer had
flown in from New Delhi and was waiting to fly the copy back to
India's capital for transmission to the United States. The newsmen were ebullient, a state brought on partly by being a part of
the first convoy to break a three-year blockade, but mainly by
the liquor some unknown benefactor had left in the press tent.

Til Durdin, of the *New York Times* was the first one finished with his story. He was always a fast yet thorough worker. As he and I stretched out in a corner, waiting for the others to complete their stories, he told me about his twelve years in China. I asked, "Don't you ever get to daydreaming about buying a farm in Connecticut and settling down?" He said, "Often," and there was a look in his eye that made me think he meant it.

After the speechmaking, General Pick snipped a ribbon stretched across a gaily decked archway that stood in front of a little wooden bridge spanning a muddy creek, the border between Burma and China. The big trucks rolled across the creaking bridge into the border town of Wanting, and continued northeast along the Burma Road toward Kunming, 566 miles away.

That night we bivouacked on a windswept hill, far from a supply of water. Two officers with the convoy had as their sole job the selection of bivouac areas. They seemed to specialize in selecting areas that were wide open, cold, and a great distance from water.

Sleeping on the ground in the mountains of China was painful. We awoke each morning covered with a thick coating of frost. Young men, hoary of hair and pinched of face, limped about with chilled, aching bones; for the first hour or two each day, everyone looked twice his age. It would have been laughable had it not been so painful. The combination of sun, wind, dust, and cold soon had all faces resembling boot leather. Almost everyone had a bad case of chapped, swollen lips as black as chunks of charcoal. Some of our lips were cracked and split so deeply that they would always carry scars.

Each day as we plunged and climbed across jagged mountain ranges and prowled through gorges of great beauty, we marveled at the downright doggedness that had built the Burma Road. Within sixteen months, some 200,000 Chinese coolies had literally scratched out the road with their fingers. The only machinery used were hand-powered drills to facilitate planting dynamite charges.

We saw maintenance being carried on in the same primitive manner in which the road was built from October 1937, until early 1939. Thousands of men, women, and children, squatting beside the route, broke boulders with small hammers. Other gangs carried the broken rocks in baskets to crouching men who fitted them into place and tapped them into the roadbed, making a mosaic. Next came great stone rollers that had been hewn by hand. Teams of men tugged them along to smooth the road. With such primitive methods they built 726 miles of road, installed two thousand culverts, and constructed three hundred bridges from Lashio, Burma, to Kunming, China.

During the building of the road, each village sent its quota of workers. They came readily enough, even though during the early stages, two hundred out of every 250 coolies died. Death came from reckless drivers, enemy bombs, exposure, and dynamite blasts, but mostly from fever, for the coolies worked on the most malarious route in the world, a distinction later claimed by the Ledo Road. The coolies did not seem to mind the bombings. They reasoned that it cost the Japanese one thousand dollars to make a bomb crater, but it cost only a few cents to fill it up.

The road was in reality a rebuilding of the ancient Ambassador's Trail, across which elephants bore gifts from the Kings of Burma to the Emperor on the Dragon Throne as early as the T'ang Dynasty (about A.D. 800). As the Silk Road, it saw long lines of coolies carrying expensive cargo from Cathay to lower Burma. Sometimes it was called the Marco Polo Road because along its route in the thirteenth century the European adventurer had journeyed to Cathay.

The Japanese captured the road in the spring of 1942. Even in the three years preceding the capture, the road was the most dangerous, most confused, and most important in the world.

More than fifteen thousand wrecked vehicles were scattered along the route, bombed to bits, burned out for lack of servicing, or smashed after sliding off one-thousand-foot precipices. Little of the damage could be blamed on enemy action; most of it was caused by incompetent driving. No drivers in the world had less ability than the Chinese. Their reflexes were poor, a condition probably caused by bad living conditions and insufficient nourishment. Their lack of contact with machinery left them unable to comprehend the potentialities and limitations of a piece of machinery.

Inability to handle and maintain vehicles was not the drivers' only fault. Having originally volunteered as patriots, they soon found themselves lured into graft—or "squeeze," as it is called in the Orient. They siphoned gas from their trucks and sold it, traded off parts from the vehicles, and carried passengers and cargo that had no military value. The easy money made on such personal ventures was spent nodding all night over rice wine in a wayside shop. The next morning the trucks careened around hairpin turns, guided by unsteady hands and bleary eyes.

The drivers were not wholly to blame for the confusion. The whole system, all the way to the top, was rotten.

The graft on the Burma Road caused some early friction between Stilwell and Chiang. The chief of supply in Burma, Gen. Yu Fei-p'eng, tried to load trucks with equipment he could sell in China during the dark days when British and Chinese soldiers were fleeing from the Japanese. His attitude was, Let the troops fend for themselves. Stilwell wanted the general shot. Somebody told him, "Forget it, Yu Fei-p'eng is Chiang's cousin."

The highway was supposed to be a military project, but was operated like a peacetime commercial venture. Private interests used it with abandon, while sixteen government agencies, each competing with the others, did a thriving trucking business. The road was so clogged with customs houses and graft that it cost between $150 and $200 in American money to move a ton of supplies from one end to the other.

The United States government saw from the beginning that the road must be directed by a single agency or individual. The Chinese did not follow that line of thought. They seemed to think that if one agency could operate the road well, then sixteen agencies could operate it sixteen times as well.

Drastic action came in February 1941, when Lauchlin Currie, of President Roosevelt's staff, visited Chungking. He made it clear to the Generalissimo that the United States disapproved of the bad odor of greed that hung over the Burma Road. The Chinese suggested, with little enthusiasm, that Dr. John Earl Baker, an official of the American Red Cross in China, be appointed czar of the road. Dr. Baker, who had a great deal of transportation experience, became known as the Inspector General. The Chinese, who resented foreign "directors" but loved foreign "advisers," soon had the good doctor so bound in red tape that he was wholly ineffective.

Other American experts joined in the farce, but none really accomplished anything before the Japanese put an end to the foolishness.

Probably the most efficient of all the specialists, and certainly the most colorful, was big Daniel Arnstein, uninhibited owner of seven thousand New York taxis. Oriental protocol and the silken manners of the East had to take cover when he stomped rough-shod into Chungking. He took a trip across the road and batted out a report as tough as a cabbie's language.

"I talked plain," said Arnstein. "When Chiang got that report, I bet it was like being hit over the head with a baseball bat."

Long after Arnstein was gone, he was spoken of as a legendary figure among China's upper crust. The story most often told about him originated at a banquet, when Madame Chiang turned to the ex-cabbie and said that she felt apologetic for the way she always harped at America for aid, but that she would continue to harp as long as China was in need.

"Don't worry, Madame," said the taxi tycoon. "We have a saying in the trucking business that it's the squeakin' wheel that gets the grease." This was translated for Chiang, who smilingly murmured over and over, "Good! Good!"

As the first American convoy rolled across the Burma Road, we wondered if Oriental "squeeze" would stage a comeback despite U.S. Army supervision. However, we were not so worried about graft as we were thankful that the Burma Road was smoother riding than the Ledo Road. When I made this comparison to a Chinese officer in Paoshan, he said, "It is like all our highways, good for ten years, bad for ten thousand. The Burma Road is still on the first ten."

The conversation with the Chinese officer took place at a banquet long remembered by Americans who attended. I remember in some detail that banquet, given on January 30, and the notes I made that day back up my memory.

In the bivouac area that morning, while my bones still creaked from frost, a delegation of news photographers descended upon me. Their spokesman, George Alexanderson, said, "Today we are going to cross the Salween River bridge. That's a famous military objective. The Japs and Chinese fought back and forth across it for two years. It has been destroyed and rebuilt I don't know how many times. We'd like to get some good shots of the convoy coming across the bridge. It'd be sort of symbolic of victory."

"Sure, why not?" I agreed.

"Here's the catch," Alexanderson warned. "The convoy is scattered over miles of the road. We'd like to have it bunch up at the Hwei Tung Bridge. If we get only one truck in a picture, it won't be very effective. If we get a bunch of trucks in each shot, the pictures we take in the Salween gorge will probably be the best of the trip."

Now, if there was one thing I had learned at Infantry School, it was to keep plenty of interval between vehicles. In that way, damages done by a bombing or a strafing could be held to a minimum.

So I hesitated to promise to bunch up the trucks. The newspaperman in me agreed with Alexanderson; the Army officer in me said, Don't do it. My answer was, "You fellows go on ahead and take your positions on the other side of the bridge. I'll plead your case before General Pick when we reach the Salween gorge. This early in the morning, when everybody is feeling cold and stiff and a little nauseated, is no time to ask favors."

As we crawled across Sungshan (Pine Mountain), I tried to phrase in my mind the plea I would make for the newspapermen. But I was distracted so often that I didn't get very far in the planning; there was so much to look at.

We were crossing one of the bloodiest battlegrounds in the history of warfare. Sungshan is a seven-thousand-foot promontory known as the Jap Gibraltar of the Salween. An enemy garrison of two thousand was destroyed there after three months of constant battling on the slopes of the mountain. I had thought Myitkyina and Bhamo were exceedingly honeycombed with foxholes and emplacements, until I saw Sungshan. It was like a sieve. To capture their objective, the Chinese had dug tunnels, loaded them with dynamite, and blown the top off Sungshan, and the Jap garrison with it. That mountain belonged to the

Kaoli Kung range, a part of the Hump on the air route between India and China.

After hours of easing our way along narrow mountain ledges, we rounded a bend to see below the rapid, sparkling Salween, twisting through an unbelievably beautiful gorge.

At the far side of the suspension bridge, way down below, I saw a group of men milling about—the movie cameramen and still photographers getting into position. Maybe it was the newspaperman in my blood that made me determined to talk General Pick into bunching the vehicles for pictures.

I stopped and waited for General Pick's jeep, which headed the convoy. While I was giving my opening arguments, the first truck pulled up. A little later, the second rounded the curve and came to a stop almost bumper-to-bumper with the first. By the time General Pick had a chance to make a reply, the front of the convoy was well bunched. But he did not seem to mind; as I said before, the general loved a favorable press.

Just as the vehicles were well bunched and about to begin their parade across the bridge, a siren sounded. American antiaircraft crews, stationed at the bridge, leaped to their guns. The officer in charge of the unit said, "We just got word that thirty-one Jap planes are headed this way. What a target this convoy will make, all bunched up in the gorge!"

I felt suddenly sick. The newsmen would photograph a battered convoy instead of a victorious one! A great publicity stunt was just about to blow up in our faces.

There was nothing for the convoy to do but pull in close to the mountainside and sit tight and wait. The larger trucks had antiaircraft machine guns mounted on them, and the gunners swung them up.

My driver and I raced down the inclining ledge and across the swinging bridge to tell the newsmen what was up. They accepted the news with a complacency and an expectancy that made me mad. Sergeant Butler and I recrossed the bridge to join the convoy. Everybody except the antiaircraft gunners had taken to the hills. I picked out a little cave and sat down in the opening. From there I had an excellent view of the bridge and the huddled convoy. I would watch the fireworks and then start planning my defense; a court-martial board would be interested in hearing why the convoy was bunched. The defense would sound thin to anybody except a photographer.

Sergeant Butler and I looked down on the Hwei Tung Bridge, and wondered whether the Japs would try to blast it, or use all their ammunition on the convoy. In their last two attempts to knock out the bridge, their bombers had missed.

The original Hwei Tung Bridge, built long before the Burma Road, was constructed by a wealthy Paoshan silver miner who wanted a shortcut between his work and his home. Since then, Americans, Chinese, and Japanese had sent many Hwei Tung bridges toppling into the swift Salween.

After what seemed like hours, but was really only thirty minutes, an all-clear sounded. My heart returned to my body and began to pound with joy. Why the Japanese hadn't struck, I didn't know and didn't much care. Tokyo Rose, in her broadcast that night, reported that Japanese planes had destroyed a good number of our trucks in the Salween gorge. I was so happy that the report was false, I could have kissed that girl for her lies—we still had all of our men and all of our vehicles!

Late in the afternoon we stirred up dust in front of the walled city of Paoshan. I asked a Chinese officer the age of the walls; he said about three thousand years. As I stood within their shadow, I found it unbelievable that they were considered ancient long before Marco Polo passed through the massive town gate.

At the gate, a military band met us, along with cheering children, exploding firecrackers, and an array of posters: "Welcome Commander Pick and His Gallant Men"; "Welcome to the Heroes Who First Broke the Blockade." We appreciated the to-do made over us, but felt a little sheepish about it.

During a speech of welcome, we learned that the Chinese officials would honor us that night at a banquet in the Temple of Confucius. Several correspondents and I decided to skip it and get to bed early. We knew we would sleep well, even though our mattresses were on a concrete floor in a warehouse.

Newsreel Wong, China's greatest cameraman, said that he knew of a good restaurant in Paoshan. Newsreel was probably familiar with the restaurant situation in every town in China. He had been covering that country for years. Until AP's Joe Rosenthal shot the flag-raising at Iwo-Jima, Newsreel had the most published picture of the war: the closeup of a lone, howling Chinese baby surrounded by the rubble of the Shanghai railroad station.

The restaurant was located on the second floor, above some dingy shops. Newsreel and a waiter got into what sounded like a vicious argument, but it was probably a friendly conversation. Things soon began to happen. Dish after dish after dish was set before us. There must have been nearly twenty courses in all.

Since the correspondents insisted that I use chopsticks, I was able to fumble only a taste from each dish before it was whisked away. I was still hungry when the bill was presented—for 9,980 dollars. Chinese dollars, fortunately. The rate of exchange was 350 to one in Paoshan at the time. In Kunming it was five hundred to one. The rate fluctuated wildly all along the road. Newsreel Wong kept us posted on the best place to exchange our Indian rupees for Chinese currency.

As we were leaving the restaurant, several Chinese policemen stopped us. They demanded, in a nice enough way, that we go to the banquet. Newsreel suggested that we take their advice. I sometimes wondered if they would have put any pressure on us, had we insisted on carrying out our original plans.

Our host at the banquet in the Temple of Confucius was Marshal Wei Li-haung, commander of the Chinese Expeditionary Force. At each of the twenty-five tables sat a Chinese general, acting as personal host to half a dozen Americans.

The Chinese waste more food at a feast than they eat. A dish is placed on the table; everyone digs in with chopsticks and hardly samples it before it is whisked away and another dish is brought on. The waiters seemed overly adept at whisking things away; they probably reasoned that the sooner the plates were taken up, the more food would remain on them, and the more food that remained, the more there was to smuggle out the back door. Most of the food was so well camouflaged that it was hard to recognize it. But the roast duck was easily recognizable because the head was still on the bird. The glassy eyes, with their cold stare, were hypnotic. Also recognizable were orange soup, chopped ham, sweet-and-sour pork, pastries, and the inevitable rice. And the inevitable rice wine.

GIs stationed in China named rice wine *"jingbao* juice." *Jingbao* means "air raid." A thimbleful of rice wine is terribly potent. *Gombay*, the Chinese expression for "bottoms up," came with frightening regularity. It all started with a Chinese general pointing to a large picture of Roosevelt and making the point that it was the President's birthday. Of course, everyone shouted, *"Gombay!"* Next a general pointed to a large picture of Chiang Kai-shek, and the cry of *"Gombay!"* rolled through the temple. Another general pointed to a picture of Churchill, and again the bottoms went up. The Americans looked around for a picture of Stalin, but there wasn't one. In those days, Americans were still supposed to love Bloody Joe. The Chinese Nationalists had already had more than their share of troubles with their own Communists. They loved to *gombay*, but they didn't love it well enough to toast Stalin.

*Gombay*s and the conversation soon became general. I realized, after the first bottoms-up, which shook me to the soles of my feet, that I needed to fake. The liquid, with the taste of wood alcohol, was burned as fuel in the Chinese trucks on the Burma Road. Smelling the fumes of that stuff coming from exhaust pipes all day, and then trying to drink it at night, was too much for me. My olfactory ducts and stomach revolted. So I clenched my teeth, faked swallowing, and poured the rice wine onto the stone floor under the table.

Word had gone around among the GI truckdrivers that it was an insult to the Chinese if you did not drink with them glass for glass. The drivers were suddenly instilled with the desire not to injure the feelings of their allies. So they *gombay*ed and *gombay*ed. And they fell flat on their faces.

Many of the drivers missed the entertainment that followed the banquet. The best of local talent—singers, dancers, and acrobats—performed for our amusement and amazement. There was one comedy act in which a local wit applied makeup to himself until he resembled Hitler, in an Oriental way. He launched into a tirade in Chinese with what was supposed to be a thick German accent. The Chinese interpreter laughed so hard he could scarcely tell us what was being said. When he did regain enough control over himself to do some interpreting, we realized that what was funny to an Oriental might fall flat for a Westerner.

Nauseated truckdrivers with bloodshot eyes and trembling hands wheeled the convoy across 150 miles of rice paddies and mountain the next day. Well after dark, the trucks halted in an open field, far from water, far from a windbreak, and far from *jingbao* juice.

General Pick held his breath that day. He saw the irony of saving his convoy from the Japanese only to lose it because of *gombay*-loving drivers. In the evening he told me to get well ahead of the convoy on the following day to discourage any celebrations. He feared that another *jingbao* juice affair would be waiting for us at Yunnani the next night.

He was right. I tried to sabotage the plans for that celebration, but trying to deter Chinese who are bent upon celebrating is like trying to beat out a forest fire with a wet broom. The Chinese of Yunnani and the American Air Force officers stationed there were not to be talked out of their party. When I told General Pick about my inability as a killjoy, he made a diplomatic decision that would keep the Chinese happy and the truckdrivers sober. He ordered the convoy to go twenty miles beyond Yunnani to bivouac on a high, windy hill, far from water. Correspondents and officers who could be trusted to enter the same room with *jingbao* juice were asked to return to Yunnani for the banquet. Everyone else went to bed early.

The affair was a repeat performance of the one in Paoshan, except that the speeches were longer and the room was colder. Each time a course was placed before us, a general stood up to give a speech, and by the time he finished, the grease had congealed.

The next night we spent on another windswept hill, far from water and far from beckoning Bacchus. Just as I was shaking billows of dust from my blankets and spreading them on the ground for the night, a liaison plane flew over and dropped a message. A few minutes later, General Pick called me to his jeep, where he handed me the message and asked, "What do you make of this?"

It was a request for General Pick to fly to Chungking, following the celebration in Kunming, to appear on a three-minute newscast to the United States. I felt foolish, merely repeating the text of the message, but that was the best I could do.

General Pick eyed me as though he believed I had allied myself with the correspondents in a deep plot against him.

"Where's Captain Farr?" he asked.

I didn't know the answer to that either, but promised to find out.

Finis Farr, who had written the script for "Mr. District Attorney" for eighty weeks before entering the service, was the senior partner of a radio team that included Lieutenant Bert Parks, network announcer. The team recorded a documentary each week for a Sunday-night radio show in the States called "Yanks in the Orient."

I found Farr trying to start a Coleman stove while Parks opened several cans from a ten-in-one ration. I briefed him en route back to the general's jeep.

Pick, in the meantime, had covered most of his sanguine face with a frothy coat of shaving soap. The lather plus his red nose, red ears, and tousled gray hair made him a reasonable facsimile of Saint Nicholas.

It was one of the few times I saw the general without his pilgrim's staff, a tall, crooked cane. The staff had long caused black troops up and down the Ledo Road to exclaim, "Here come Pick, the man with the stick!"

The general handed Farr the message and asked, "What do you make of this?"

While Farr stalled for time to think up an intelligent answer, Pick turned to the rearview mirror that jutted from the windshield of his jeep. He began to scrape at his whiskers, which gave way with the crackling sound of a dry brushfire. Farr, although he had developed his imagination writing detective yarns, could not think of a more intelligent answer than mine. He too simply repeated the text of the message.

Pick turned on Farr with suspicion in his pale blue eyes. The whole thing didn't make sense and was getting embarrassing. Then he began to give us reasons why he would not be a part of the broadcast. He repeated the words "three minutes" so often that I judged he resented being asked to speak for such a short time.

As he finished shaving and turned to a plate of stew that someone had prepared for him, he gave us a lecture on the historical importance of the convoy. The lecture was unnecessary, because at that time all of us had exaggerated ideas of the Ledo Road's importance. And since the project was Pick's baby, he was naturally a little more warped on the subject than were the rest of us.

I often wondered how the old fellow felt when, a few months later, politicians and some military men in Washington began to wonder whether the road was really worthwhile. Such doubts were prompted by *Time*'s description of the project as "the million-dollar-a-mile road." Pick rushed the theater public-relations officer to the States to prepare a defense for his baby. I supposed all was forgiven and forgotten with the end of the war.

Pick closed his lecture to Farr and me with a gruff order: "Get ready to go on into Kunming tomorrow to see if you can help with any arrangements. We'll bivouac a few miles from the town tomorrow night, and come in for the parade Sunday."

We left General Pick sitting atop a jeep fender with a plate of stew in his lap. That picture often popped into my mind during the next few months whenever anyone said, "I hear Pick flew to Kunming and left the rest of you fellows to go the hard way." Even back in the United States, I was to hear the same unfair rumor. Whenever I said, "General Pick went every mile with the convoy. He roughed it as much as anybody," my informant would look at me as though doubting that I had made the trip. Gossips resent losing their favorite cynical anecdotes.

The next day in Kunming I bumped into another rumor that strengthened my theory that very little information reaches us that is not false or distorted. The rumor had its roots in the fact that Farr, Parks, and I stopped on the outskirts of Kunming to give a lift to two American officers who were evidently having jeep trouble. Two Chinese girls climbed out of the back of the jeep and also boarded our weapons carrier. We drove them into the city. By night the rumor was around Kunming that the first truck of the convoy had arrived and that the Americans had adopted the system of carrying "comfort girls" with them, a system that had official sanction in the Japanese army. The rumor kept making the rounds for a long time.

FIVE

T here was no need for Finis Farr, Bert Parks, and me to arrive early. All plans for the official welcome had been taken care of. Each time the word went around that Generalissimo Chiang Kai-shek had declared a national holiday in honor of the convoy, more flags went up.

We were pleased, though, that General Pick had sent us into Kunming ahead of the convoy, because that night rain came down in torrents.

The next morning we watched dozens of carpenters put the finishing touches to a large stage at the terminus of the Burma Road. Nearby, an arch festooned with colored streamers spanned the road; at about neck height, a white ribbon stretched from post to post on the arch.

The lead jeep carrying General Pick stopped at the arch, where the general snipped the ribbon, the last of a long series, and mounted the stage to join the array of brass. Those of us with the convoy crowded around, and humanity filled all available streets, balconies, and rooftops as far as we could see.

Pick made the last of his many booming speeches. Like all of the rest of them it began, "I have a convoy. . . ."

A Chinese general announced that the Generalissimo wished the Ledo-Burma road to be known as the Stilwell Road, a belated honor for the man the "G-mo" had demanded be kicked out of the CBI. When Stilwell heard the news, he declined the honor, but the name stuck. As far as Pick was concerned, that choice of names must have cast a shadow across the day of jubilation. All the way along the road, the truck following the general's jeep had attracted attention because the canvas cover bore the words THE FIRST CONVOY ACROSS PICK'S PIKE. Even the correspondents who were Stilwell fans felt that the road should have been named after Pick.

While American and Chinese generals stood on the stage at the terminus of the Ledo-Burma Road and talked on and on, Lily Pons, the opera star, and her husband, Andre Kostelanetz, the orchestra director, who were on a USO tour of the Orient, stood there and beamed approval.

With speeches finished, the convoy troops mounted their jeeps, trucks, and weapons carriers for the last time to begin a parade through Kunming's main thoroughfare. The over-crowded and filthy city was the new home of a million refugees from Japanese-held eastern China. It seemed that every one of the million crowded the sidewalks and rooftops to welcome us.

Bands played; school children waved pennants; merchants gave the thumbs-up gesture and shouted, *"Ting hao,"* meaning "You're the best." American missionary nuns waved so hard their wimples went askew. Firecracker-men beamed through the din and smoke, thrusting out poles ten feet long, with thousands of sputtering firecrackers coiled about them. This is the highest form of welcome China can give, similar to New York's ticker-tape parade, but having firecrackers pop in one's face is not a Westerner's idea of welcome.

Across town we turned over the vehicles to Ordnance and returned to the press hostel to get ready for the governor's party. We washed our faces and combed our hair, but had to wear greasy field jackets, dusty ODs, and clumsy combat boots be-cause those were all we had. Almost all major American in-stallations in China were located in Kunming; many of our countrymen came to the party dressed in their well-pressed best, but that night the sloppy, soiled appearance was the smart thing, the mark of the honored guest.

As we entered the garden, a Chinese girl pinned a flower on each of us; the color of the flower determined the section of the garden in which we would dine. There sat my driver, Sergeant Butler, observing all with watchful eyes. I asked what he would be doing next, and he said that tomorrow he would fly the Hump back to India and from there go by ship to the States, having put in more than enough time.

Our host, Lung Yun, governor of Yunnan Province, welcomed each of us. The solemn little man, scarcely five feet tall, wore a brown military uniform; his military cap with its oversized visor gave him the top-heavy silhouette of a mushroom. Although his name meant "Dragon Cloud," he had the features of a ferret, and movements to match. Stilwell once described him as a "comical little duck."

His loyalty to the central government was even then under suspicion; it was being whispered that he was pro-Japanese. Suspicions must have continued to accumulate, because within less than a year of our meeting, Chiang Kai-shek deposed the little warlord.

That may have been the most fortunate thing that ever happened to Lung Yun; maybe it saved him from assassination. His own officers were turning against him. One day while he and his wife were taking a walk on the outskirts of Kunming, someone took a shot at him; the little governor and his lady jumped into an Army truck and fortunately found a machine gun on the floor, with which Lung sprayed the rebellious soldiers until they retreated.

The governor's popularity declined as the hardships of war grew more acute. He got the blame for the extremely high cost of rice, a topic that had first priority in every conversation, and people wondered whether Lung Yun was contributing to the war fund or stuffing his own pockets.

With the trip and the celebration behind us everyone felt let down the next day. Ian Fitchet, of the *London Daily Express*, and I decided to go to bed early. Just as we were congratulating each other on our intelligence, Captain Farr entered the vast dormitory, bearing a bottle of rum. Soon Fitchet was sitting up in bed, waving a canteen cup full of rum and reciting, "I met evil on the way; he wore the mask of Castlereagh."

Farr was reciting gems of American verse when Parks came in, unlimbered a typewriter, and began pounding the mechanism out of it. Manohar M. Nerurkar, an Indian correspondent, entered, sat cross-legged on a bed to read from a thick black book that resembled a Catholic priest's breviary, and now and then grunted over a passage.

An excited Chinese correspondent, Eddie Tjung, burst through the door holding aloft a diamond ring. He had just broken his engagement with his fiancée. The breakup came when the girl refused to go out to dinner with him in the company of two American war correspondents. I tried to reason with him. "The girl hasn't seen you in several months. She has a right to expect to spend an evening alone with you. I don't blame her for not wanting a couple of newspapermen trailing along."

"That's not the reason," said Eddie. "She will not go out with me because they are foreigners. She is anti-foreign. I told her that I have too many good American friends to throw them all over for her. If we can't see eye-to-eye on this, we might as well quit."

For the first time in my life I realized I was in a country where I was considered an inferior. I told the anecdote to Martha Sawyers, the *Collier's* artist, and her artist husband, Bill Reusswig, several months later in Burma; they said they had noticed that attitude in Chinese communities in the United States.

Brigadier Shelford Bidwell, the British historian, wrote in *The Chindit War:* "Contempt for 'foreigners' is a Chinese national trait, and the Chinese officers had a full measure of both national and military arrogance which made it impossible for them to accept that the Americans knew better than they did."

When our room was filled with smoke and the smell of rum, Fitchet began punctuating the din with, "Who in hell ever said this room was a clubhouse!"

Kunming was the home of many American characters who came around to the press hostel for long hours of conversation. I spent one morning with a sergeant from the Sino-American Horse Purchasing Bureau, a lieutenant who had flown with the

Doolittle raid on Tokyo, and a colonel who had fought with Chennault's Flying Tigers.

In some ways the sergeant had the hardest job. For one thing, nobody knew about him, no correspondents publicized him, and nobody thought of him as glamorous. He would go up into the far northern mountains to buy horses from the Tibetans and from the Chinese Lolo tribesmen. In telling about it, he stressed the feasting and the drinking in a way that reminded me of the truckdrivers in Paoshan, who kept saying, "You gotta drink with 'em, Lieutenant, or else they lose face!" The sergeant assured me that unless he drank the potent stuff and ate unattractive food, the horse sellers would not even talk to him.

After completing a deal, he and several other Americans from our western states began their six-week journey down mountains covered with ice and deep in snow. Handling wild, unbroken ponies under such conditions could be harrowing. The shaggy, ill-tempered little beasts were kicking and biting all the way. I told the sergeant it reminded me of the refrain of a song the muleskinners sang at Fort Riley:

> *Wild and wooly and full of fleas*
> *And never been curried below the knees*

In Kunming the Americans would turn over the animals to the Chinese army and, after a few days of rest, would return to the wild country, starting once more that strange journey.

The sergeant was pleased to hear that I had come to the CBI to run mule trains through Burma. He said, "Wingate was right, American-bred mules are better than these damn ponies." He was referring to Orde Wingate, the British commander of the Chindits, whose story I would soon be learning in some detail.

The sergeant continued, "Wingate believe that mules are even better in the jungle than bullocks; they more faster. He held only one thing against them; as he said, 'Mule meat is not too savory if you are forced to eat it.' But when the Japs had them Chindits on the run, they ate it!"

The lieutenant who had flown with Doolittle said that he would never forget April 18, 1942. On that day, sixteen B-25s flew to Japan from the carrier *Hornet*, 650 miles out at sea. At noon the bombers came in at treetop level, then pulled up to 1,500 feet to release their bombs and fly on to China.

One airman was killed in a crash, four drowned, and of the eight captured, three were executed, one died of malnutrition, and four lived on as prisoners of war.

The seventy-one survivors were decorated by Madame Chiang Kai-shek in Chungking. That ceremony and everything about General Doolittle's raid got plenty of publicity. That daring raid and the exploits of General Chennault's Flying Tigers were among the few bright news stories during the dreary months immediately following Pearl Harbor.

Until Kunming I had met mostly ground troops who admired Stilwell, but now, coming to know those who fought in the air, I learned that they did not all hold Vinegar Joe in high regard.

A colonel who had fought with the Flying Tigers repeated several times, "We were over here even before Stilwell." After all, the colonel was one of Chennault's boys.

When Stilwell arrived in Burma, early in 1942, the Flying Tigers were doing well in the air, but much was going wrong on the ground beneath them. The Chinese had two armies, seven divisions in all, up north near the China-Burma border; eventually one division went down to the battle line, four hundred miles to the south. There the British were confronting the Japanese with two divisions and a brigade of tanks. Between Rangoon and Mandalay, the Japanese were just too much for them.

Sitting there in the press hostel in Kunming, the colonel recalled the early 1930s, when Chennault and two other pilots worked together in an act called Three Men on a Flying Trapeze. Their breathtaking precision flying did not impress the generals who believed that the bomber was the future of air power. Chennault admitted that the dogfight was a thing of the past, but insisted that fighters working as a team could be effective. He recalled the success of the Flying Circus, led by Baron Manfred Von Richthofen, the German ace in the Great War. Chennault's argument carried such little weight that in 1936 the Army Air Corps' program in fighter tactics was dropped.

Partly out of annoyance and partly because of ill health, Chennault retired from the service in 1936. A restless soul, he was much pleased at being invited to serve as an adviser to the government of China.

Upon arriving in China, in May of 1937, he found that the Chinese air force needed advice galore. For one thing, of the five hundred planes listed, only about ninety were fit to fly. Chennault urged Chiang Kai-shek to buy more planes, and Chiang asked the cities to raise funds. During a fund-raising rally, a plane would land and the city's name would be painted on it. Later the name was painted out so that the same plane might land at another rally to be christened with that city's name.

Chinese pilots, Chennault found, were an even greater problem than the shortage of planes. As the sons of wealthy families, they could not be washed out of a training program; if they were, they would lose face. Because of pilot ineptitude, the airfields of China were littered with the wreckage of bad takeoffs and landings.

To get the fighter planes they needed, Chennault bought one hundred P-40 Tomahawks that the British had rejected, saying their pilots found them too clumsy to use against the Germans.

Chennault longed for American pilots. Since he and Madame Chiang Kai-shek were close friends, he urged her to see what she might do about getting permission for Americans to volunteer. Her brother, T. V. Soong, China's chief lobbyist in the United States, pulled enough strings to get President Roosevelt's permission for Chennault to hire Americans for China's air force. All of this had to be hidden beneath some sort of cover, because the United States was not yet at war. So when 112 pilots resigned from the Army, Navy, and Marine Corps, they came to China under the guise of workers for an aircraft maintenance company. Chennault was pleased to observe that they were more interested in a chance to fly combat missions than in their pay, which ranged from $600 to $750 a month, with a $500 bonus for each enemy plane destroyed.

Chennault studied the strengths and weaknesses of the P-40s and developed tactics especially for them. He knew the Tomahawk was clumsy compared with the Japanese Zero. At a blackboard, diagramming tactics that showed his pilots how to fight in pairs, he would say, "In a P-40, never, never, try to outmaneuver and perform acrobatics with a Jap Zero. Use your speed and diving power to make a pass. Shoot and break away."

The volunteers soon became known as the Flying Tigers. They flew their first mission on December 20, 1941, two weeks after Pearl Harbor, intercepting ten twin-engined Mitsubishi bombers that had bombed the terminus of the Burma road hundreds of times without opposition. Now fourteen fighter planes, with noses painted to resemble grinning sharks, bore down on them. The Japanese jettisoned their bombs and turned back toward their home field in Hanoi, but only one reached the airstrip. All of the Flying Tigers returned to Kunming.

On February 25, 1942, nine Flying Tigers took on 166 Japanese planes that were en route to bomb and strafe Rangoon. In shooting down twenty-four enemy planes, the Tigers lost three. The next day the Japanese lost eighteen of two hundred planes while raiding Rangoon; all six of the Tigers returned safely. That night an artist worked late, painting miniature Japanese flags beneath the canopies of the P-40s. Back toward the tail on some planes there was a Bengal tiger with wings, designed by a Disney artist.

To make the Japanese think the Tigers had more planes than they really possessed, the artist kept changing the numbers on the fuselages and repainting the noses of the planes with different colors. Pilots kept changing their voices over the radio giving orders to imaginary squadrons hoping to strike fear into the Japanese.

Airfields were widely scattered throughout China, and so the three squadrons—Hell's Angels, Panda Bears, and Adam and Eves—were much on their own. Chennault wanted it that way; he was developing aerial guerrilla warfare.

After the fall of Rangoon, on March 7, 1942, Chennault pulled his planes back into China to protect the convoys on the Burma Road. When the road also fell to the Japanese, the Tigers provided air protection to the cities of western China.

The Flying Tigers were credited with having destroyed some three hundred planes by the time they—the American Volunteer Group—were inducted, July 4, 1942, into the Army Air Forces unit called the China Air Task Force. They provided the nucleus for the Task Force's 23rd Fighter Group, which became part of the U.S. 14th Air Force in March of 1943. By the end of the war the old Tiger pilots were credited with 1,200 enemy planes and seven hundred probables.

Although the Flying Tigers existed as a unit for only seven months—December of 1941 until July of 1942—they provided Americans with something much needed in those dark days: something to brag about. The press, burdened with dark news from Europe, the Philippines, and Burma, made sure the public saw the American volunteers as larger than life.

Although the Tigers never had more than fifty-five planes in operation on any one day, their victories over the Japanese were impressive even while the results on the ground were dreary. In a way, this was unfortunate for Stilwell; it made Chiang believe in Chennault's arguments that air power could defeat Japan. Stilwell argued that the main job had to be done by foot soldiers. Chiang loved Chennault's idea: Fight the war with planes and let the ground soldiers rest, saving themselves for the fight against the Chinese Reds.

Sitting there in the press hostel in Kunming, I told the colonel who had fought with the Flying Tigers that I had seen General Chennault at one of our speechmaking celebrations along the Burma Road. The colonel observed that even though Chennault's face looked as though it were chopped out of granite with a dull hatchet, he had enough charm and diplomacy to soften his blows. Stilwell, he said, had just as much toughness but lacked the diplomacy, and he concluded, "That's why he's gone and Chennault's still here."

The colonel stepped into a beat-up jeep that would take him to 14th Air Force Headquarters. From the side yard next to the press hostel, he eased into a swollen river of humanity that was like every street in Kunming. He did not know, of course, that within a few months Generals Marshall and Arnold would push Chennault into retirement.

Driving a jeep through downtown Kunming was a drunkard's dream. The streets seethed with rickshaws, pony pack trains, water buffalo carts, coolies toting buckets of human excrement on the ends of poles, incompetent Chinese drivers, wild GI drivers, and irresponsible pedestrians. Ponies kept falling beneath their too-heavy burdens and were beaten and hauled to their feet. Chinese and GI drivers roared through the undulating tide of humanity to the blast of impatient horns. Pedestrians, when moving from the edge of the street to the center, didn't look around to see if anything was coming.

If there was one thing worse than driving a jeep in Kunming, it was riding a rickshaw through the town. A coolie gave me thrills as he dogtrotted down the main thoroughfare. Without looking back, he dashed out in front of Army trucks with abandon. The danger doubled my discomfort. Even under better circumstances, I always felt like a heel while riding in a rickshaw; it was using a human being as a beast of burden.

Before climbing into the wayward rickshaw in Kunming, I asked the coolie the price of the trip; we were warned never to hire any transportation in the Far East without settling the cost in advance. The coolie said two hundred Chinese dollars. At the end of the trip I gave him three hundred. He whined. I gave him another hundred, double the asking price, but he still whined. It is part of the game.

One day while writing a letter in the Red Cross club, I saw a Chinese coolie, a sweeper, looking at pictures in *Life*. Suddenly he began to chuckle, then laugh, then roar. His glee was unbounded. Curious to see what he considered so funny, I slipped around behind him and glanced over his shoulder. He was looking at a four-color ad that showed a battered, blood-smeared American soldier with an arm or a leg blown off. It was one of those "He gave—did you?"

This was mild compared with some anecdotes Americans told about Chinese humor. An American officer witnessed a shocking display of Chinese horseplay while flying the Hump. As a C-47 droned above the Himalayas, carrying a cargo of troops from China to India, one nosy soldier stuck his head out of the open door to get a good look at the scenery below. One of his fellow soldiers slipped up from behind and shoved him from the plane. As the victim plunged toward the jagged mountaintops without benefit of a parachute, the remaining soldiers burst into gales of laughter.

A captain friend of mine told me of a similar incident he had experienced during his first days in Burma. While bouncing along the Ledo Road in a jeep, he spied several Chinese soldiers looking down a stone well and laughing at what they saw inside. Out of curiosity he stopped the jeep to have a look. A Chinese soldier in the well was trying without success to climb out. The captain returned to the jeep and got a chain. When he started to let down the chain, the soldiers poked the muzzles of their rifles into his ribs and forced him back into the jeep. As he drove away he heard a grenade explode in the well. It was not so much the explosion as the laughter that followed that made him shudder.

An officer had warned us of this incomprehensible sense of humor during the first lecture we attended in Ledo. He had been a liaison officer with the Chinese Army for two years. On several occasions he heard Chinese roar with glee when one of their fellow *bings* (soldiers) had his head blown off by an enemy shell.

Parks, Farr, and I could have taken a leave of absence in Kunming, but we so disliked that chaotic city that we were eager to return to Burma. Of all places, Burma! We decided to hitch a flight westward to Chabua, in India, and then hitch another eastward to Myitkyina, in Burma.

At the Kunming airport a sergeant said, "No flights today. Too much weather. Takes a lot of weather to ground us. As they say around here, 'It's so bad right now that not even the birds are flying.' "

Bad weather was the norm for flights across the Himalayas. One night, for example, thirty-one planes circled the field in Chabua with a fog fifteen feet deep clinging to the ground. An old hand, Capt. Hugh Wild, talked down nineteen, but seven crashed and five crews bailed out when their planes ran out of gas.

The Hump flights covered five hundred miles from China to India, across the Shantsung Range, which rises to fifteen thousand feet. The greatest enemies in that remote vastness were not the Japanese, but freak winds, monsoon torrents, and wild turbulences that flipped over planes and caused them to drop three thousand feet in a minute.

Farr and Parks had done a radio documentary about the Hump, and so they spoke of it with some authority. They expressed the hope that we would not draw a C-46; so many of those had crashed on the Hump that pilots called a certain stretch of rough country "the aluminum trail." Everybody standing around in a small room cloudy with cigarette smoke in Kunming airport agreed that the most serious defect of the C-46 was that it was prone to fuel line breaks, which would spew gasoline over hot engines, causing mid-air explosions.

A young lieutenant, with his officer's cap crushed at both sides to give him the look of a Hump pilot, chain-smoked and listened with nervous intensity. He said he thought fatigue as much as bad weather caused accidents. It was not unusual for a crew to work sixteen-hour shifts, flying three round trips a day. The lieutenant said that a pilot needed 650 hours of Hump time to qualify for rotation home, and so, to hurry along the great day, some flew too many hours a month. A lot of the long hours also had to do with the need in the closing months of the war for more than six hundred planes to fly the Hump each day.

The sergeant who had told us we would not be flying that day said that he had worked on airplane maintenance for a year. Whenever they could reach a wreck, they would cannibalize it and bring back parts for further use. In India during the heat of summer, the sun made metal too hot to touch, and so the sergeant's maintenance work was carried on mainly from sundown to sunrise. He spoke of how helpful elephants were in loading planes; one elephant could do the work of eight Indian bearers.

The sergeant must also have worked on maintenance for the Flying Tigers. He told of how they used to put dummy planes on an airstrip to attract the attention of enemy bombers, while the real planes were being repaired under nearby trees. The ground crews even carried tommy guns to fire at low-flying Japanese planes.

Whenever they were interviewed, the Flying Tigers always praised their mechanics. Those ground crews worked around the clock. The planes went into combat as many as eight times a day, and were usually outnumbered by the Japanese eight to one.

I pointed to a stack of cartons that held some engine parts manufactured in upstate New York. I estimated that they had crossed the States two thousand miles by train, then had gone twelve thousand miles by sea, then fifteen hundred miles by rail across India—shifted often because of four different railroad gauges—and finally five hundred miles over the Hump to China.

"Yeah," said the tense young lieutenant, "now that you guys have opened the road, those things will have to travel more than a thousand miles by truck across the Ledo-Burma Road."

I asked when the Hump flight had begun, and Farr, having written a script on the subject, said it was in April of 1942. The Japanese, racing northward, had taken the Burma Road, cutting the supply line to China. Flights across the mountains then carried supplies from India to China. The eighty tons a month that the planes carried at first grew, in a year, to four thousand a month, but this was still far too little.

The trickle of supplies was one of the things that caused disputes between Chiang Kai-shek, Chennault, and Stilwell, disputes I would hear a great deal about in months to come. Chiang wanted supplies to save for his conflict with Mao after the big war had ended; Chennault wanted most of the supplies for his air war against the Japanese; Stilwell needed them if he hoped to train and equip Chinese armies so that they might fight westward from China into Burma to reopen the land route through China's back door. (The Air Transport Command got 650,000 tons of cargo across the Hump during the war. The distribution was always a matter of dispute.)

When Farr and Parks and I returned to Kunming airport the next day, the sergeant said, "We have to fly tonight. We ought not. Bad weather. But we have to. You want to go?"

Our dislike for overcrowded Kunming was evident when we agreed to fly that night.

Farr recalled that the Japanese began attacking Hump flights on October 14, 1943; they shot down four planes that day. Night flights became more popular, and sometimes P-40s were escorts.

I said that having less-than-benign weather over the Hump had advantages: Japanese fighter pilots wouldn't go hunting in bad weather. Parks and Farr accused me of being a Pollyanna.

The sergeant gave us parachutes and instructed us on what to do in the event we had to bail out. He listed the medical supplies and the food we carried with us. After a jump, we were to rally around the pilot and he would be in command of the party.

The three of us climbed into a C-54, a four-engine transport, and picked our way through motors that were being flown back to India for repairs. As we settled into bucket seats, I said, "I like to look out the window and see four motors."

Farr said, "When I look out the window, all I see is one wing."

A little, yellow-haired flight officer climbed into the plane; he had the look of a cheerleader at a high-school basketball game. When we realized that this kid was to be our pilot, we lost some of the desire to shake the dust of Kunming from our GI boots. His greeting—"This weather is strictly *bu hao!*"—didn't help any. A final dramatic touch came when we began to taxi down the runway, and sleet started to tap at the windows.

We did not get a very good look at the Hump, a wartime graveyard of about six hundred planes. Storms forced us up to nineteen thousand feet.

The heating system in the plane went on the blink, and the temperature at that altitude above the Himalayas must have been well below zero. The air got thin at about 10,000 feet, and sometimes the temperature dropped to minus forty degrees Fahrenheit. We were not dressed for it. The short hoses on the oxygen masks did not permit us to stir about to increase blood circulation. We thought we would freeze to death on that three-hour trip.

The boyish pilot decided to drop us off at Myitkyina to save us the bother of flying back from India. He stopped just long enough for us to get off, and then left for Chabua or Dinjan or some other landing field across the border. A sergeant at the airstrip, with the dramatic gestures of a Barrymore, cried out, "Everybody's gone! Gone to Bhamo!"

In late January, Northern Combat Area Command and the Tenth Air Force had moved to Bhamo, a hundred miles down the Ledo Road. The forward headquarters of Detachment 101 of the OSS had moved to a Shan village five miles south of Bhamo.

We slept at the airstrip that night, and early the next morning boarded the theater commander's plane, called Sultan's Magic Carpet, for the short hop to Bhamo. Its furnishings were swanky: leather chairs, wine-colored rug, blue-quilted walls, blue curtains. Surely it was not so fancy when Stilwell used it!

The first time General Stilwell flew in Gen. Lewis Brereton's personal C-53 in India, he stared at the luxurious interior and, according to Gen. Frank Dorn, "His lips tightened with disapproval as he looked around the pastel-tinted cabin, at the upholstered chairs and specially made desk. But when his eyes dropped to the fine Persian carpet, cut and patched to fit the narrow compartment, he blew through his lips and threw his campaign hat on the floor."

Forty-two letters awaited me in Bhamo. One of them, from my sister, said, "I read in the paper that the Ledo-Burma Road is about to open. Maybe you will have something to do with it."

SIX

Why the intelligence officer instead of the personnel officer gave me my next assignment, I never knew. Everything was done in such an offbeat way in Burma; as the supply sergeant said, it was "a chancy war."

Anyway, when Col. Joseph Stilwell, Jr., heard that I had once taught in a college and had written field manuals at the Infantry School at Fort Benning, he assigned me to write the history of Northern Combat Area Command, explaining that before long the War Department would be expecting to receive such. I wondered, but did not ask, if the colonel knew I had come to Burma as a muleskinner.

"Where do you want to go to write?" he asked.

"Someplace where nobody will bother me," I answered, meaning a tent for myself amid the rubble of Bhamo.

The colonel sent me to a deserted Buddhist monastery on the banks of the Irrawaddy. The monks had fled during the month-long battle that destroyed Bhamo. All that was left of the monastery was a two-story teak framework, and a courtyard lined with great statues of the Buddha. Army engineers had

wrapped yards of burlap around the framework and capped it
with some corrugated metal.

I began my new assignment by reading bales of situation
reports, studying maps, interviewing people, and, in time,
traveling. Piece by piece, large chunks of combat history began
fitting together like pieces of a jigsaw puzzle. Soon I was writing
one of the strangest stories that the United States Army had to
tell, a story about Americans, Chinese, British, Kachins,
Karens, Nagas, Shans, Gurkhas, and Indians.

It told of heroism, petty jealousies, bungling, and clashes with
a ruthless enemy. And the accomplishment of the "impossible."
Ordinary people were doing extraordinary things. The boy who
had left his plow in Missouri and the young man who had
drydocked a fishing sloop in Maine found themselves in a land
they had never heard of, or that, at best, had been just a liver-
colored splotch in a sixth-grade geography book. Those who had
been accustomed to pronouncing such names as Boise, Akron,
and Rochester found names like Shingbwiyang, Shaduzup, and
Myitkyina rolling from their tongues.

Nobody correctly guessed how to say *Myitkyina*. When a GI
asked Father Stuart how to pronounce it, the missionary said,
"In Ireland, when you play hooky from school, it is called
mitchin'. To that, add *awe*. *Mitchin-awe*, that's how you say it,
lad."

GIs quickly picked up such phrases as *hao bu hao*, "how are
you"; *ting hao*, "very good"; *bu hao*, "no good"; *baksheesh*, "gift";
and *gombay*, "bottoms up." The tribesmen augmented their own
vocabulary with "Hey, Joe," and "okay."

The changes that the Americans wrought among the natives
were noticeable and a little disheartening. Tribesmen whose
customs, dress, and ways of life were the same at the beginning
of the war as those followed by their ancestors the night that
Christ was born, soon began wearing olive drab caps, khaki
shirts, and GI shoes, and eating from cans.

Before the Americans cut the Ledo Road through northern
Burma, the tribesmen had a philosophy of *htonzan*, which meant
that they must follow the well-worn path of custom and live
exactly as their ancestors had lived. They were opposed to *s'taing
ga*, which meant "change" or "style." But *htonzan* slipped a few

notches and *s'taing ga* lost some of its stigma after the GIs arrived.

The land was almost as strange to the Chinese as it was to the Americans. Many a *bing* who had never been away from his Yunnan Province rice paddies or who had known only the crowded streets of Kunming was lost in the wilds of Burma.

The jungle was wild and beautiful, with a savage heart. Delicate orchids, flaming poinsettias, huge banyan and teak trees furnished a haven for such pests as buffalo flies, leeches, and mosquitoes. Death moved across the scenic hills in the guise of malaria, dysentery, and typhus.

Americans who had never seen wild animals except in the zoo or circus found themselves in the midst of some of the finest big-game country in the world. Their neighbors were elephants, tigers, black leopards, cobras, pythons, and monkeys.

Men who had never seen mangoes, lemons, and bananas grow were soon using those fruits to supplement their rations.

As they played out their roles on this strange stage, soldiers frequently asked each other, "Why are we fighting for Burma? Why should even the Japs want this damn country?"

The Japanese had a good reason for wanting the land of sprawling ranges and dark jungle topped by the towering mountain mass of central Asia known as the Himalayas, the Roof of the World. Seizing Burma would accomplish two purposes: first, the supply line to China from the west would be cut; second, that wedge of land between India and China could be used to invade India and to pry open the back door to China. The Japanese accomplished the first mission when they took the Burma Road; they were less successful in accomplishing the second.

In my early research, George Weller, a correspondent for the *Chicago Daily News,* was a great help. He dropped by the Buddhist monastery one morning and, hearing I was from Notre Dame, asked if I had ever read the *Review of Politics,* which had been started at the university shortly after my graduation in 1937. I had not yet seen a copy. Weller said, "It's a first-rate magazine, even if it did give my book a bad review."

I told him about being assigned to write the history of the Northern Combat Area Command, and wished I knew more of what had happened in Southeast Asia before NCAC existed. Weller pulled a beat-up map from his knapsack, spread it across the olive drab army blanket on the bunk, and started a lecture on how war had come to that remote part of the world.

He started with Chiang Kai-shek, explaining, "If you are writing about NCAC, you are writing about Stilwell; and if you are writing about him, you are also writing about Chiang. After all, why is Stilwell no longer among us?"

George Weller saw Chiang Kai-shek as an inflexible man of tremendous pride, so excessive in his unbending ways that he was doomed by what the ancient Greeks called *hubris*, the pride that precedes a fall.

Chiang, born in 1887 on a small farm in Chekiang Province, lost his father when he was nine. His mother, a strict woman, reared him in what he called "a miserable condition beyond description."

At age eighteen, the youth cut off his pigtail, a symbol of subservience, to dramatize his rebellion against the Manchu government. His mother's discipline, which he had considered a disadvantage, turned into an advantage when he went to Japan for military training. There he was inspired by a man who gave direction to his life, Dr. Sun Yat-sen, the Chinese Nationalist leader, who was in Japan raising funds to overthrow the Manchus.

At age twenty-four, Chiang returned home to organize a freewheeling rebellion, attracting enough attention to rise in the ranks of Dr. Sun's Nationalist Party, the Kuomintang. The party sent the young officer to study Soviet institutions in Lenin's Russia. He ended by hating Russia as much as he had hated Japan; he always hated foreign things, an attitude that caused friction when he worked closely with Americans.

When Dr. Sun Yat-sen died, in 1925, Chiang began to play the role, at age thirty-eight, of leader in a party that was soon eliminating rivals, mainly warlords and Communists.

In his rise to power, his wife, Soong Mei-ling, was most influential. The charming, vivacious girl brought with her the prestige of a famous family; her father had grown wealthy printing and selling Bibles. Her two sisters were wives of powerful men: H. H. Kung, a direct descendant of Confucius, and Dr.

Sun Yat-sen. Her brother, T. V. Soong, a wealthy financier, traveled the world telling foreign governments of China's needs.

The Japanese annexed Manchuria in 1931, giving warnings of things to come. In 1937, they started taking over China piece by piece—Peking, Tientsin, Shanghai, Nanking, Hankow. When they cut off supplies along the coast, they forced the Chinese to build the Burma Road. Supplies would arrive at Rangoon, move by rail and river to Lashio, and then cross the 681 miles to Kunming.

With the Japanese moving at ease in eastern China, stopped only by the vastness of the country, Chiang Kai-shek began moving his Nationalist government westward, to Nanking and Hankow, and, in the fall of 1938, up the Yangtze to Chungking. There, he and a million refugees were safe enough as long as a dense winter fog covered the city, but on May 4, 1939, Japanese bombers attacked Chungking, and within three years, three thousand tons of bombs fell on the city. In the early bombings, about five thousand victims died in each attack, but in time there were only about fifty victims per attack, for they learned to give early warnings and to build caves and tunnels for protection.

Since the old section of Chungking was built of bamboo, firestorms destroyed it again and again. After each destruction, the Chinese rebuilt with speed and patience. To rise again was an ancient habit with them, a theme in Chinese history from time out of mind.

Chiang ordered his armies to give way before the aggressive Japanese, saying he was trying to gain time, to get aid from the United States. Madame Chiang and her brother, T. V. Soong, and other Chinese lobbyists were more effective than was the military: they got nearly two billion dollars in Lend-Lease aid and various financial credits.

No matter how victorious the Japanese were, Chiang always seemed more concerned about the Chinese Communists. In 1925 a split had developed between Nationalists and Communists. This split, plus the uneasy relationship between Nationalists and warlords, had given Japan the courage to occupy Manchuria in 1931. At that time Chiang showed a tendency that he would exhibit time and again, one that would annoy Stilwell no end: Instead of attacking the invader, he felt he must first deal with the enemy within, especially the Communists in Kiangsi Province in southern China. He kept at them until in 1934 they retreated on the six-thousand-mile "Long March" to the remote mountains of Shanshi Province. Twenty divisions of Chiang's troops kept the Reds detained there in the northwest.

Members of Chiang's own party wanted him to form a united front with the Communists and drive out the Japanese. When he refused, his colleagues kidnapped him, holding him captive for thirteen days in 1936. When he was released, the Nationalists did form an alliance with the Reds, but it was too vague to amount to much.

All through World War II, the Generalissimo kept his best troops in the northwest to keep an eye on three million Communists who waited for peace to make their decisive move. Being deprived of the best troops annoyed Stilwell; he wanted to use them to help recapture Burma.

George Weller carried on his orientation lecture as we walked from the Buddhist monastery to the officers' mess, a hundred yards away. The hall, long and narrow, and crowded with long, narrow tables, was enclosed with brown burlap walls.

Weller said that he thought Stilwell had got involved with China in 1921, because he was attracted to the offbeat, and because life was dreary in Army camps and forts in the United States just after the Great War. During his first tour of duty he had studied the language in Peking and served as a construction engineer on a road the American Red Cross was building for famine relief in Shanshi province.

Stilwell came to know China at several levels. While living with peasants he developed some feel for Chinese psychology. While traveling with soldiers, in 1927, watching them fight a civil war, he learned the ways of the military. Later, during the early years of China's war with Japan, he served as military attaché to the American Embassy in Peking, where he came to know the Chinese of high rank.

He developed an undying respect for the Chinese people and clung to it even when they disappointed him during World War II. For instance, when his senior aide-de-camp, Frank Dorn, said, "I'd hate to have them as my enemy. They're so tenacious," the general agreed, "You're right. They've lasted as a nation for over four thousand years and, in one way or another, have licked all comers."

Stilwell was getting bored with peacetime assignments when suddenly the whole world changed on December 7, 1941. That Sunday morning, several officers and their wives had gathered at the Stilwell home in Carmel, California. As they ate sandwiches and drank coffee, 353 Japanese planes sank five American battleships and three destroyers at Pearl Harbor, and put out of action three other battleships and three cruisers, while disabling 150 of the 202 naval planes on the base and seeing to it that few of the 273 Army aircraft survived. More than two thousand men died that morning, and 946 suffered wounds of various degrees of graveness.

Stilwell's daughter was listening to a radio broadcast of popular music when an announcer broke in: "The Japanese are bombing Pearl Harbor!"

No American knew, that morning, that the man behind the attack had been opposed to going to war with the United States. When Grand Admiral Isoroku Yamamoto, commander-in-chief of the Japanese navy, had visited America, in 1910 and in 1925, he found Americans admirable and stood in awe of their industrial power.

Yamamoto became unpopular among Japan's military men because he persisted in repeating that Japan did not have a chance in a war with the United States. He wrote, "To start a war with America would be the worst disaster to befall Japan."

When he accepted the responsibility of getting crews ready for the 353 dive bombers and torpedo planes, he put them through intensive training, morning, noon, and night. By October they were ready, but he wrote, "I am determined to do my duty, which is completely opposite to my personal convictions." This must have been a bitter assignment for a man who, a year before, had nearly retired "to grow vegetables and take care of the chestnut trees."

When the pilots returned from their highly successful attack on Pearl Harbor, Yamamoto gave them scant praise. He said to high-ranking officers, "America is an enormous country. Train more pilots."

Everyone in the Stilwell garden, that morning of Pearl Harbor, knew all too well that the United States military was poorly prepared because Roosevelt had not been able to unite the country the way Yamamoto was to unite it through the attack on Pearl Harbor. Some of the officers were speaking of that very condition of unpreparedness when the dark news arrived. Stilwell later wrote in his diary that if the Japanese had landed "after our handful of ammunition was gone, they could have shot us like pigs in a pen."

Rumors kept the West Coast jittery. Whenever Japanese planes were reported in the sky over California, they turned out to be American planes; when the Japanese fleet was reported to be steaming toward Monterey from 150 miles out, the boats belonged to fishermen hurrying back to California.

Stilwell, as commander of the Third Army Corps, which consisted of the Seventh Division, the 40th Division, and Corps Troops, had his headquarters four miles from Carmel, at the Presidio of Monterey. He was responsible for the defense of the coast from San Luis Obispo to San Diego.

Winifred Stilwell, on the day of Pearl Harbor, must have looked at her husband and wondered what role he would play in the war. Although he was nearing his fifty-ninth birthday, he seemed in good health; his greatest ailment was boredom with the peacetime Army.

What about his eyes? Defective vision caused him to squint, giving him the sour look that was partly responsible for his nickname, Vinegar Joe. An explosion of an ammo dump in the First World War had severely damaged his left eye; the right one from then on required strong lenses. Winifred knew that her husband felt some concern, wondering if his eyes would last out his career.

The answer to what he would do began to take form on Christmas Eve of 1941, when he arrived in Washington and was told to organize an attack in North Africa. His friend, Gen. George Marshall, explained that the objective of the campaign was to protect the Mediterranean sea lanes so that convoys might quadruple British shipping.

No one had any idea about when, where, or how the campaign should be conducted. Stilwell was supposed to reach into all of that confusion and come up with a definite plan. After two days of chaos in Washington, he wrote to Winifred that somebody with a loud voice and a mean look and a big stick should yell, "HALT, you crazy bastards. SILENCE, you imitation ants. *Now* half of you get the hell out of town before dark and the other half sit down and don't move for one hour."

That Christmas the British, Dutch, and Australians were in Washington deciding what ought to be done about China. Since Chiang Kai-shek was complaining about lack of attention, Churchill felt he should be given enough supplies to keep him in the war, but not enough to turn China into a military power. He did not add that he feared China might take over Burma and India.

Stilwell was puzzled to hear, on New Year's Day of 1942, that Wavell had refused to accept 100,000 Chinese troops that Chiang had offered to send into Burma. Such an uneasy relationship between the British and the Chinese would plague Stilwell for the next three years, but of course that never crossed his mind while he was working in Washington to plan a North African campaign.

Someone from the military was needed to represent the United States in China. Stilwell's aide, Frank Dorn, suggested Gen. Hugh Drum, commander of the First Army of New York, and Stilwell made the recommendation. Neither Secretary of War Henry Stimson nor General Marshall felt easy about appointing Drum; they reasoned that Stilwell, with his ten years of experience in China, was a better choice, and Roosevelt agreed.

Stilwell was never a Roosevelt fan. After his visit to the White House, February 9, 1942, he wrote in his journal: "F.D.R. very pleasant and very unimpressive. . . . Just a lot of wind." He felt that the Navy was the apple of Roosevelt's eye, and that the Army was a "stepchild." Later, in the privacy of his diary, he called Roosevelt "a rank amateur in all military matters" and feared he was apt to act on sudden impulses. Feeling that the President had been "completely hypnotized by the British who have sold him a bill of goods," Stilwell wrote, "It took the disaster of Hawaii to stop the flow of all our stuff to the Limeys." Once Stilwell said, "The Limeys have his ear while we have the hind tit."

When George Weller and I returned from lunch, we went upstairs in the Buddhist monastery to plot the opening months of the war in Burma on a map of Southeast Asia. Whether Weller had ever taught, I do not know, but certainly he had the skills of a great teacher. That big, competent man, with his quiet power, was clear and definite while processing information through a strong, well-organized mind.

Weller spoke of the amazing things the Japanese had done within a few months. As he spoke, he pointed out areas they had occupied—French Indochina, Thailand, Malaya, Singapore, Sumatra, Borneo, Java, the Celebes, New Guinea, Timor, Hainan, and the Philippines.

"Look at how small the Japanese islands are," I said. "And how vast the area taken! In the history of warfare, was there ever anything more dramatic?"

Weller and I were now willing to give the Japanese credit, something we might not have done three years earlier. By February 1945 the war had turned against them, and everyone felt less bitter.

Weller said that the Japanese had moved into Lower Burma shortly after Pearl Harbor and had advanced with some deliberateness, always making sure that their supply lines were intact. They seemed to sense that the British would sit and wait for something to happen rather than take action. Whenever the British set up a defense, the Japanese knew its weakness. Nobody could have predicted that the enemy would move from Lower Burma into Upper Burma even before the monsoon arrived in the spring.

The British military in Burma were not a fighting force, but more of a police force, an army of occupation. They could take care of unruly natives, but not hold their own against fierce professional fighters. The British did not know how to fight over undeveloped land and in the jungle, something the Japanese knew well. Instead of specializing in light weapons, as did the Japanese, the British depended on roadbound vehicles. So right away the Japanese developed a roadblock tactic in which a small unit dropped trees across roads behind retreating British units, and then used crossing machine-gun fire to cause havoc. The

British allowed the Japanese to dictate when and where the fighting would take place. Such passivity caused both physical and psychological breakdown.

The Burmese were another great help to the Japanese. For years they had resented the lackadaisical British Raj, and now was the chance to get even. They shouted "Asia for the Asiatics," and acted as spies and saboteurs, even forming their own military units. Buddhist monks, very anti-British, became effective saboteurs and spies, so effective that at times Chinese soldiers took to shooting at any yellow robe in sight. Bandits, known as dacoits, had for years caused the crime rate in southern Burma to be one of the world's highest; now they began raiding British camps.

Weller created a disquieting mood that would cling as I listened to more technical matters. He put together parts of the conflict in a way that helped me see and feel the tragic unfolding of events. He was showing me how to give it all order and wholeness.

On December 23, two weeks after Pearl Harbor, the Japanese bombed Rangoon. It was clear from then on that they intended to cut the supply line to China and to seize its great oilfields, abundant rice crops, and rich mineral mines.

Japanese soldiers, invading Burma from Thailand, were seasoned troops filled with the high morale that came from winning victory after victory. The 33rd and 55th Divisions had enjoyed success in China, Malaya, and Singapore, and now found weak resistance in Burma. As for the Allies, the first Burma Division and the 17th Indian Division were below strength and poorly trained. When British, Indians, Kachins, Karens, and Chins, about 25,000 of them, tried to stop the enemy at the Salween and Sittang rivers, they failed.

In Rangoon, the British were their own worst enemies. For one thing, some troops moving from India to Rangoon were stopped on the way and sent to Singapore, where they arrived just in time to be captured in the surrender of sixty thousand British troops garrisoned there. Other troops stopped just outside of Rangoon because some official had assured them that the city was doomed and that they could not be of much help. The British Seventh Armored Brigade, disembarking at Rangoon, suffered taunts from refugees who said the soldiers should be going in the other direction. When the city seemed lost, British officers ordered it burned, and American officers set fire to 980 trucks scheduled for delivery to China across the Burma Road.

In those early months the only good news coming out of Burma was of victories in the sky. General Chennault's American Volunteer Group and the British Royal Air Force inflicted heavy losses on the Japanese air force. In time, though, the Japanese sent the American flyers back to China and badly damaged the RAF.

On March 8, only three months after Pearl Harbor, the Imperial Japanese Forces occupied Rangoon.

Stilwell had reached India a few days earlier. His promotion to lieutenant general caught up with him on February 27 in Calcutta. In Washington he had been put in charge of a small mission to China. He was to oversee the distribution of Lend-Lease material, meaning he was to find out who was stealing things—some supplies were being lost to personal greed, and some were being stored for use against the Reds after the war. Stilwell was also to serve as head of Chiang Kai-shek's Allied staff, but at that time no Allied troops were being sent to China. Chinese troops were to go on the offensive against the Japanese, and Stilwell was to make sure they knew how to use American arms, but after the fall of Rangoon, weapons were no longer reaching China. Chiang's troops were said to number about four million, but many were "phantom soldiers," just names kept on a list so that commanders might collect pay for them.

Right off, Stilwell observed that the chains of command were awkward. In December 1941 the China-Burma-India Theater had been established with a split headquarters—the British in New Delhi and the Chinese in Chungking. The British commander of the Imperial defenses of India and Malaya was Sir Archibald Percival Wavell, the desert warrior. The commander of the China Theater was Generalissimo Chiang Kai-shek.

Stilwell flew across the Himalayas to Chungking, where, on March 6, 1942, he met with Chiang Kai-shek. The high regard in which they held each other that day would soon fade. Stilwell was in agreement when Chiang complained about the British in Burma, saying they were too ready to retreat. The Generalissimo did not want his troops in Burma under British command, and so, to the American's delight, he asked Stilwell to command the Chinese Fifth and Sixth armies in Burma.

Stilwell wrote to his wife that although this was the hardest job ever handed him, he was delighted because "now I don't have to wake up in a blue funk every morning and wonder what the hell I can do to justify my existence." He felt so kindly toward Chiang that he wrote, "He has a lot of good sense in his talk." If in the future he reread that sentence, he surely flinched.

Stilwell collected a chaotic assortment of duties: as chief of staff of the China Theater he was responsible to Chiang, and as commander of the Chinese in Burma he was not only responsible to the G-mo, but also to Generals Alexander and Wavell, who were, in turn, responsible to Churchill. As commander in chief of any American military men in China, India, and Burma, he was responsible to the U.S. War Department and to Roosevelt. To add to this complexity, he was in charge of all Lend-Lease material for China. In theory it was possible for Chiang to order him to do one thing and for General Alexander to command him to do something else, and for the U.S. War Department to require something entirely different.

From Chungking, General Stilwell flew to Maymyo, in Burma, a picture-postcard town with aromatic gardens, charming homes, and tree-lined streets, the kind of town the colonial British created with love and tended with care. At British headquarters he met Gen. Sir Harold R. L. G. Alexander, the British commander in Burma who would be Stilwell's superior officer in the field. Both men took an instant disliking to each other. Alexander had been a hero in the Great War and had done a remarkable job commanding the British rear guard during the evacuation of Dunkirk, but Stilwell felt he lacked an aggressive spirit.

Stilwell thought highly, though, of Lt. Gen. William J. Slim, commander of the British First Burma Corps, which consisted of the 17th Indian (Black Cat) division and the First Burma Division. Slim's troops were mainly Asiatics: Gurkhas, Sikhs, Rajputs, Karens, Kachins, and Chins. Only four battalions were composed of British troops.

Stilwell admired Slim because he, too, was aggressive. Slim

thought well of Stilwell even though he thought him "sometimes as obstinate as a whole team of mules."

Slim's willingness to fight grew, in part, from his concern that the Japanese might invade India. He knew that the Indian soldiers captured at the fall of Singapore were being trained as the Indian National Army, one that might win the hearts of Indians who wanted to be rid of British rule, something Mohandas K. Gandhi and his Congress Party had been promoting for years.

Slim and Stilwell both wanted a campaign directed at recapturing Rangoon. Before they could get it started, though, the front collapsed and chaos engulfed central Burma.

Stilwell realized immediately that he was commander of Chinese troops in name only. Chiang and the Chinese generals kept strings tied to everything. Although Chiang promised Stilwell the Fifth, Sixth, and 66th armies, he allowed only the 200th Division of the Fifth Army to go far enough south to face the Japanese. When the 200th got into difficulties, Stilwell wanted to move other divisions southward to help, but Chiang refused.

As far as Stilwell was concerned, Chiang was a juggler, making promises and breaking them, playing off warlord against warlord, general against general, the wealthy against the peasant. All the while he was haunted by an awareness of the Red Army that would eventually sweep down from the north.

While Stilwell built up resentment, Chiang Kai-shek was doing the same. He was convinced that Stilwell was working against him, believing that as his chief of staff the American general could get the guns, trucks, planes, gasoline, and tanks from the United States if only his meanness did not stop him from trying. The G-mo did not want to admit that with war flaming out all over the world in that spring of 1942, China was near the bottom of the list when it came to supplies, and was going to stay there for some time.

Perhaps what hurt Stilwell's pride more than anything else was having the G-mo constantly trying to tell him how to deploy Chinese troops. Chiang said that it would take three Chinese divisions to defend against one Japanese division, and on the attack the ratio would have to be five to one. Chiang also told Stilwell that he was all wrong in grouping Chinese divisions for defense; the Chinese way was "defense in depth," which meant stringing out the troops, one small unit behind another, for fifty miles.

By late March, General Stilwell was considering resigning. Chinese officers were not carrying out his orders. He felt caught between the British and the Chinese, who hated each other, and he hated both. He felt caught in the mood swings of Chinese officers. Whatever he ordered them to do was not given consideration; they always wondered what the Generalissimo was thinking. The frustrated Stilwell wrote in his diary, "I can't shoot them. I can't relieve them; and just talking to them does no good."

For example, when the Japanese were on the way to Lashio, where the Burma Road started, Stilwell wanted to rush the 200th Division to stop them. He asked Gen. Yu Fei-p'eng to let him use some of the seven hundred trucks under his command to carry troops to Taunggyi, a hundred miles south of Lashio. Yu, who was using the trucks to carry his black-market goods to China, sent only twenty-two trucks. Stilwell wanted to have Yu shot until someone said that he was Chiang's cousin.

Stilwell felt convinced that Generals Tu Yu-ming, commander of the Fifth Army, and Lin Wei, Stilwell's chief of staff, disregarded his orders because behind his back they were receiving conflicting orders from Chiang. Each treated the American with less than courtesy. When Stilwell came to see Tu, the Chinese general would sometimes lock himself in a room and refuse to come out. On at least one occasion, Lin Wei took off to put great distance between himself and the front.

Stilwell lost faith in Chinese officers, but continued to feel that if Chinese troops were properly motivated, they could be real fighters. To demonstrate this, he offered troops of the 200th Division 50,000 rupees if they recaptured Taunggyi by five in the afternoon. They recaptured it by four.

April was a month of horrors. The war just south of Mandalay turned into a nightmare. The Burmese began decapitating Indians, something they had long wanted to do because Indians, more disciplined than the Burmese, had practically taken over the economy of southern Burma; what the Indians did not own, the Chinese merchants did. The Burmese began mutilating Chinese soldiers, too, and often started forest fires and field fires around Chinese camps, trapping the soldiers until they were overcome by smoke or consumed by flames. The bandits treated everybody with a meanness beyond description; rape, murder, beatings, and theft were rampant.

April is also the hottest month in central Burma. Soldiers learned that one could go without food for days, feeling only discomfort, but a lack of water for even a short time brought on madness.

The only bright piece of news to come out of Burma during those dark times was the story of how Lt. Gen. Sun Li-jen rescued the British First Burma Division. When the Japanese cut off the British with a roadblock, Sun's 38th Division broke through to free them.

From that day on, the British and Americans called Sun the best of the Chinese generals. Although the English never fully trusted the Chinese, they so admired Sun that they made sure he received the Order of the British Empire. Sun was still being called the best Chinese general three years later when he gave that field party for the war correspondents near the junction of the Ledo and Burma roads.

On April 4 the Japanese bombed Mandalay. The fire, aided by a west wind off the Irrawaddy, destroyed the lovely city. No one had prepared for any emergency. The fifth-columnists were fierce in their looting. For twenty-seven days Mandalay burned.

Chiang Kai-shek and Madame Chiang, accompanied by General Stilwell, flew into Maymyo, a few miles up the road from Mandalay. With them was Gen. Lo Cho-ying, a first-rate soldier who had proven himself at home and in Shanghai. He was now in Burma to serve as Stilwell's executive officer and make sure orders were obeyed. The Generalissimo called a meeting of high-ranking Chinese officers to tell them that anyone disobeying General Stilwell might well be executed. With Oriental courtesy they bowed to their American commander.

The real blow came April 17. The Japanese, now reinforced, struck the British at Yenangyaung and practically destroyed the First Burmese Division.

At the same time the Japanese thoroughly destroyed the Chinese 55th Division of the Sixth Army at Pyinmana, halfway between Rangoon and Mandalay. Gen. Chen Li-wu showed remarkable ineptitude in stringing out his troops for miles in a thin line along the road, while he remained many miles to the rear. The Japanese, moving along the road, mowed down the Chinese as they went, until the last of the soldiers took off into the hills to vanish so completely that never again was there a 55th Division listed on the rolls of the Chinese Army.

When the Chinese 55th vanished like a mist in the hills, the Japanese hurried toward Lashio, the town where the Burma Road began. They had captured one more major objective!

Stilwell was swinging from despair to hope and back again. For instance, when he had his picture taken with the Generalissimo and Madame Chiang in Maymyo, on April 7, they felt close in spirit. That day, everybody in the photograph, including Generals Tu Yu-ming and Lo Cho-ying, agreed on the plan Stilwell had promoted for a month: Attack! But three days later Stilwell complained that Chiang was "welshing on [the] agreement."

On April 25, Stilwell and Alexander met a few miles south of Mandalay and decided that the Allies had better flee before the Japanese cut off the routes of escape. During that dreary meeting the Japanese dropped bombs within a hundred yards of the conference site. Everybody fled to cover except Alexander and Stilwell, who stood in the garden, acting as though nothing unusual were happening.

Now plans for retreat were replacing plans for attack. The campaign was disintegrating fast.

When General Slim saw that he must retreat, he ordered the destruction of the vast oil fields at Yenanyaung. Some five thousand oil wells and a large power station went up in flames.

The Japanese were not going to permit an orderly withdrawal. As the British retreated to the northwest, in the direction of India, the enemy repeatedly cut them off. The route, really just a trail, was cut by rivers, which always brought up the question of how to get across. As the mangled units built whatever would float, the Japanese kept them under fire. Finally the British abandoned all equipment and retreated with all possible speed. The Japanese, for some reason, failed to follow. The British made the ninety-mile march westward through what became known as the Valley of Death.

Stilwell had hoped to withdraw his Chinese troops along the Burma Road, on up into Yunnan province. When the enemy captured the road, Stilwell, too, turned westward toward India.

What a mess it all was! Chinese officers refusing to obey their own superiors, civilians defying the military, refugees clogging the roads, the civil administration vanishing into thin air. Panic everywhere! When British and Chinese commanders met, one of them said, "My men are simply afraid of the Japanese." The others nodded.

On April 30, Stilwell asked the War Department whether to take troops to India or China. But it was too late for an answer.

In mid-December, when he had been overwhelmed with false alarms about Japanese invasions of California, he had written in his diary, "Nothing is ever as bad as it seems at first."

Now, four months later, things seemed about as bad as they could get.

SEVEN

The details of General Stilwell's flight from Burma were given to me by three men who were a part of it: Gen. Frank Merrill, Lt. Paul Geren, and Lt. Col. Gordon Seagrave.

Merrill was a major at the time of the flight. He had been a military observer with the British when they were suffering heavy losses in Burma, and before that he had studied the Japanese language while serving as a military attaché in Tokyo. Geren, after receiving his doctorate in economics at Harvard, had volunteered to teach as a missionary at Judson College in Rangoon. When the Japanese captured the city, early in 1942, he hurried northward to join a medical unit organized by another missionary, Dr. Gordon Seagrave, whose father and grandfather had been missionaries on the China-Burma border.

On May 1, 1942, Mandalay fell. Stilwell's authority over the Chinese troops had vanished, and all Allied forces were on the run. Now it was just a matter of keeping supplies from falling into enemy hands, and of saving one's own neck.

The Japanese were dropping British and American bombs

captured at Rangoon. Frank Dorn said, "Aren't they ever going to let up on us?"

Stilwell answered, "Not while they have us on the run. And if the shoe was on the other foot, we'd do the same thing to them."

Stilwell tried to get two dozen Americans from Mandalay to Myitkyina over a single-track, narrow-gauge railroad while soldiers of several nationalities were fighting among themselves to board the same train. In the confusion, two engines collided head-on, and that took care of that. The general decided at that moment that either he walk to India or be captured by the Japanese.

The idea of being chased by the enemy was repugnant to the general's aggressive nature. He saw nothing to recommend the flight of the Allies, and so he fumed when he heard, on May 4, that London radio had called General Alexander a bold and resourceful commander who had fought "one of the great defensive battles of the war." He added in his notes, "and a lot of other crap about what the Limeys have been doing." He was incensed again when a British communiqué said, "The masterly conduct of the withdrawal from Burma was one of the bright spots of the war."

Stilwell wanted to withdraw to Myitkyina, but decided, on May 5, that that was impossible; the Japanese were nearer the town than he was. The chance to organize an orderly retreat was past. Some refugees had reached the Myitkyina airstrip in time to be flown to India by American pilots working with the Chinese National Airways Corporation. Flights continued as the airstrip was bombed and strafed, until enemy troops reached the edge of town. Many of the pilots later joined the United States Air Corps and flew the Hump from India to China as members of Air Transport Command.

A C-47, sent by United States Army Air Force chief Henry H. "Hap" Arnold, landed in Shwebo, northwest of Mandalay, with orders to bring out Stilwell. He refused to be rescued. After ordering most of his staff onto the plane, he stood there watching the last flight out of Burma.

The general gathered together twenty-six Americans, thirteen British, sixteen Chinese, some civilians, and several Indian cooks and mechanics. Since Seagrave and his nineteen nurses and seven English Quakers, conscientious objectors from an ambulance unit, were to be a part of the walkout, Paul Geren was invited to come along. He recalled Stilwell's warning the 113 refugees that they would have to walk to India through some of the worst country in the world, and describing the coming monsoon, the shortage of food, and rampaging rivers that were almost impassable. If everybody was determined enough, he said, they might make it.

The refugees started their flight for India in worn-out jeeps and trucks, which failed one by one and were set afire where they stopped. Even the start was enervating, because Stilwell's group was engulfed by starving refugees. Finally, one night the general said, "We're ahead of the mob. But we've got to keep moving." The refugees and the Japanese were always threatening to catch up.

Just beyond Mansi, near the Chaunggyi River, the convoy reached a place where the only way forward was over a bridge made of bamboo and rope across a deep ravine. No truck could make it across, but jeeps might. Everyone carried supplies over the bridge, and then courageous drivers eased eleven jeeps across. Not far beyond, even the jeeps had to be abandoned, for the terrain was just too rough.

An English planter offered Stilwell some elephants, but the general did not accept them because elephants would not be able to climb the steep hills, of which there were many up ahead.

Just as the jeeps were abandoned and the elephants refused, the tinkle of a bell came from the mountainside. Twenty stunted mules and two Chinese muleteers came around a curve in the narrow trail. They carried no load, the muleteers said, because they were en route to India to pick up supplies—probably opium. Stilwell offered a handsome fee if they would help transport things, and the muleteers were delighted.

Stilwell was a fierce disciplinarian all the way, for he realized that only intense self-discipline would get his refugees to India alive. He was also demanding of himself, even in small ways. For instance, whenever food was given out, he ate last, following the admonition often heard at Officer Candidate School at Fort Benning: "Officers should always stand at the end of the mess line." Instructors told candidates that the Infantry School's slogan was "Follow me!" but it only applied to combat.

No matter how tired and dejected the refugees felt, Stilwell demanded that all of them keep up physical appearance. Once, when events were exceptionally disheartening, he snapped, "Colonel Huston, get those men shaved and cleaned up. They'll feel better, and so will I." Stilwell began shaving, and as Frank Dorn said, "With every few strokes of the razor he glanced out the corners of his eyes to see if others were taking the hint."

When the general heard that Colonel Holcombe had collapsed on the trail, he snapped, "He'll have to go on. This column will not stop for anything."

But it did stop for one thing—a rogue elephant. Paul Geren said, "I came around a turn in the trail, and there stood Stilwell with his tommy gun. I didn't recognize his silhouette and said, 'How goes it, bud?' He said, 'You'll soon find out if you don't watch out!' The elephant blocked the way. Natives had put a bell around his neck, to mark him as a beast that had killed someone." When the beast withdrew, Stilwell moved ahead at the regulation Army pace of 105 steps a minute, and men half his age had trouble keeping up.

With a loud groan, Maj. Frank Merrill fell facedown into the mud at the edge of a stream. It was the first of several heart attacks. Stilwell directed Paul Geren and two of the English Quakers to inflate an air mattress and use it to tow the major downstream. Merrill was so stoic and noncomplaining, said Frank Dorn, that he gave some strength to others who were about to stumble and fall along the way.

"Christ, we're a poor lot," Stilwell grumbled. "We've got to average fourteen miles a day, and we haven't made five."

The general was pleased with the way the native nurses held their own. He wrote, "I thought we'd have to gear the march to *their* short steps." They kept up the pace and the spirit with their Protestant hymns and lovely peals of laughter.

One evening after an especially bad day, the nurses began a hymn, and Doc Seagrave added his fine baritone, and before long everybody was singing. At the end of the song, Stilwell said, "I wish our people would sing more often on the march. When I was with the French Army in 1918, they always sang.

But so far, all I've heard is a lot of griping and I've seen some pretty poor physiques."

During the long days on the trail, Stilwell and his aide, Lt. Col. Frank Dorn, sometimes talked about the tragedies of war. The general said, "It can break down the moral fiber and sense of decency of individuals who have been forced by circumstances to fight it."

Dorn observed that an urge to loot comes over men at war. Time and again he saw soldiers take things that would later be cast aside as too heavy to carry. "They leave a trail of litter, denuded homes, and a 'liberated' people wondering if liberation had been worthwhile."

One day Stilwell saw a bulging bedroll lashed to a mule; a lieutenant's name was stenciled on the canvas. The general ordered someone to spread the contents along the beach—several blankets, sheets, a mattress, a pillow, underwear, socks, towels, a couple of uniforms, and shoes.

Vinegar Joe had the whole party lined up along the bank, and with his walking stick he lifted item by item, giving a furious oration about how selfish some people could be. He did not speak the nervous lieutenant's name, but threatened to deal with him in India.

In recalling this incident years later, Dorn, by then a general, said that had the lieutenant been in the Chinese army—where military "justice" was swift—he would almost surely have been shot right there, and his body left to rot on the beach.

Dorn described such "justice" with an anecdote about the time a group of Chinese soldiers hijacked a convoy of supplies that several Americans were taking to Chinese headquarters. The commander of those soldiers guaranteed the Americans that there would be punishment, and to prove his good faith, he sent the American commander a severed hand. Days later he invited the Americans to the compound at his army headquarters, where five hundred Chinese soldiers huddled against a stone wall. Machine guns fired until all five hundred were on the ground, covered with blood. There had been no trial of any kind.

At the Uyu River, the head man of a village supplied the refugees with thirteen unsafe rafts that were at least floating for the time being. Seagrave's nurses made little houses for the rafts by splitting bamboo into fine strips, weaving them together, and covering the framework with broad leaves. As the refugees pushed off into the river and the rafts began to spin, Stilwell said to Dorn, "We might have made better time hiking, but this should give our weaklings a rest before we tackle the mountains."

While they were poling along the river, worried about their need for food, a British plane flew over and dropped bundles. Naked, dark-skinned mountain people ran from the jungle and scooped up everything before the refugees could reach it. Fortunately the plane made another pass and dropped corned beef, hardtack, and biscuits near the refugees.

Rain came lashing down, the wind blew, and the rafts began falling apart. When things were exceedingly bad and everyone felt dejected, Paul Geren exclaimed, "What a cursed life this is!"

"But this was no complaint," wrote Jack Belden, the correspondent for *Time*. "It was a simple fact. It impressed everybody so that they began to laugh, cook, servant, soldier, nurse, doctor, ambulance driver, and war correspondent were shaken by laughter like a fever. It rattled the rafts, beat hollowly against the house shelter, drowned out the sound of the rain."

After a hectic forty-eight hours on the river, the ride ended at Homalin, where all the rafts seemed to disintegrate at once. Stilwell had been hoping that food would be waiting in Homalin, for just before starting the march he had sent a radio message asking that supplies be stored there. Now he learned that the British official had departed on the last steamboat and had left nothing.

Stilwell bought four ponies so that those with the most dangerously blistered feet might ride. Things were going so wrong, Dorn said, that everybody began showing an ugliness of temper not evident before as they went stumbling about their tasks.

Now there was only enough food left for three meals. Eight days of walking stretched ahead. Stilwell made the self-evident observation, "If we cut down to one meal a day, we'll still have five days with no food."

Things seemed on the verge of disintegration. A thick blanket of fog hugged the ground in the early morning, giving the surroundings a ghostly appearance. Monkeys and birds were annoying with their angry noises.

How to get across the wide, rapid Chindwin River? That was the immediate worry. Just as Stilwell reached the bank of the great river, five dugout canoes and a freight boat came around the bend. Everyone shouted with joy, and a Protestant minister dropped to his knees to give thanks to God. A few at a time, all of the refugees were ferried to the far shore and stood a little closer to India. Stilwell said that if Japanese gunboats had not caught up with them at the Chindwin, chances were they would not, but this did not solve the food problem. Once more he repeated, "Let's keep ahead of the deluge," referring to the thousands of refugees staggering toward India.

The monsoon began on May 14, and it was a lulu. The downpour was so heavy and the wind so severe that it was painful; even the nurses whimpered and the strongest men went off balance and fell. The mules brayed in terror and formed a stubborn circle to give each other protection.

Suddenly, in a clearing stood five *basha*s surrounded by half-naked men. Stilwell stepped into one of the huts to find a gigantic, blond Englishman with a broad welcoming smile.

"I'm Tim Sharpe, president of the Manipur Durbar. General Wood sent me. He's in command of supply in Assam. I've been on the trail from Imphal for five days. Coming up behind me are five hundred porters with food, cigarettes, and whiskey. A doctor with medical supplies is a day behind me. Hundreds of pack ponies are on the way. Your messages and recommendations all got through. I've been instructed to guide you to Imphal."

Once more the Reverend Breedom Case was kneeling in the mud, his gaunt face raised against the driving rain, giving thanks to God. Dr. Seagrave led his nurses in prayer. That night the nurses sang hymns and everyone joined in, especially with "Onward Christian Soldiers," and "The Battle Hymn of the Republic."

It was still a long way to the British corps headquarters at Imphal. For the next six days the general forced his refugees to cover twenty-one miles a day.

On May 19, several British officers watched a long line of ragged people struggle up the valley. At the head of the line was a skinny man wearing a campaign hat, and at the end was a group of native nurses.

"How many did you lose?" asked a British officer.

"Not a one," said Stilwell. "Not a single one!"

The officer said, "I'll wager you a quid to a dollar no other party crosses those mountains without some loss of life."

Some twelve thousand British troops ended their nine hundred-mile retreat from southern Burma at about the same time. They looked so wraithlike that the first Indians to see them fled in terror. Thousands had died along the way, and many died shortly after reaching India. They received such an unfavorable reception that it seemed to kill what little spirit that was left; they received no encouragement, no welcome, but were treated as though everyone was ashamed of them, like a team that had lost badly.

The Chinese reached India at Ledo, in Assam, north of Stilwell's refugees. They had hoped to fight their way back to Yunnan province, but the Japanese drove northward so fast toward Myitkyina and Bhamo that they cut off all but a few units that managed to reach their homeland.

What was left of the Chinese armies wandered northwesterly through the dread Hukawng Valley. Only General Sun's 38th Division fought its way to Assam, each soldier carrying two or three rifles or machine guns that had been abandoned by others.

The greatest horror of those dark days of spring 1942 could be found among the 900,000 civilian refugees. Soon the trails across two thousand miles were covered with hundreds of thousands of bodies, as starvation, fatigue, and disease caught up with them. The British colonial administration was criticized for not having stockpiled food and medicine along the way. To add to the horror, at some places the Burmese poisoned wells, and at rivers they burned boats so that the refugees could not cross.

The traumas that Stilwell had suffered in a two-month period set the mind reeling. From March 11, 1942, the day he arrived in Burma, until May 19, when he reached safety in India, he had suffered incredible pressures on his body, mind, and spirit. He knew the fatigue, danger, and hunger of the common soldier and the mental and spiritual anguish of a foreign commander confused by an Oriental culture, fighting a losing battle with ill-trained, undernourished troops. That he could still be filled with determination is almost beyond imagining.

The praise that the press showered on Vinegar Joe annoyed him. War correspondents made it sound as though he might retake Burma in short order. When they asked him for a news conference, he held one in the Imperial Hotel in New Delhi, and closed with a much-quoted statement carried May 26 by the Associated Press. When a British correspondent said that both General Wavell and General Alexander had described the retreat as "an heroic, voluntary withdrawal" and "a glorious retreat," Stilwell snapped, "In the first place, no military commander in history ever made a voluntary withdrawal. And there's no such thing as a glorious retreat. All retreats are as inglorious as hell. I claim we got a hell of a licking. We got run out of Burma and it's humiliating as hell. I think we ought to find out what caused it, go back, and retake Burma."

Stilwell began making plans to go back and retake it, refusing time off to recover from exhaustion and various ailments. Right away he spoke of things he had planned during long hours on the refugee trail: Across the hills and through the jungles of Upper Burma the Allies should build a road and lay a pipeline all the way to the Burma Road; they should clear the enemy from Upper Burma while fighting into western China, and from there fight eastward, pushing the enemy into the sea; use the eastern coast of China to launch air raids on the Japanese homeland; and train troops on the coast for an amphibious invasion on Japan.

As commander of the China-Burma-India Theater, General Stilwell had headquarters in New Delhi and Chungking. Frequently he made the dangerous 2,100-mile Himalayan flight between New Delhi and Chungking, and often flew the 450 miles from Chungking to Kunming, terminus of the Hump flights and center of most American activities in China.

In Chungking his headquarters were in a house of modern design, clinging to the side of a hill above the Chialing River. Of the twenty-nine servants in residence, he soon got rid of most, believing that they were spies, especially after catching them ransacking his desk. The trick to catching them, he said, was to return to the office, walking quietly, shortly after leaving it.

Chiang gave Stilwell permission to train the nine thousand

Chinese soldiers who had fled from Burma into India. Stilwell convinced Chiang that the planes returning across the Hump to India from China should not return empty, but ought to bring recruits to train with the refugee soldiers in Ramgarh. Chiang also agreed to let Stilwell send Americans into Yunnan Province, in southwest China, to train soldiers in a unit called Yoke Force, which, in time, might move into Burma to fight westward until meeting up with the Ramgarh troops fighting eastward to China. More of this in due course.

The British did not like the idea of bringing Chinese to India, because Chinese had a way of settling down to take over all trade and power wherever they happened to strike. The British had seen it happen in many parts of Burma, and since they were already badly bowed beneath the white man's burden, they did not want any more troubles in India.

Because of the Chinese, the British were also against building the Ledo Road. They looked into the future and envisioned a road that would make travel easy from China into Burma and India. They envisioned the sandaled feet of Chinese soldiers kicking up the dust of the road as they marched westward toward India under a new crusade of Asia for the Asiatics. And, above all, they saw the road as a threat to postwar shipping monopolies.

Rapport between Stilwell and Chiang had begun falling apart in that depressing spring of 1942, when the Japanese were running everybody out of Burma, and now the decline in their relationship continued. In his diary, Stilwell referred to the G-mo as "the peanut," "insect," "stink in the nostrils," "dope," "little squirt," and "the world's greatest ignoramus." He sinned against Oriental courtesy time and again; for instance, he came right out and told Chiang how terribly the Chinese had performed in Burma. Afterward, even he admitted that perhaps he had been a little too forceful.

Chiang believed that Stilwell lacked loyalty to the Chinese cause, or else the CBI would not be at the bottom of the list in every way. If Stilwell would only make the effort, Chiang believed, he could get whatever China needed from the United States.

When Chiang became angry about anything, it would reflect

in his relationship with Stilwell, even if the general had nothing to do with the event. For instance, the Generalissimo was furious, in the summer of 1942, when American air units were withdrawn from India to help in the fight against Rommel in the Middle East. He hinted that he would defect from the Allies unless the United States sent him five hundred planes, five thousand tons of supplies a month across the Hump, and three U.S. fighting divisions. Right away!

Chiang promoted the slogan "Beat Japan First!" Stilwell believed that Chiang did not want too much attention focused on the Germans until they had defeated the Russians, for he feared having at his door at war's end a powerful Russia. The Russians might back the Chinese Communists then blocked in northern China.

When Stilwell began expressing admiration for the Russians, the gap between him and Chiang widened. The general often contrasted the Russian and Chinese approaches to war, praising Russia's unity, pride, and determination, and showing disdain for China's intrigue, propaganda, and corruption. In writing about China's flaws, he found the words "cesspool" and "skulduggery" coming readily to hand.

General Chennault was a major cause of the rift between Chiang and Stilwell. Chiang believed in Chennault's theory that air power instead of ground combat would win the war. Stilwell said that Chiang wanted to believe such nonsense because he wanted to fight a cheap war, saving his troops to face the Communists after the armistice.

Stilwell and Chennault were bound to collide, for they were two strong-willed men holding opposing views. Chennault believed that if only he were given what he asked for, he could defeat the Japanese in the air, at sea, and in their homeland. Even his critics had to admit that he had worked miracles with a few bombers and several dozen worn-out fighter planes. He had a way of getting things done; for example, he kept his forward bases supplied under conditions that would have caused many commanders to call the situation impossible. Often those bases waited eight weeks for supplies to travel the four hundred to seven hundred miles from Kunming, coming by trucks that broke down and sat at the side of the road for days, and sometimes the aviation fuel arrived by oxcart and even by Chinese coolies rolling drums of it over nearly impassable roads.

Stilwell's main argument against Chennault and Chiang was that without the protection of ground troops, airfields would soon be in enemy hands. He used the Doolittle raid to demonstrate how the Japanese would react. After the bombers continued on into China after their raid on Japan, several crashed in Chekiang Province, where the crews were well cared for. To teach a lesson to all concerned, the Japanese sent battalions of infantrymen into the province to plow up airfields, destroy villages, and kill a quarter of a million Chinese.

Chennault was a better salesman than Stilwell. Perhaps as a result of his Southern upbringing, he promoted air power with diplomacy; Stilwell promoted ground troops with abrasiveness.

Chennault saw Stilwell as an infantryman determined to fight his way back through the jungles of Burma to wipe out memories of an embarrassing defeat. Stilwell could have made a similar psychoanalysis by observing that Chennault, having fallen into disfavor with his superiors, wanted to prove the rightness of his opinions by winning a war with air power.

Wendell Willkie helped widen the gap between these two able men. In 1942, Willkie, who had lost to Roosevelt in the last presidential election, went on a forty-nine-day world goodwill tour at FDR's behest. In October 1942, Chiang Kai-shek, probably thinking that Willkie might win the election in 1944, treated the politician from Elmwood and Rushville, Indiana, as though he were a head of state.

The Chiangs put on an impressive show. Police tore down the huts of peasants along the roads that Willkie traveled. Schoolchildren lined miles of the parade route to cheer; soldiers marched with the goosestep that German officers had taught them; bunting flapped in the breeze, and firecrackers filled the air with noise and smoke. Willkie was even taken to "the front," a wide river separating Chinese from Japanese troops. Stilwell, in an undiplomatic way, told Willkie and everyone else present that this was just a marketplace where Japanese and Chinese soldiers come together daily to bargain. Later the general wrote in his diary, "He hardly spoke to me. Utterly indifferent."

Again Chennault proved himself the better diplomat, so

charming and convincing that Willkie offered to deliver a letter to Roosevelt outlining Chennault's opinions. In the letter the general claimed that with 105 modern fighters, thirty medium bombers, and twelve heavy bombers he could destroy the industrial cities of Japan, and suggested that he be made American military commander of China.

When Roosevelt showed the plan to George Marshall, the general called it "nonsense." Although the President respected Marshall's opinions, he was also haunted by the idea of winning an easy war.

A month after Willkie had delivered the letter, Madame Chiang came to the White House as a guest. She used her days there to assure Roosevelt that her husband favored Chennault's plan. To add to this promotion, Joseph Alsop, the newspaper columnist who served as public-relations aide to Chennault, sold the plan to Harry Hopkins, Roosevelt's adviser.

General Marshall, although he favored Stilwell's ideas, had to give his friend discouraging news. Not only was the Chennault plan getting undue attention, but the CBI could expect little in the way of troops and supplies because the focus was on North Africa.

The year 1943 dawned with Stilwell in a dark mood. When Chiang told Roosevelt that this was not the right time for the Chinese to fight, Stilwell wrote in his diary, "What a break for the Limeys. Just what they wanted. Now they will quit, and the Chinese will quit, and the goddam Americans can go ahead and fight."

Stilwell had an unhappy sixtieth birthday in March; it was then that Roosevelt lifted Chennault's spirits by dissolving the old China Air Task Force and approving a new 14th Air Force in China, promoting the brigadier with another star, and putting him in charge. Now Chennault was independent of Gen. Clayton Bissell, commander of the Tenth Air Force in India, but was still subordinate to Stilwell—at least on paper, if not in spirit.

The disagreements between Stilwell and Chennault became so disruptive that Roosevelt ordered them to Washington in May 1943, to plead their cases at the Trident Conference. When the two met at the Kunming airport to fly to the United States, the atmosphere was frigid.

At the Trident Conference the American chiefs of staff agreed with Stilwell that the Japanese would capture China's airfields unless infantrymen defended them. While Stilwell was feeling good about that opinion, the British chiefs spoke against his determination to recapture Burma, saying that, at best, he would have to wait until the end of 1943. Churchill agreed, saying that perhaps Burma should be bypassed in an effort to recapture Singapore.

Roosevelt held a private meeting with Stilwell, and another with Chennault. After that, he brought the two together to ask their opinions of Chiang Kai-shek. Chennault praised the Generalissimo as a great military and political leader; Stilwell called the G-mo an "old scoundrel."

Roosevelt decided that seven thousand tons of supplies a month must cross the Hump during the summer, and the total must reach ten thousand a month by the end of 1943. About half of the tonnage would go to Chennault, for he was promising to sink Japanese merchant ships galore. Roosevelt further showed his preference when he told Chennault that he might communicate with him directly and no longer need go through channels.

Stilwell was not long back in China when he had the bitter assignment of decorating Chiang Kai-shek as chief commander of the Legion of Merit, the highest decoration that the U.S. government can give a foreigner. To make the occasion even more unpleasant, Chiang showed up a half hour late for the ceremony. Stilwell wrote to his wife, "When I grabbed his coat and pinned it on, he jumped as if he was afraid I was going to stab him."

At the Quebec conference, in August 1943, Stilwell began to have renewed hope. Roosevelt and Churchill, supported by their military advisers, decided that the Japanese should be cleared from Upper Burma and that the Ledo Road to China should be completed. The troops to carry this out would be British, Chinese, various tribesmen, and Americans. Stilwell was pleased to be promised some American infantrymen.

Stilwell was also pleased, at least in the beginning, with the appointment of Lord Louis Mountbatten as Supreme Allied Commander, Southeast Asia Command. At the Cairo Conference, in November, Mountbatten presented a plan for the invasion of Burma.

At Cairo, Chiang Kai-shek, attending his first top-level meeting, told Roosevelt and Churchill that the British must make an amphibious landing in the Bay of Bengal, cut the enemy's supply lines at sea, and attack Mandalay, to take the enemy pressure off of Yoke Force, getting ready to move into Burma from western China. Admiral Mountbatten gave serious consideration to making an amphibious landing, but said he could not make an attack on Mandalay. Chiang balked time and again at Cairo, but eventually he was talked into promising the use of the Yoke Force.

Chiang's vacillations at Cairo made the top brass realize what Lord Louis and Vinegar Joe were up against. Toward the end of the conference, Roosevelt told the Generalissimo and Madame Chiang what they wanted to hear: the British would make an assault from the sea on the southern coast of Burma.

A week later, however, at the Teheran Conference, Stalin demanded, and Churchill concurred, that there must be a cross-channel invasion of Europe in 1944. Landing craft meant for Burma would have to be sent to England for the Normandy invasion.

Roosevelt, when forced to withdraw his pledge to Chiang, asked Stilwell to go to Chungking to break the bad news. Vinegar Joe had to renege on something, face to face with the man he had so often accused of breaking his promises.

Chiang, of course, was furious, but something had happened that assuaged his anger somewhat. On the way home from Cairo he had stopped in India to inspect Chinese troops training at Ramgarh. He was so pleased with what the Americans had done in training Chinese soldiers that there was a good chance he might use Yoke Force when the time came.

Yoke Force grew out of Stilwell's attempt to organize into thirty divisions the most promising of the four million soldiers who made up the inept, disorganized three hundred divisions of the Chinese Army.

Frank Dorn, Stilwell's aide, was promoted to general and

assigned to organize and train Yoke Force for combat as the Chinese Expeditionary Force. Six thousand American officers and enlisted men arrived in Kunming, via the Hump, to set up training courses in Yunnan Province. They started schools for infantry, artillery, and staff, and provided hospitals and aid stations for Chinese troops. American engineers supervised sixty thousand Chinese men and women in working the Burma Road for two-way traffic from Kunming to the Burma border, and in building a new bridge across the Salween to replace one destroyed by the Japanese.

Stilwell hoped to move Yoke Force westward along the Burma road at the same time that his Ramgarh-trained Chinese fought westward from India until the two forces would eventually meet. Yoke was an ironic code name, for with the passing of months it became a heavy yoke for the general to bear; he got an abundance of promises, but little action.

Stilwell did well in training Chinese in India. To bolster the two refugee Chinese divisions that had fled from Burma, he flew recruits across the Hump from Kunming to Dinjan, and moved them to Ramgarh. When American instructors arrived in India, a unique experiment began in which the soldiers of one country were trained by officers of another country within the boundaries of a third country.

Top army men of every country had doubts that the Americans would succeed. The Germans and the Russians had both failed at one time or another at making soldiers out of Chinese coolies. The only thing the Chinese army seemed to remember from that early training was the German goosestep. Would Americans be able to teach a gang of apathetic coolies? Would Chinese officers take suggestions, or would they consider it a loss of face to take advice from a foreigner?

As to the number of Chinese recruits that flew the Hump to India, the figure ranges from 45,000 to 66,000. Medics rejected at least half of them because of various diseases. This was easy to understand, considering that the recruiting officers in China often seized peasants, bound them together with ropes, and dragged them off to the army. Fewer than sixty percent of these reached their units; the rest either deserted or died. On many days the recruits that were supposed to depart Kunming for India failed to show up at the airport. About 23,000 eventually formed X Force in India.

American instructors hated the Ramgarh assignment. In trying to turn peasants into soldiers, they could not understand how anyone could be so inept at handling trucks, tanks, radios, and rifles; they even had to instruct nine thousand *bing*s in the difficult use of artillery.

Americans, paired off with Chinese student-interpreters, were in charge of instruction; Chinese officers were in charge of administration and discipline. There was plenty of friction. The Chinese officers resented having foreigners telling them what to do, and were especially resentful when the Americans paid Chinese soldiers individually out of suspicion that Chinese officers might take their cut of the payroll.

Chinese soldiers seemed to enjoy life at Ramgarh. They were eating better, gaining weight, and getting good medical care. They were playing soldiers with wonderful new weapons and getting paid to do it—directly from the paymaster.

Stilwell always thought highly of the Chinese soldier. In a talk on Chungking radio, he paid tribute to him: "He endures untold privations without a whimper. He follows wherever he is led without question or hesitation. And it never occurs to his simple and straightforward mind that he is doing anything heroic."

But Stilwell and Chiang Kai-shek both lacked respect for Chinese officers. Chiang said that if anything could possibly go wrong, Chinese officers would see that it did, and one must think of every possible mistake that they could make, and warn them in advance.

All in all, it was a dark eighteen months from the time Stilwell walked out of the jungle promising to "go back and retake it" until he was ready to do just that. He was sure that commanders in the CBI had more abrasive jobs than other commanders in the war. Not only were they at the end of the longest supply line and at the bottom of every list; worse still, they rarely agreed among themselves. It was not just American, British, and Chinese disagreeing at the top level, but bickering went on at all levels.

Even Japanese officers began fighting among themselves, a rarity. Perhaps everybody got on everybody else's nerves when

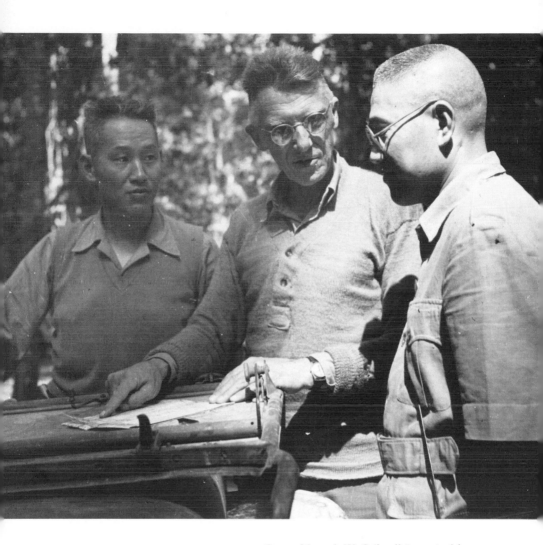

General Joseph W. Stilwell *(center)* with two Chinese commanders, Lieutenant General I. J. Sun *(left)* and Major General Lico *(right)*.

American and Chinese troops march together on the Ledo Road.

General Merrill *(right)* congratulates an Army sergeant who helped build the Ledo Road and who also conducted a band.

Merrill's Marauders could average ten miles a day when the Ledo Road was as good as this. Most days the going was rougher, especially when they were ordered to go off into the jungle and circle in behind enemy lines.

Above: When the rains came what a mess it was! Here a pack pony has fallen into the water while traveling along the Ledo Road. It took four of Merrill's Marauders to rescue him.

Left: Mules and Merrill's Marauders relax during a difficult march over the newly cut Ledo Road.

General Stilwell visits combat troops on the Ledo Road.

Father James Stuart, an Irish missionary, became a legend among troops in Burma. General Stilwell said, "The biggest mistake the Japanese made was in not taking Father Stuart prisoner." General Merrill called him "the bravest man I have ever known."

American medics often gave attention to ailing Burmese civilians. Here Sgt. Robert Dunkin of Texas uses his medical skill to treat a Kachin boy, assisted by Karing Naw, an interpreter.

An American radio team packs equipment on their horses as they move from an occupied area near Inkangahtawng.

Lt. Gen. Daniel Sultan, who succeeded Stilwell as commander of the India-Burma Theater of Operations, rides a mule to inspect combat troops near the Burma Road.

When Adm. Lord Louis Mountbatten *(right)*, commander of SEAC, lands in Burma, Lt. Gen. Daniel Sultan *(left)* is at the airport to meet him. Sultan had just taken over Stilwell's command of American forces in the theater.

A group of U.S. soldiers prepares for an attack on a Japanese machine gun nest that has held up American troops in the jungle for two days.

Two GIs search a Japanese foxhole on the road to Walabum.

P-40s taxi out for takeoff from an airstrip cleared from the jungle.

Above: At Myitkyina airstrip, ox carts collect rations and ammunition to be brought to the edge of the town where American and Chinese troops were hammering at the Japanese defenders. The C-47 transport in the background was wrecked in earlier fighting.

Above left: Kachin guides lead Marauders over a secret route to Myitkyina.

Below left: Cpl. Leslie C. Wilson scans the ration slip of Burmese refugees who have come to draw their family allowance of supplies from the U.S. warehouse at Myitkyina.

Above: For four weeks the Japanese held this desolate area; then the Chinese, after four hundred casualties, took it from them. This is the high ground where the ferry road meets main street in Myitkyina.

Above left: When American and Chinese troops fought their way into Myitkyina town they came upon the ruins of what had been attractive homes. This one had been owned by a Persian jewel merchant who had fled to a refugee camp organized by the U.S. Army.

Below left: At Myitkyina, a temple on the banks of the Irrawaddy overlooks a dug-in position of Chinese troops.

Capt. Edward Fischer in 1945.

facing such terrible conditions—dense jungle, wide rivers, monsoons, killing heat, tropical diseases, and lack of supplies.

During those awful eighteen months, Stilwell put pressure on everybody except Gen. George Marshall. He avoided asking his friend for preferential treatment, for he knew that Marshall had to worry about the way the war went all over the world. More than once, Stilwell said that Marshall must be free to make unpressured decisions. He was especially grateful when his friend made the unpressured decision to send American infantrymen to Burma.

EIGHT

One morning when I entered the press room in Bhamo, Bert Parks said, "Gus Raynaud is at the warehouse, drawing supplies. I got a jeep—let's go!"

I understood all of the unspoken sentences. What he was really saying was that Sgt. Jules Raynaud was drawing supplies for Gen. Daniel I. Sultan, commander of the India-Burma Theater, and that if our jeep happened to be standing at the warehouse door, Gus would deposit in it a case of something or other, such as grapefruit juice.

Before the war, Jules Raynaud had been a celebrated chef at the Stork Club in New York. He had been Stilwell's cook until after the change of command, and now he was Sultan's. I had gained respect for Raynaud in a Bhamo bazaar when Lily Pons and Andre Kostelanez raved about his artistry. Miss Pons kept saying to Gus, "Your lentil soup! I'll never forget your lentil soup! And the guinea hen!" All Gus said was, "You got gypped," pointing to the trinkets the opera star had bought from the natives.

When we returned to the press room, Parks, with a flourish, pulled right up to the entrance. In stepping out of the jeep, I found myself face-to-face with General Sultan coming through the door. Since I was blocking him from view, Parks felt free to yell to a captain coming down the street, "Hey, Cipriano, come see what we got at the warehouse. Gus Raynaud put it in the jeep!"

Sultan knew that whatever Gus drew from the warehouse belonged to the commander of the India-Burma Theater. He stood looking me in the eye, giving no hint of what he was thinking. Finally, Parks stopped in the middle of a sentence and hurriedly cleared the doorway. He and I were embarrassed and were thankful that Sultan made no point of the fact that we had supplies that belonged to him.

Inside the press room, a war correspondent asked how my history was coming along. I said I was gathering reports to make sure they were not destroyed when various units began closing down. He said I ought to focus on interviews, since the people who had been around for the action would soon be gone.

"For instance, go down to Detachment 101 headquarters and talk to them. And there's a British officer there just now who knew Wingate. Talk to him."

A disgruntled correspondent growled, "Why send him to 101? Those OSS guys won't talk. A tight-mouthed bunch."

"Yeah, but he's a historian. They know he won't publish anything until after the war." He turned back to me with more good advice: "Go down there for dinner. They eat well."

As I approached the Shan village, the location of Detachment 101 headquarters, it reminded me of the kind of native village found on the back lot of a Hollywood studio, neat, charming, romantic—not at all like the Kachin villages, with their primitive, cluttered look. Five tough-looking Kachin Rangers broke the mood by stopping me with the muzzles of their tommy guns. An American officer had to come out of the village to say it was all right for me to enter. We walked along a shaded street lined with bamboo *basha*s. Shan women cooked over open fires; children played among the flowers. The soft sound of cooing came from a hut that bore the sign PIGEON MESSAGE CENTER.

The American officers were not dressed very GI. Some wore bright green or yellow cravats of parachute silk; some sported

125

jaunty bush hats with the wide brims turned up at one side and bright feathers tucked in the hatbands.

We sat down to a dinner of grilled steak, fried onions, browned potatoes, beets, and chocolate pudding. My hosts were former schoolteachers, stockbrokers, lawyers, missionaries, and merchants; all had volunteered for the job because the sense of adventure was strong in them.

They opened the conversation with amusing stories. One concerned a box of Whitman's chocolates airdropped behind enemy lines. The box featured a colored picture of the New York skyline. The Kachins stood in awe of it, saved the box, and spoke long and often about the great pagodas in America.

The OSS officers laughed over a problem that had embarrassed them. It had started when they sent a message to an officer behind enemy lines, saying, "You will receive food cma ammunition. . . ." The officer forgot that *cma* was the abbreviation for *comma*, and thought it was a military award. He told his Rangers about it and radioed back how excited the Kachins were to hear that they would be decorated with the CMA award. This caused anxious moments at headquarters; to tell the Rangers the truth might lower morale. Someone suggested that *CMA* could mean Citation for Military Assistance. Someone else suggested that Detachment 101 strike such a medal. To this day, in *basha*s deep in the jungle, are probably found green ribbons with embroidered peacocks on them, attached to silver medals bearing the imprint of an American eagle and the letters *CMA*.

The Americans spoke highly of the Kachins, a warlike tribe whose very name meant "robber," and whose customs, language, and features showed a marked Tibetan influence. Kachins looked down on peaceful tribes like the Shans and Karens as effeminate and soft; they hated the Japanese, who treated all natives like dogs, but they liked the white man because missionaries had been kind to them.

I asked the OSS officers about Gen. William "Wild Bill" Donovan. They spoke well of him and were especially pleased that he had visited them behind enemy lines. Donovan, the chief of the Office of Strategic Services, had commanded the Fighting 69th in the Great War. He and General MacArthur were the only soldiers to wear the nation's three top medals: the Medal of

Honor, the Distinguished Service Cross, and the Distinguished Service Medal.

Detachment 101 of the Office of Coordinator of Information (later called the Office of Strategic Services) was activated on April 14, 1942. The number 101 was probably selected by the unit's first commander, Capt. Carl Eifler, who said, "It sounds like the unit has been around a long time."

Eifler was another larger-than-life character, the kind who often ended up in the CBI. William R. Peers, Eifler's successor, described how he felt when he reported to Eifler for the first time: "To say I was in for a rude shock would be the understatement of a lifetime. After an exchange of salutes, he offered his hand. I could see it was strong and the way he grabbed my hand was proof. He proceeded to crack every joint, smiling all the time. Back of what he was doing was a message. Danger? The next thing, as if it were entirely habitual, he took a stiletto-type dagger and drove it to a good two to three inches into the top of his desk. He looked pleased. I was confused. I had never had anything like this happen before and all I could think was, 'What's next?' "

Eifler was the kind of man General Donovan needed to train Americans in irregular warfare. The two agreed that if Burma was to have guerrilla fighters, they ought to be trained in espionage, sabotage, propaganda, and other aspects of clandestine operations.

The first members of Detachment 101 went to the Catoctin Mountains in Maryland, to a place later taken over by President Roosevelt for a mountain retreat, Shangri-la, which President Eisenhower renamed Camp David, after his grandson. Up in the mountains, members of 101 studied a variety of skills including cryptography, secret writing, resisting an interrogator, dirty fighting, and the use of explosives.

From the twenty members of OSS who had arrived in India in July 1942, the group had grown to 250 officers and 750 enlisted men by the time I visited their headquarters two and a half years later. The Kachin Rangers now numbered 10,800. Twenty-seven Americans and 338 natives had lost their lives; five thousand Japanese had died at their hands.

The officers told me they had demolished fifty-seven bridges, derailed nine trains, and captured 272 Japanese vehicles. They seemed proud that they had been able to capture sixty-eight Japanese, not an easy task. But they were most proud, it seemed, that they had led to safety 425 airmen who had bailed out behind enemy lines or had crashed onto the Hump.

The officers spoke of how they had trained aircrews in jungle survival. One of them said, "We told them, for instance, that the tendency was to follow a stream downhill, but they should do just the opposite. Downhill leads to the Burmans, who will turn you over to the Japanese. Uphill leads to Kachins; they'll risk their lives for Americans."

During training, many crews lived in the jungle for a week on scant supplies. When they came out, they had a confidence that, in time, could save their lives.

That part of the conversation closed when someone said that it was not unusual for a parachutist to get hung up in a tree and suffer a slow, agonizing death. An officer said that he had once come upon a skeleton hanging in a tree; ants had eaten away the flesh.

An OSS officer told with amusement an anecdote about Chiang Kai-shek. When some Kachins, working for the OSS, destroyed several Chinese villages in retaliation for forays the Chinese had made into Burma, the Generalissimo sent a personal memorandum to Colonel Peers, now commander of Detachment 101, demanding payment of 500 million Chinese Nationalist dollars for damages. Years later, Colonel Peers wrote, "This would amount to 25 million United States dollars, hardly payable out of the wages of a colonel."

The officers I dined with believed they would be tortured if captured, and so they carried pistols. Some had suicide pills. They said that if the Japanese captured an officer from Merrill's Marauders or one of the Flying Tigers, they would not expect him to know any far-flung plans, but they would think that an OSS officer should have some idea of the "big picture."

The men I talked with had parachuted into the Japanese-held territory to radio back information, rescue airmen, and organize the Kachins for guerrilla warfare. They learned early that guerrilla teams work best when they are kept small, six members at most, preferably three or four. One of the main assignments was to blow bridges and destroy railroad tracks using Composite C, an explosive more powerful than dynamite or TNT. Each charge was planted with a tiny mechanism that would delay the explosion from a matter of minutes to as long as twenty-four days.

A major assignment was to send radio messages reporting enemy movements along roads, rivers, and trails. Kachin agents tended to report Japanese strength at three times the actual figure; a training program stressing how to estimate enemy strength got the figures more reliable by the summer of 1944. The Chinese were inclined to exaggerate tenfold, but no one tried to teach them greater accuracy, fearing that correcting them would cause them to lose face.

A typical coded message might read, "Quit blowing up bridge 23. The Japs rebuild it each day just so you will bomb it. The one they use is a hundred yards downstream and a foot underwater."

The language barrier was a problem. For instance, in one unit neither the American officer nor his Karen radio operator could speak Kachin. So the American spoke to the Karen in English, the Karen translated the English into Burmese, and a third party translated it into Kachin. Of course, that often caused confusion. When Father James Stuart dropped by to visit some of his Kachin parishioners, he helped solve that unit's language problem temporarily.

Father Stuart was also interpreter when Wild Bill Donovan visited Burma in November 1943. The general flew in a light plane to an OSS base 150 miles behind the Japanese; he wanted to confer with Kachin headmen. From that day on he spoke with enthusiasm about having the Kachins on the Allied side, saying that success in Upper Burma might well be impossible without them.

On that trip, Donovan observed that Capt. Carl Eifler's health was not good, and so he relieved the colorful commander of his duties. Col. William Peers, one of the most efficient officers in the CBI, assumed command of Detachment 101 in December 1943.

From the beginning, members of the detachment made an effort to learn the culture of the people of Burma. They sought instruction from Dr. John Christian, a man who would later be of help to me. Christian had lived in Burma and had written books about that country.

Despite good intentions about learning the culture, things would go wrong from time to time; Americans could not fully understand the Kachin soul. For instance, for quick recovery, wounded Kachin guerrilla fighters needed the feeling of being "at home." Americans were not doing them a favor by flying them out from behind enemy lines to a U.S. hospital; there, their recovery was slow because hospital food was too bland for their fiery taste, and, worse still, they were unable to talk with the nurses and doctors. So the OSS built its own hospital, staffing it with Kachin cooks and native nurses, and the patients responded to treatment much better.

The OSS officers told me that they sometimes bartered with opium. Paper money meant nothing to Kachins; silver had some value because it was used to make necklaces, but opium bought food, favors, and information.

I said to the Americans that to live deep in the jungle with only Kachins as companions must be a lonely life. They admitted that it was, and said that whenever one of them began to crack up—such a breakdown was detected by the tenor of the radio messages—a liaison plane was dispatched to bring him out from behind enemy lines. And yet some Americans so enjoyed the life that when, after eighteen months of service, they were eligible for a leave in the States, they asked to stay on.

OSS officers lived as well as it was possible to live in the jungle. Natives sometimes treated them like white gods.

Although the best of supplies arrived by airdrop, they learned to eat roots, berries, wild fruit, monkey, elephant, tiger, fried termites, white bees, and paddy rats. An officer said, "We never learned to relish K rations, but the Kachins did."

The day that I dined with them in the Shan village, I sensed that the American officers felt that time was running out for Detachment 101. A few months later, on July 12, 1945, its work done, it ceased to exist.

At the end of dinner in the headquarters of Detachment 101, I asked the only British officer present if he cared to take a walk.

The burly fellow, who had wiry red hair and a bristling mustache, said he would be delighted. We took off on a trail that seemed to circle the village. I asked him to recall what he remembered about Maj. Gen. Orde Wingate and his Chindits.

Anyone speaking about Wingate was apt to use the words *genius* and *fanatic*. He was a madman who at times performed with brilliance and at other times failed dramatically.

As a young British officer in the 1930s, he had trained guerrilla fighters in Palestine to help the Jews against the Arabs, and in Abyssinia he had helped Haile Selassie against the Italians. Although he had accomplished much with few men, the morose Scot sometimes felt he had failed, and fell into deep depression. While recovering from one such dark fatigue in a Cairo hospital, he had slashed his throat. For the rest of his life his voice was raspy, and whenever he wanted to turn his head to the side, the rigid neck muscles required that he swing the whole of his upper body.

Orde Wingate was often compared with Lawrence of Arabia; he became known in the press as the Lawrence of Judea, of Ethiopia, of Burma. This made him angry; he was very much himself, and did not want to be thought of as somebody else.

Gen. Sir Archibald Wavell, an admirer of Wingate's wild imagination and fierce courage, brought him to Delhi to make plans for guerrilla fighting in Burma. The Scot promoted "long-range penetration" (LRP), a matter of landing troops behind enemy lines to cause havoc. Most officers in Delhi thought Wingate's ideas unreasonable, but General Wavell liked what he heard.

Wingate organized the 77th Indian Infantry Brigade and called the troops "Chindits," a mispronunciation of the Burmese word *Chintha*, the grotesque lionlike animal that guards temples in Burma. The Chindits were mainly British, especially the officers, but the ranks also included men from the Burma Rifles, the Royal West African Frontier Force, Chinese from Hong Kong, and Gurkha riflemen from Nepal.

The three thousand Chindits entered Burma in mid-February of 1943. One column turned south, hoping to divert the enemy's attention, the way a magician seeks to distract with one hand while the other brings off the trick. The secret column moved eastward, aiming at the important railway linking Mandalay with Myitkyina.

The Chindits were successful at first; they cut the railroad in seventy-five places, destroyed bridges, and set booby traps galore. Whenever they met the Japanese they fought with some viciousness, seeming to prefer hand-to-hand combat.

Then Wingate made a mistake. He crossed the mile-wide Irrawaddy River. An enemy reconnaissance plane spotted this, and the Japanese trapped the Chindits with the Irrawaddy between them and India. For several weeks the troops kept on the move, trying to hide from the enemy. When supplies failed to reach them, they ate mules, rats, monkeys, and locusts.

The British officer who walked with me around and around the Shan village had as his recurring theme, "It's a cruel land!" The terrible density of some jungle, he said, made seeing even a few feet ahead impossible; enemies might pass each other only yards apart and not be aware of it.

Wingate talked incessantly, quoting the Bible, lecturing on Medieval art, and extolling the merits of preserving the classics. His main problem, though, was to recross the Irrawaddy unseen by the enemy. As one of his men said, "We returned to India in dribs and drabs after he divided us into small groups, a few dozen men in each."

Those unable to turn westward and recross the river kept going eastward to eventually reach China. All in all, the Chindits walked 1,500 miles through "a cruel land." Dysentery and malaria weakened them; some were in such helpless condition that they were left behind to shift for themselves. Of the 3,000 troops, 883 did not return.

When the Chindits walked out of the jungle, badly defeated, Wingate said that his campaign was just a rehearsal for the real show. But at British headquarters in India, practically everyone thought the effort costly and mad.

"The effort of the Chindits had some value," said the red-haired British officer. "England had a need to cheer about something. The propagandists stressed how the 77th Indian Infantry Brigade had penetrated well behind enemy lines and had destroyed many installations. Yes, back home it gave them something to applaud."

Churchill was impressed. He wanted to put Wingate in charge of the campaign to recapture Burma. The Scot had convinced him that deep-penetration units should not serve as aids to conventional troops, but ought to be the main force, building airfields and establishing strongholds behind enemy lines.

The officer impressed on me that Wingate was the star when Churchill brought him to the Quebec Conference in August 1943. For the first time the United States and Britain began giving serious consideration to the invasion of Burma. The chiefs of staff, both British and U.S., and President Roosevelt paid close attention to the wild Scotsman. Even the levelheaded George Marshall was impressed with Wingate's ideas.

The British high command in Delhi, however, was unhappy. No one wanted to turn over so much equipment and so many men to an officer who acted so crazy. In their opinion, his career in Palestine, Abyssinia, and Burma had been anything but impressive.

Stilwell was pleased that Burma was at last getting attention, but he was worried that Wingate might soon be running the whole show. Marshall tried to calm his friend by saying that at times each of us "must eat some crow."

Some order finally came out of chaos: General Slim would lead regular British Forces; Wingate would lead Chindits; Stilwell would command some Americans and also the Chinese who were training in India. The campaign would be conducted by a new organization, the South East Asia Command, with Lord Louis Mountbatten as Supreme Allied Commander. SEAC included Burma, Malaya, Sumatra, Ceylon, Siam, and French Indochina. As of November 16, 1943, Mountbatten became responsible for operational control of all allied forces in that area.

Things began to happen when Orde Wingate and the American Col. Philip Cochran were brought together to plan a campaign in Burma, one that would make things easier for Stilwell's American and Chinese troops moving eastward. The Wingate-Cochran plan was to get behind Japanese lines to destroy railroads, riverboats, bridges—anything that would stop supplies coming up from Rangoon and Mandalay—and, in general, raise hell with the enemy's equipment and morale.

Wingate and Cochran were so different that it is surprising they worked together as well as they did. The mad Scot thought of war in global terms—freedom for all—and held a fierce view of existence similar to that of the Old Testament prophets, while Cochran, no global thinker, was highly practical, focusing his thoughts on the next enemy plane to be shot from the sky. Wingate wrestled with abstract ideas and a moral conscience; Cochran just wanted to get the show on the road.

Perhaps the two of them got along because both were men of action. Cochran had noticed that the British were great planners, given to compiling vast stacks of paperwork, and that the Americans took the attitude, "When do you want it done? Let's go!" So when he found a British officer with wild ideas—a man of action, willing to take risks—he felt some kinship.

To cement this partnership, Gen. "Hap" Arnold, chief of the USAAF, was generous in providing planes: one hundred CG-4A Waco gliders; one hundred light planes, mainly L-5s with a few L-1s; thirty P-51A Mustang fighter/ground-attack aircraft, twenty B-25H Mitchell medium bombers; twenty C-47 Dakota and twelve UC-64 Norseman transport planes; and six Sikorsky helicopters.

The bases that Cochran and Col. John Alison selected were in Assam hill country along the India-Burma border—Lalaghat for gliders and tow planes; Hailikandi for headquarters, fighters, and bombers.

To hide the planes, native workers cut down some trees in the jungle and had their elephants move the logs. To firm the ground so that the planes would not sink in, mahouts walked elephants around and around at six dollars a day per elephant. Wingate and Cochran planned on opening the campaign by landing four hundred men in gliders in two clearings—Broadway, midway between Myitkyina and Bhamo and just west of the Irrawaddy, and Piccadilly, about forty miles from Broadway. Once the original four hundred had secured the clearings, transports would bring, within a week, about twelve thousand men, mainly Scots of the Black Watch; they would also include West Africans, and Indians who were mostly Gurkhas.

All of this by the light of the moon. In 1944, March 5 brought a full moon, and so that was selected as Burma's D-Day. Eighty gliders, airborne at dusk, would land by moonlight, forty at Broadway and forty at Piccadilly. To divert the enemy's attention from the two clearings, Wingate had a few soldiers land early in an area where his troops had been the year before. Patrols then went from village to village, asking where they might get food for six thousand men and fodder for six hundred mules. The playacting worked so well that natives passed along the false information to the Japanese.

Wingate's order of the day for March 5 was filled with sentences biblical in feeling: "We have all had the opportunity of withdrawing, and we are here because we have chosen to be here: we have chosen to bear the heat and the burden of the day. . . . Comfort and security are not sacrificed voluntarily for others by ill-dispositioned people. Our motives, therefore, may be taken to be the desire to serve our day and generation in the way that seems nearest to our hands. . . . Finally, knowing the variety of man's efforts and the confusion of his purposes, let us pray that God may accept our services and direct our endeavours so that when we shall have done all, we may see the fruits of our labours and be satisfied."

Colonel Cochran looked his pilots in the eye and spoke a few firm sentences: "Tonight your whole reason for existing will be jammed into a couple of minutes." He closed with, "Tonight you will know that you have a soul."

Later a Southern lieutenant drawled, "We shore did!"

A few hours before takeoff, a photographer, much against orders, flew over the clearing and found Piccadilly covered with teak logs. Did the Japanese know? (The logs had been placed there by native woodsmen as part of their work, but Wingate did not know this at the time.)

At the last minute, plans were revised so that all landings would be on Broadway. This change delayed takeoffs only by one hour. At sundown, at 6:40 P.M., two planes each towing two gliders took to the air.

Right off, things went wrong. In trying to get over the mountain, two gliders broke loose, and landed near where they had taken off. Soon another pilot returned, explaining that halfway to Broadway his two gliders had broken free and crashed in the jungle. Another reported the loss of his gliders over the Chindwin River. Two more pilots returned early to report the loss of gliders.

Why were the gliders so sluggish getting over the mountains, and why, when cut loose, did they land at such excessive speed? Perhaps because Wingate's troops had smuggled extra equipment and supplies on board. They remembered that Wingate's jungle campaign the year before had run short of everything. So everybody brought extra cartridges, grenades, and rations, without realizing that the added weight would change the behavior of the gliders.

An hour and twenty minutes after the first plane had taken off, Cochran quit expecting one plane to tow two gliders. He ordered one glider per transport. From then on, none broke loose en route.

It was a long night of horror. Most of the first group of gliders, carrying a pathfinder team, crashed. The ground was rougher than anyone realized, for dense grass had concealed deep ruts from the camera's eye. Glider after glider crashed into the wrecks of those that had crashed before.

In India, Wingate and Cochran heard the radio crackle the word they most feared: Soyalink. It was the name of a sausage made of soya beans and sent by the United States to British troops, who detested it. The code word meant, "Halt the operation. Send no more."

Forty-five of the eighty gliders had departed, and by now most were wrecks. Cochran was inclined to send the rest, but Wingate said, "We must not attempt to snatch victory from defeat."

Troops ran around in the darkness of Broadway, directing landings to various lanes. When the lanes were filled, the pathfinders shifted the lights so that other gliders would go beyond the litter of wrecks. The shouts of the troops giving directions, the sounds of crashing gliders, and the screams of the dying turned the clearing into a terrible place.

Back in India, at the airstrip in Lalaghat, officers crowded into the radio shack, waiting for a sign that somebody was in charge.

At dawn the voice of Col. John Alison came through in fragmented sentences with a brief, dark report.

Amid the chaos on Broadway, the British Brig. "Mad Mike" Calvert, seeing Col. John Alison's dismay, said to the American, "Johnny, we've got the gliders stopped. Everything will look better in the sunshine. Let's have a cup of tea and get some sleep."

While Calvert's batman was making tea, the sound of a tow plane's motor approached the jungle at treetop level. The men on the ground tried to signal it away, but failed. A glider hit the trees with a terrible crash, and two men and a bulldozer popped out without injury or damage.

Mad Mike, sipping his tea, said to Alison, "If we are licked, we might as well admit it." He was in favor of bringing in light planes to evacuate the wounded, and let everybody else spend weeks walking through the jungle back to India.

Alison said, "Let's wait until daylight. Let's see how bad things are."

At daylight they learned that Captain Casey, commanding officer of the engineers, was dead. Alison said to Lieutenant Brackett, of the Airborne Engineers, "We've got to get a strip for small planes. One for large planes would be better. How long would it take to build a field for large transports?"

"I think we can do it by this afternoon."

And they did! Across the terribly furrowed ground, covered with wreckage, they built a long strip for transports.

That first morning, patrols of a dozen men each fanned out in a five-mile radius. No Japanese. No natives. Before noon, Alison radioed Cochran that troop carriers could land by nightfall. Cochran was so relieved that he cried. Wingate showed no emotion.

Light planes came in all day to carry out the injured. By nightfall, nearly a mile of runway was ready for transports. Although the moon was still full, a portable electric light system helped night landings. The first time a helicopter ever went into combat was that night in Burma, when one flew in and out of a place too small for a light plane to land and, in time, evacuated eighteen wounded.

Things had taken a turn for the better. Within hours, gliders were once more in the air, carrying troops to seize a second base behind enemy lines, fifty miles from Broadway, in a clearing called Chowringhee, named after Calcutta's main street. A news story went out that the first glider to land at Chowringhee was piloted by Jackie Cooper, a former child movie star and former husband of Betty Grable, but Cooper was second in, not first.

Mad Mike Calvert led Wingate's Chindits twenty-seven miles west of Broadway to cut a railroad line and a highway in the sector of Mawlu and Henu. The 2,500 Chindits concentrated there and began attacking Japanese lines that carried troops and supplies to the base at Bhamo. Hit-and-run tactics gave way in time to a more traditional way of fighting, until finally the Chindits even built a formal fortified position.

On March 8, Wingate's order of the day: "Our columns are inserted in the enemy's guts. . . . Let us thank God for the great success he has vouchsafed us and press forward with our sword in the enemy's ribs to expel him from our territory of Burma."

On March 12, Wingate sent Mountbatten a message to be forwarded to Churchill: "At a total cost of 120 all ranks, approximately twelve thousand men of Special Force are now within a circle of fifty miles radius centre Burma area."

Nineteen days after the chaotic night at Broadway, Wingate was flying back to Lalaghat, in India, when his B-25 suddenly crashed and exploded on a hill just west of Imphal. What caused the wreck nobody ever knew. The crash site was so remote that it took search parties two days to reach the wreckage. The only thing recognizable was Wingate's pith helmet, the one he had worn during the war in Ethiopia.

Wingate's death was kept secret for weeks; the British feared the Chindits' morale would suffer. The story became public when Wingate's wife put an obituary notice in a London newspaper.

At the time of Wingate's death, on March 24, 1944, American and Chinese troops, moving eastward across upper Burma, were beginning to meet serious opposition. They needed all the help the Chindits could give them in destroying Japanese routes of supply from the south.

After taking a long walk with the British officer who was

familiar with Wingate's ways, I left the Shan village, where Detachment 101 had its headquarters, and decided to stop for a brief visit with the Sawbwa of Hsenwi. I had come to know him and his family through Lt. Paul Dodge, whose job was to compile data on all the trails, bridges, and rivers in whatever part of Burma our troops were advancing. Dodge, who frequently visited the exiled Sawbwa of Hsenwi to gather information, always went bearing gifts, such as a box of hard candy, an overseas edition of a popular novel, a cake of soap, or a mosquito net. Such simple things probably bought a lot of useful information.

The Sawbwa, a member of Burmese royalty, was in his upper forties, a slight, wiry man with sharp features, who looked dapper in his black beret and GI suntans. When the Japanese reached Hsenwi, he and his three wives and his sister hid in caves until they were able to escape through enemy lines. The Japanese confiscated all of his possessions, including two Dodge cars and two Chevrolets. Now the ruler of the Upper Shan states lived in exile in a village near Bhamo.

The Sawbwa's wives appeared to be mere children, although the youngest was twenty-two. Her Shan name meant "Millions of Politeness"; the number-two wife, twenty-four, was "Beautiful Moonstone." I did not recall the name and age of the oldest wife, a princess, the daughter of the Sawbwa of Hsipaw.

The Sawbwa's sister was a delicate and charming woman who had been reared by Catholic nuns in a convent in Mandalay, and spoke excellent English. It seemed strange to hear a girl who wore wraparound *lungyis* and wild jungle flowers speaking about such books as *Gone with the Wind*, *A Tree Grows in Brooklyn*, and *Magnificent Obsession*.

When I returned to the Buddhist monastery press room in Bhamo, the war correspondent who had given me good advice was sitting in the doorway, admiring the moonlight. I told him that I had been given some good information about the Kachin Rangers and Wingate's Chindits.

"That's good," he said. "Now you have some idea of what was happening to the south of Merrill's Marauders and the Chinese troops. Now go talk to somebody who went through that hell up in the north."

139

NINE

When I began writing about the grand assault to recapture Burma, some Americans who had experienced Stilwell's campaign were still around Bhamo. That was fortunate, because records kept by Merrill's Marauders were scarce; troops fighting in the jungle behind enemy lines were not apt to burden themselves with paperwork. Besides, a Japanese shell had blown sky-high a mule carrying records of Merrill's headquarters.

Some Americans in Bhamo recalled how Wingate's Chindits and also the Kachins, under the OSS, had used hit-and-run techniques to distract Lieutenant General Tanaka so that his tenacious 18th Division could not give full attention to Marauders and Chinese moving across upper Burma to open a route between India and China.

One morning at breakfast, an American officer from head quarters of Northern Combat Area Command told me how Admiral Mountbatten had nearly ruined Stilwell's plans as late as January 1944, only days before the campaign was to start. The admiral had wanted to cancel the ground war in Upper Burma and delay everything until the end of the year, when landing craft from Europe might be available for an assault from the sea.

High-ranking British officers in SEAC stood behind Mountbatten, saying the Allies did not have enough troops for a successful attack across Upper Burma. Whenever they said this, Stilwell would needle them by dropping the name of Clive into the argument: Robert Clive had established British imperial dominion over India with only 123 men.

The idea of an assault from the sea pleased Chiang Kai-shek, for Chinese troops would not be involved. General Chennault liked the plan because if it was carried out, many of the supplies scheduled for Stilwell's troops might be turned over to the Air Force.

The admiral's assault by sea did not get the approval of Roosevelt or of the Joint Chiefs of Staff. So Stilwell finally got his chance, the one he had been planning for ever since walking out of Burma nearly two years earlier.

The three thousand GIs of the 5307th Composite Unit (Provisional), made up the first American ground combat unit to reach the Asian mainland. It was called "composite" because its volunteers were drawn from various services and "provisional" because it was to be temporary, to exist only for a ninety-day campaign. Its code name was Galahad.

The unit got a new name when, on January 1, 1944, Stilwell named Gen. Frank Merrill as Galahad's commander. A war correspondent called the unit Merrill's Marauders, and the nickname stuck.

Although Merrill's assignment was now with the infantry, his affection was still with the cavalry. His knowledge of the Japanese language was an advantage; his defective heart, which had caused difficulty during the walkout, was a disadvantage.

Tough fellows were plentiful among the three thousand volunteers from Guadalcanal, New Guinea, Trinidad, Puerto Rico, and the United States. Some knew well the insides of guardhouses, and so it was understandable that their commanding officers might "volunteer" their services for an assignment that would take them far away on what was called a "hazardous mission."

When the three thousand volunteers disembarked on October

31, 1943, at Bombay, they were but a small percentage of the 95,000 troops in the CBI.

Their morale was low when they arrived, and it never rose to great heights.

A major complaint was the lack of furloughs. Every man who volunteered for the secret mission had been promised a furlough, they said. Instead, the Caribbean volunteers flew to Miami and crossed the continent by rail to assemble with Stateside volunteers at San Francisco. Later, these joined volunteer veterans of the South Pacific at Noumea, New Caledonia, and those from the southwest Pacific at Brisbane, Australia. All without furloughs.

Discontent increased when the British took over the Americans in Bombay, hurrying them to a British camp at Delolai to be trained under the direction of Gen. Orde Wingate. Living conditions at the camp were terrible. After having had lunch at a British officers' mess, an American officer said, "Ever since that meal I have understood the origin of the term 'mess' for the place in which an officer eats." The living conditions at Delolai were so vile that Col. Charles N. Hunter, senior officer among the volunteers, sent a potent letter to New Delhi describing the situation, a letter that got the Americans moved to Deogarh, where things were more favorable.

Still the GIs resented the fact that the British were supervising their training. They reasoned that if Wingate directed their destinies, they would get all the nasty jobs that the British didn't want.

Before long, some of the Marauders took over a train and went AWOL. They leaned out of the windows, taking potshots at cows and chickens and even at the feet of Indian coolies, just to watch them dance. The Absence Without Leave list usually stood at ten percent. An Englishman wrote, "They kept the military police busy, the neighboring natives in a state of terror, and their own guardhouse full."

The first time Stilwell saw them, he called them "a tough-looking lot." He resented Wingate's intrusion, for he had fought hard to get American infantrymen into the CBI; it was not easy for him to see someone else take over their training. Especially a Limey. He complained, and to his surprise the American unit was turned over to him with scarcely a struggle.

Stilwell's return to Burma had begun when the Chinese 38th Division crossed the border late in 1943. Gen. Su Li-jen, an able commander during the dark days of 1942, was senior Chinese commander for the reconquest. Immediately his Ramgarh-trained troops ran into soldiers of the Japanese 18th Division, efficient professionals who had acquitted themselves well at Singapore and Rangoon.

The Chinese dug in and refused to fight. Stilwell went into the jungle to give some Chinese officers a tongue-lashing, one that surely made them lose face. To embarrass them further, he led a Chinese platoon, a lieutenant's job, against an enemy position. He once wrote in his journal, "Told them to fight or I would go and stand in the trail up front. This makes them move and it is the only thing that does." General Sun asked that Stilwell avoid getting too near the front, because if anything happened to him, the Chinese officers would be held responsible.

On Christmas Eve of 1943, Stilwell made a favorable entry in his diary: "All things considered, Chinese did a good job. The men are fearless and the junior commanders did O.K. Very tough going to get Japs out of this jungle." The next day he wrote about some Japanese killing themselves, and about capturing one of their wounded officers.

Early in 1944, when the Marauders were ready for jungle fighting, the Chinese were showing signs of combat ability. The Chinese enjoyed their first real jungle victory on February 1, when they captured Taipha Ga in the Hukawng Valley; from here on they would work as a team with the Americans.

Just as Uncle Joe was beginning to enjoy a few bright days, the Japanese launched an offensive on February 4, down south in the Arakan region of the India-Burma frontier. They wanted to cut off the British from Stilwell's troops up north and sever supply lines, and even move far enough into India to encourage a native uprising against the Raj.

Air superiority saved the British. When the enemy overran a British unit, General Slim asked Air Transport Command to move a division into the Arakan. This angered Chiang, for it meant the planes were diverted from carrying supplies across the Hump. The planes, helping Slim to break the enemy's offensive, rained from the sky ammunition, food, and equipment. The

Japanese, with only ten days of food, fought at the end of a long, thin line stretching far back into Burma.

When the Japanese withdrew, Slim conferred with Stilwell about Wingate's airborne brigades, scheduled to relieve the pressure early in March from Chinese and Americans moving across Upper Burma. As described earlier, gliders crashing in the moonlight seemed to doom Wingate's plans, and yet in six days 250 planes flew 650 sorties to transport 9,000 men and 1,300 mules deep into Burma behind the Japanese lines.

When the Marauders arrived by train at Ledo, General Merrill said he would march his men at least one hundred miles into Burma. Colonel Peers of the OSS tried to talk him out of this, urging the general to send them by truck as far as possible. Peers explained that the human body became exhausted fast in the jungle, and it took a long time to renew one's strength. Merrill marched his troops anyway, saying it would be good for their conditioning and would give the muleskinners a chance to know their newly arrived animals.

In his book, *Behind the Burma Road*, Peers wrote, "I remain convinced that this act had much to do with the later tragic events that overtook Merrill's Marauders."

A Chinese-American tank unit joined Chinese and American infantrymen. The ninety light and medium tanks were under command of an American, Col. Rothwell Brown. The tanks, of course, could not strike off across hills and through jungles the way foot soldiers could; they had to work their way along old trails and through new ones cut by the engineers. Colonel Brown said that the route into Burma was always tougher than anything he could imagine.

Waiting in the jungle of Upper Burma were between forty and sixty thousand Japanese who had done well in all their battles. While the Americans numbered only three thousand, the three Chinese divisions trained in India had a total of fifty thousand men.

The mountains and rivers of Burma tend to go north and south, and so, when Stilwell set out from west to east from India toward China, he was confronted by great natural barriers. To get from one place to another, as shown on the map, always took longer than expected. One mile an hour in the jungle was a good pace. Stilwell wrote to his wife, "Yesterday, on a cut trail I took three and a half hours to go three miles, tripping and cursing at every step."

The Marauders entered the Hukawng Valley on February 19. Two Chinese Divisions, the 22nd and the 38th, moved down the valley, applying pressure on the Japanese while the Americans swung wide to the left through jungle and rugged mountains, marching sixty miles in eight days, to come in behind the enemy at Walabum. There they held while the Chinese hammered against the trapped Japanese.

In this, their first victory, some of the fighting was bayonet against bayonet. Here the Americans learned how easy it was to become disoriented in jungle warfare. Nobody knows where anybody else is; turn around twice, and you are confused. There is no church steeple to serve as a landmark, and you cannot orient yourself by the scar on the red clay hill or by the lone pine tree, as was done in field maneuvers at the Infantry School at Fort Benning.

From March 4 to 8 the Marauders killed some eight hundred Japanese while suffering a loss of eight dead and thirty-seven wounded. Ten Americans broke down mentally and were sent back to Ledo, along with 136 severely ill. About 1,500 Chinese died in action.

When Mountbatten visited Walabum and smelled what a British major called "the heavy, sweet stench of death," he observed that a great advantage of sea battles was that "one is spared all of this." He said to the Marauders, "We will supply you by air. If the Japanese get behind you and cut you off, stay put. We will reach you by air."

The fight at Walabum was the first combat in which American and Chinese troops worked together. American liaison officers had been with Chinese troops for some time, but had served as advisers, with no command function. Their greatest use to Stilwell was to let him know, over their own radio channel, when the Chinese were reporting fiction instead of fact.

At Walabum, one American adviser was unable to keep a Chinese regiment from becoming too cautious, and so the main body of the Japanese slipped away through the jungle. The American did not know that there was a tradition in the Chinese military of always allowing the enemy a way out, for a trapped enemy was too dangerous. Some OSS guerrillas ambushed stray Japanese fleeing Walabum, killing 150 while losing only one wounded Kachin.

Once again, when Stilwell thought that things were going his way, Lt. Gen. Renya Mutaguchi, commander of the 15th Army in Burma, invaded India, to the south. The old pro—he had commanded the Japanese regiment that started the war with China at the Marco Polo Bridge near Peking in 1937—was as much of a gambler as Stilwell, and as dramatic as Wingate. Later he admitted he had enjoyed daydreams of "riding through Delhi on a white horse."

Mutaguchi believed that the jungles and mountains of western Burma were impenetrable, until he learned from Stilwell that they were not. He learned the lesson so well that he invaded India, aiming to capture Imphal and Kohema and to cut the railroad at Dimapur. He wanted to sever any lines supplying Stilwell's troops, now moving with effectiveness across upper Burma, and he hoped to encourage native mobs to continue tearing up railway tracks, cutting telegraph wires, and killing white men in their revolt against colonialism.

When Mutaguchi invaded India on March 16, aiming first at Imphal, Stilwell wrote, "This ties a can to us and finishes up the glorious 1944 spring campaign." He knew that if the British retreated and the Japanese cut the Assam-Bengal railroad, his troops would have to retreat from Burma for lack of supplies. To complicate matters, the rice crop had failed in India, causing millions to die of starvation; to relieve the tragedy, transportation carrying food to civilians left the military short of supplies.

The bright spot was that the Japanese would be facing the British 14th Army, commanded by General Slim. Stilwell admired Slim, but knew that the British had been having morale problems; the disillusioned troops had lost too many fights in the past two years. Not only were they run out of Burma in the spring of 1942, but in the fall of that year they lost again. That happened because the British felt they needed something favorable to point to. They could not afford a major offensive, but if they could win a minor one, they might brag about it until it seemed major. So, in the fall of 1942, they decided to take

Akyab, saying that they could establish a base there for attacks on Rangoon.

Everything went awry. The British, thinking the Japanese had a small detachment, went after it with the 14th Division, and might have won had they advanced through the jungle instead of down roads where they were exposed. The Japanese attacked, protected by the jungle, and once more the British retreated, leaving behind 2,500 dead.

Morale fell so low among British troops that many men deserted. Others avoided taking antimalarial drugs, feeling it was better to suffer a fever in the hospital than to fight in the jungle. They dreaded the jungle and feared the Japanese.

Day after day, Slim visited units. Standing on the hood of a jeep, he assured his men that the jungle and the Japanese were less dangerous than they believed. He stressed personal discipline, speaking in several languages to units that included Indians, Gurkhas, and Africans.

General Dorn had once said, "Then General Slim arrived. He was not afraid of anything and looked it." Coupled with that indomitable spirit was a memory that never forgot any lesson learned in an ill-fated campaign, and so he never made the same mistake twice. Suddenly, in the spring of 1944, he inspired the British troops until they fought as they had never fought before in Southeast Asia.

But it wasn't that way right off. In mid-March the Burma front was chaotic, with bands of British troops intermingling with bands of Japanese. For a time the only thing that kept Slim's campaign going was a brilliant airlift flown by British and American pilots. In this the C-46, despite its unfavorable reputation, was more useful than the C-47 because it had nearly twice the capacity.

By the end of April it became evident that the British would, in time, drive the Japanese from India. Mutaguchi's troops at Kohema were in terrible condition, exhausted and cut off from supplies. Of the 155,000 who had crossed the border, 65,000 were now dead. Those who had been so victorious two years earlier now left their own to rot along the trails on which thousands of refugees had died in the dreadful spring of 1942.

While the Marauders were moving across Upper Burma, the

Japanese were also moving freely in China. They were out to destroy air bases of planes that were attacking Japanese shipping lanes. In moving from Changsha to Kweilin, a large American military center, the enemy nearly cut China in two.

Since Stilwell was using Chinese troops with some success in Burma, the U.S. government put pressure on Chiang Kai-shek to give the general direct command over all troops on the China front and even to allow him to bring Communist troops down from the north to use against the Japanese.

Stilwell was not too worried about the enemy's gains in eastern China; the country was so vast—about one third again as large as the United States—he was willing to buy time with space. The Japanese might well stretch themselves too thin and collapse. He hoped eventually to take units of Northern Combat Area Command all the way to China, join Yoke Force, and then push the Japanese in eastern China backward into the sea.

His troubles with Chiang and Chennault started anew. For one thing, Chiang was not willing to allow Communists to come down from the north. Vice-President Henry A. Wallace even visited Chungking to ask Chiang to help get Mao Tse-tung's three million troops training in Yenan to fight against the Japanese, but Chiang never gave such a request any consideration.

It finally became evident that Chennault's 14th Air Force could not stop the enemy ground troops in their marches toward air bases. Chennault wanted Stilwell to get more planes, fuel, supplies of all sorts, and even arms for Chinese foot soldiers. When Kweilin and Liuchow fell, Stilwell felt this proved he had been right all along in insisting that air bases could not continue to exist without ground troops to defend them. He was also pleased that General Marshall was getting annoyed with Chennault's persistence, for Marshall had now decided the Hump flights were absorbing equipment and supplies that might better have been used to hurry along the war in Europe.

Mountbatten asked Roosevelt to put pressure on Chiang to get him to start Yoke Force moving from Yunnan Province into Burma to help Stilwell's troops on the move eastward. Chiang refused, saying he needed Yoke Force in China because the

Communists were too threatening and the Japanese were about to start an offensive north of the Yangtze.

Since Roosevelt had gotten no results, Stilwell decided to try, but he had little hope of success. In Chungking, on March 27, he heard all over again that Chiang would not make a truce with the Communists, allowing them to move southward against the Japanese, and that Yoke Force would not move westward into Burma.

Chiang, however, did promise two divisions to reinforce Stilwell's NCAC troops, and he kept his word. In late April two divisions, the 14th and the 50th, reached India by way of the Hump, and in eight days were outfitted and flown to staging areas in the Hukawng Valley.

Yoke Force continued to be a matter for disagreement. General Dorn, Stilwell's former aide, was a commander of the American Liaison and Advisory Group of Yoke Force, with headquarters in Paoshan. He kept telling Stilwell and anyone else who would listen that the troops in western China were ready to fight. Finally, on May 11, when 72,000 men made bamboo rafts and crossed the Salween, Yoke Force, now called the Chinese Expeditionary Force, began moving toward Burma. But they did not reach Burma until several months later.

The Marauders' victory at Walabum gave Northern Combat Area Command control of the Hukawng Valley. The next mission called for the Chinese to move down the Mogaung Valley while Americans made two more left hooks through the mountains and returned to the valley to set up roadblocks behind the Japanese, serving once more as anvils while the Chinese pounded away from the front. The First Battalion of the Marauders was to block the road at Shaduzup, and the Second and Third at Inkangahtawng.

The First Battalion got off to a good start, covering twenty miles in two days. But then they began meeting small Japanese units; the fighting was especially severe whenever the enemy blocked trails with crossing machine-gun fire and artillery. Fortunately, Kachin guerrillas, led by Lt. James Tilly of Detachment 101, were behind the Japanese, ambushing them enough to

149

cause confusion. Soon Tilly's fifty Kachins took over as guides for the Americans.

The Marauders found it a scary experience to look at a high, steep mountain, covered with dense wilderness, and realize that it must be crossed. Such a wilderness demands arduous hewing and chopping; on one occasion it took two days of sweat with kukris and machetes to get four miles. The troops not only cleared trails for themselves, but cleared spaces for airdrops.

Because of the surrounding hills, the C-47s had to unload cargo at high altitudes. Light planes flew in low to drop smoke bombs, and "kickers" inside the open doors of transports aimed at the smoke. The Marauders often lost free-dropped grain, but they usually located in the hills anything that floated down by parachute.

As had many soldiers in Burma before them, the Americans learned that a lack of water was far worse than a lack of food. Whenever troops were trapped on high ground, planes dropped drinking water to men and mules. On March 20, several Kachin guides for the First Battalion began "excited jabbering," as the Americans called it. Scouts at the head of the column thought the natives wanted food and cigarettes, and gave them both; the Kachins thought they were being rewarded for their information, which had to do with a Japanese machine gun just ahead. The machine gun killed one Marauder and injured two. The incident taught a lesson: Whenever Kachins begin "nervous jabbering," hurry an interpreter to the head of the column.

The First Battalion soon found Japanese blocking every trail, so they began cutting through more dense jungle. By avoiding the easy routes, they surprised the enemy time and again. For instance, they came upon a group of Japanese lounging beside newly dug foxholes. By creeping forward with caution, they were able to kill seven and take over the foxholes, so that when a counterattack came, they were able to kill still more Japanese.

That they might surprise the Japanese when slipping behind them at Shaduzup, the Marauders avoided contact on the way. The going was rough as they kept moving cross-country. On March 23 and 24 they hacked through what at first seemed impenetrable growth; at each steep hill they unloaded mules and hand-carried supplies upward. It was a slow five miles, but they met no Japanese and so it was worth the effort.

The Kachins reported that about three hundred Japanese held Shaduzup and that five or six hundred more were up north, in the vicinity of Jambu Bum, where the Chinese waited to begin their attack southward as soon as the Americans were in position behind the enemy.

To fake the Japanese out of position, a rifle platoon of Marauders made a feint just north of Shaduzup, and when the enemy reacted, the rest of the battalion cut across the road four miles south of the town. At three in the morning, in silence and with caution, troops waded the Mogaung River and struck at dawn. Not even a sentry was in sight. Early risers were cooking breakfast at small fires. With fixed bayonets, Marauders rushed the camp. Naked Japanese scattered, but bayonets, grenades, and tommy guns killed many of them. With high-strung elation, the Marauders changed into clean underwear found in a truck, and ate the rice and fish cooking over the breakfast fires.

A counterattack started at seven o'clock, when enemy snipers moved into position. By nine, Japanese artillery shells were pounding the area.

All of this activity diverted much attention from the Chinese 22nd Division advancing down the road from Walabum to Jambu Bum, at the threshold of the Mogaung valley, ten miles north of Shaduzup. The Japanese kept pulling back to cope with the Americans behind them, and so the Chinese moved southward with some ease.

By afternoon the Japanese were counterattacking from several directions, but the Americans stopped each attack and inflicted heavy casualties. At night the enemy ceased ground attacks to make heavy use of artillery; the Marauders, lacking artillery, responded with mortars and grenades whenever they heard a suspicious sound along the front. The Japanese and Chinese finally settled into an artillery duel while the Americans rested and listened to the distant rumble.

The First Battalion completed its mission at Shaduzup, but behind schedule. It counted eight of its own dead, and three hundred Japanese. For rest and treatment for its thirty-five wounded, the Americans withdrew a mile up the Chengu River to a Seagrave hospital unit.

General Merrill ordered the First Battalion to leave Shaduzup and rejoin the rest of the Marauders. This meant a trip across the Kumon Range, one so rugged that in ten hours the troops covered scarcely a mile. They were out of touch with headquarters for several days because a sack of grain, dropped from a C-47, had smashed the unit's only long-range radio.

While the First Battalion had been making its fifty-mile hike to Shaduzup, the Second and Third Battalions, followed by one Chinese regiment, were making a wider and deeper sweep of about eighty miles with a mission to block the Kamaing Road at Inkangahtawng, south of Shaduzup. These battalions crossed a series of sharp ridges that changed elevation as much as 1,600 feet in four miles.

Near Inkangahtawng, Col. Charles Hunter's men kept running into fortified positions and were sometimes surprised by Japanese attacks. For instance, they held off a heavy attack from a stand of *kunai* grass eight feet tall; but they were running out of ammunition, and to make things worse, they were nearly cut off from the rear while Japanese trucks carried reinforcements up from Kamaing.

Colonel Hunter, not knowing that the First Battalion was behind schedule at Shaduzup, wondered why the Japanese seemed so free to concentrate troops around Inkangahtawng. Only when he intercepted a radio message from the First Battalion to General Merrill did he learn of the delay at Shaduzup. Since the First Battalion did not put in the roadblock at Shaduzup until March 29, the Second and Third Battalions were forced out of the area around Inkangahtawng on March 25. The ineffective preliminary move of the Marauders on Inkangahtawng cost the Marauders two killed and twelve wounded; the Japanese dead numbered two hundred. The Second Battalion carried its wounded on litters as it withdrew eastward through torrential rains and over rough terrain. Finally the unit reached a clearing large enough for small planes to land to carry out the wounded.

Merrill ordered Hunter to retreat northward as far as Nhpum Ga. Since the trails were wide enough, the Japanese pursued the

Marauders in trucks, until air strikes on the enemy's column delayed the pursuit somewhat.

An I-and-R platoon with some riflemen attached did a remarkable job of covering the Second Battalion's retreat; those relatively few men held off a sizable enemy force for two days without suffering any casualties. Japanese artillery finally found its range, and shells searched the trail that ran along a narrow ridge, a trail uphill and ankle deep with mud all the way to Nhpum Ga. As the order to move faster ran up and down the column, mules began falling, calls for medics came from the rear, and everyone hurried at an awkward run.

The exhausted troops reached Nhpum Ga, a village of five huts 2,800 feet above sea level. It was evident that the Japanese might well use the trails on each side, isolating the Second Battalion while hurrying to face the First Battalion at Shaduzup. The Third Battalion could not be of much help, for it was at Hsamshingyang, four miles to the north, defending the airstrip and being ready in event that the Japanese were determined to continue northward.

Soon both battalions were busy fighting the Japanese, who seemed everywhere at once. Artillery attacks and ground attacks kept the exhausted Second Battalion on Nhpum Ga from resting. Kachin guerrillas were of great help; by constantly ambushing small units, they gave the Japanese the idea that the Marauders numbered more and controlled a larger area than they really did.

After a few days, living conditions atop the knoll became insufferable. Of two hundred horses and mules, about seventy-five had been killed, and their carcasses began to putrefy; the wind shifted and brought with it the odor of decomposing Japanese corpses.

When the Japanese captured the water hole, the Marauders knew they were surrounded. In the few swampy pools still available, dead mules added the taste of decomposing flesh to the water. In desperation the Marauders asked that five hundred gallons of water be airdropped in plastic bags.

On April 1, the beleaguered Second Battalion received some favorable news: The First Battalion had finally captured Shaduzup, and the Second Battalion was given credit for contributing to that success, for it had kept the enemy distracted at In-kangahtawng. Everybody hoped that the Japanese would now withdraw to regroup well to the south, but that did not happen.

After seven days of siege, the situation at Nhpum Ga was desperate. The wounded could no longer be evacuated, and so several died and were buried in that miserable, confined space.

By now Colonel Hunter commanded the Marauders. On March 28, when he had returned from Nhpum Ga to Hsam-shingyang, he found General Merrill unconscious from another heart attack. Stilwell ordered Merrill flown to the hospital at Ledo, and put Hunter in charge.

Before volunteering for hazardous duty, Colonel Hunter had been in charge of weapons instruction at the Infantry School at Fort Benning. There I had come to know and respect him. While writing a field manual, I had asked his advice about the tactical placement of certain weapons in the field, and he had given me help in simple, direct language that I translated into some jargon that the committee on field manuals in the Pentagon would accept.

Hunter, small and compact, had the build and movements of a gymnast. His hands were large and strong, and his forearms were covered with dense blond hair. Whenever he handled a weapon, he did it with a deftness that had about it a certain beauty. He was a professional, all right. While observing all of life with a penetrating eye, Hunter was what Will Rogers used to call "a close chewer and a tight spitter."

Merrill was no sooner in the hospital in Ledo than he decided that the Marauders needed artillery, and so he sent two 75-mm howitzers with instructions on how to assemble and use them. Colonel Hunter found several infantrymen who had been with a pack artillery unit in New Guinea. Instead of using guns for indirect fire, the artillerymen-turned-foot soldiers usually pre-ferred to fire point-blank at Japanese bunkers.

Colonel Hunter decided that the Third Battalion at Hsam-shingyang would have to break through the Japanese force that encircled the badly mauled Second Battalion at Nhpum Ga. He planned various tricks to fool the enemy; for instance, he had a fake message dropped by plane so that it would fall behind enemy lines, announcing to the Second Battalion that a parachute battalion would land south of Nhpum Ga. The enemy must have seen through the fake, for no Japanese units seemed to withdraw from the Nhpum Ga encirclement.

There followed five days of the heaviest fighting of the war. Time and again the Third Battalion tried to break through to cover the four miles from Hsamshingyang to Nhpum Ga, but always the Japanese stopped them. Machine guns, mortars, and artillery made life in that relatively small area a hell on earth. The men who survived had anecdotes of bravery to repeat through the years. For instance, Lieutenant Woomer, leader of a weapons platoon, worked his way to within twenty-five yards of two enemy machine guns that were holding up the attack. From this position he directed the fire of a mortar unit until the shells were landing just beyond the target. His next order was: "Deflection correct. Bring it in twenty-five yards. If you don't hear from me, you'll know you came this way too far. Then shift it back just a little and you'll be right on it." The next rounds knocked out the enemy guns.

Everyone still alive atop Nhpum Ga on Easter Sunday, April 9, 1944, will always remember that day. Just before dawn, patrols moved down the trail from Hsamshingyang to Nhpum Ga without any opposition. The Japanese had retreated.

The Marauders were too exhausted to give chase. They spent the day cleaning up the scene of the siege—burying dead Japanese, scattering lime to disinfect the area, and using flame throwers on dead animals to rid the place of swarms of flies.

Fifty-seven Marauders lost their lives at Nhpum Ga, and 302 were wounded. The Japanese dead exceeded four hundred.

By the time Colonel Hunter took over the Marauders, it was evident that General Wingate was correct in preaching that no unit could retain its efficiency in the jungle beyond ninety days. Although the Americans had not been there that long, they were getting "jungle happy" in a country they called Green Hell.

"Combat in Southeast Asia is more depressing than that in Europe," an officer at NCAC said. "Americans grow up accustomed to open spaces and to towns and to fast movement, all a part of Europe's environment. But the jungle brings a hemmed-in feeling with slow movement and heat, rain, and humidity. It all makes everything depressing."

Upon returning from a trip to Europe, a correspondent for the *CBI Roundup* said to me, "This CBI patch got me free drinks in Europe. Over there they know about the horrors of a jungle. Some have scribbled on their trucks, 'Don't send me to the CBI.' "

When General Marshall requested volunteers for a secret mission in Burma, he asked for men "of a high state of physical ruggedness and stamina." Many fell short of that, according to a medical report: "We expected picked troops. Instead we found many chronically ill men, also numerous psychiatric problems."

Marauders ate less than the three thousand calories a day that the medics believed were needed to keep a soldier in condition, and energy declined and disease had its way. Malaria, the number-one enemy, was joined by dengue fever, mite typhus, cholera, scabies, yaws, and fungi. Rotting was prevalent; feet flinched upon touching the ground, and the body flinched when touching anything, especially a heavy pack and a rifle.

Nature, as cruel as the enemy, caused constant uneasiness. The continuous whir of mosquitos announced that this was the world's center for malaria; leeches latched on to exposed flesh and sucked blood; swarms of angry black flies would sting and burn until men and mules were near madness, and snakes slithered against the body in the night.

In open country, temperatures reached well above one hundred. Clothes were always damp, even in the dry season, and weapons rusted unless oiled daily. During the monsoon, from May to September, over three hundred inches of rain fell in some parts of Upper Burma, and then fields turned to lakes, trails and roads ceased to exist, and all the world was gray and waterlogged. Rain came early in 1944—twelve days of it in January, eighteen in February, ten in March, and ten in April. Although this was not officially the monsoon, a driving rain was depressing no matter what it was called.

Their combat fatigues were always wet and sticking to their bodies. A Marauder wrote home, "Since there is no place to sit, we eat the stuff standing in the mud with rain beating on our helmets and water running down our backs."

A packet of rations opened in a heavy rain instantly turned to soup. Soon food became boring, then disgusting; some soldiers retched at the sight of it. Diarrhea was severe. Sometimes the rain lashed so hard that one could not see a step ahead. Exhaustion was a blessing when time came to fall asleep curled up in the mire. Upon awakening, those terribly aching bones were waiting.

Nature conspired in so many ways. Bamboo thickets, for instance, were often so dense that a soldier had to tunnel through them, learning at first stroke that bamboo was exceedingly hard to cut. A certain variety of bamboo, *bullaca*, was from four to six inches thick, growing in clumps from ten to fifteen feet in diameter; the Japanese would burrow under a clump, come up in the center, and be in practically a concrete barricade, protected against rifle and artillery fire. Tall stands of elephant grass might be a welcome relief, except that the blades were as sharp as razors. Streams, wide, deep, and swift, were also problems; soldiers had to take material found in the jungle and lash it together to form foot bridges strong enough to hold in place until the last man and beast had crossed. Stilwell wrote of "this bitching jungle."

A mile an hour in the jungle is good marching. An officer said that even this required "a great mental effort to put one foot in front of another."

At first, mules bore much of the burden; small mules carried 125 pounds, and large ones carried 200. Each day something happened to a mule or two. They went lame, or took sick, or slid off cliffs—and then their burdens were transferred to human backs.

Seven hundred Marauders acted as muleskinners. Some had volunteered for the job, and others had been ordered to it when mules joined the unit shortly before entering the jungle. Those who handled mules soon saw them as more trouble than they were worth; it was annoying to have to take care of an animal while other soldiers were slumped on the ground, resting. The Americans were fortunate, though, in being spared a problem that Wingate's Chindits faced: they had to try to lead mules into a C-47 and keep them calm during flight, when the beasts would try to throw themselves down or kick the sides out of the airplane.

Americans were also spared the agony suffered by the Chin-

157

dits who sometimes shot their own wounded rather than let them fall into Japanese hands. Somehow or other a light plane could always land near enough to carry out wounded Americans. The Marauders learned early in combat what soldiers everywhere learn: The sight of the severely wounded is more unnerving than the sight of the dead.

The Chinese also helped lower morale because they specialized in making Marauders mad. A concern for hygiene, for instance, did not exist in the Chinese soldier's mind, but it had been harped on in every phase of U.S. military training. So GIs got annoyed whenever they came across an area made squalid by Chinese who defecated wherever they pleased, encouraging the spread of disease. Americans also got annoyed whenever they felt the Chinese were getting first choice in equipment; a GI might be stumbling around a bivouac area in the dark and come across a *bing* lighting his way with an olive drab GI flashlight. Another thing that Americans resented was the way Chinese stole from them; at an airdrop *bings* often rushed forward, grabbing things not meant for them and sometimes pointing rifles at anyone who objected.

Stilwell lowered morale among the Marauders whenever he made a decision favoring Chinese over Americans. For example, when an American sentry challenged a Chinese officer for the password and the officer spat in his face, the sentry knocked down the officer and went to the stockade for it.

After the Marauders and the Chinese broke the blockade at Nhpum Ga in mid-April, Stilwell decided he must capture Myitkyina before the monsoon, less than a month away. Otherwise all of that combat in the Hukawng and Mogaung Valleys was just so much sound and fury.

If he captured the Myitkyina airfield, the Japanese could no longer use it as a base for planes attacking cargo flying the Hump; besides, the Air Transport Command could use the airstrip when carrying supplies to China and so reduce traffic over the main Hump route, with its great heights, greater distances, and terrible weather. With the Myitkyina area in friendly hands, the Ledo road and pipeline could be extended well toward a linkup with the Burma Road.

The secret march to Myitkyina, called End Run, began

April 28 with 1,400 Marauders, 4,000 Chinese, and 600 Kachins. Since the Americans had lost 700 men killed, wounded, or sick, Stilwell added Kachins and Chinese to bring the Marauder strength up to 7,000. These troops were divided into three combat teams called H Force, M Force, and K Force.

Now the Marauders faced terrain far worse than anything covered in the three hundred miles since leaving Ledo. The weather was supposed to be clear for two more weeks, but in 1944 the monsoon struck on May 1, and from then on the jungle was a great pressure cooker.

Even the Kachins, who seemed undaunted by anything in the jungle, said that the Marauders would never be able to cross the Kumon Range, shaped like a six-thousand-foot razorback hog. To make matters worse the ancient trails had practically ceased to exist for lack of use in the past ten years. The going was so steep in places that soldiers hacked steps into the mountainside and even crawled upward on hands and knees. Muleskinners unburdened their pack animals and manhandled their loads up dangerous inclines. The lead combat team lost fifteen mules when the naturally tough, surefooted beasts died of exhaustion or plunged over precipices, carrying ammunition and weapons with them.

On the ninety-mile march, the men were often so near exhaustion that they just didn't care anymore. Climbing steep trails high in the mountains is an agony for the muscles, but, even worse, in the thin air breathing becomes labored, followed by weakness and nausea. At times the men were so weak and sick that they stumbled and fell, indifferent to the nearness of death.

Anger kept them going. They kept telling each other that they had volunteered for one dangerous mission: Wasn't that Walabum? Or Shaduzup? Or Inkangahtawng? To put it another way, they had volunteered for a ninety-day mission, and that time would be up May 7.

They complained that the Chinese got the best assignments. The Chinese moved through valleys, while Americans had to climb mountains on long end runs to get behind enemy lines. Officers of the Marauders could not think of any way to give their men some semblance of pride, for they too resented that

Stilwell spent so much concern on Chinese that he neglected Americans. Vinegar Joe was a heroic figure to many soldiers in Southeast Asia, but not to the Marauders. One of them bragged that he had held Stilwell in the sight of his rifle and "came damn near shooting the sonofabitch."

A few things pleased them. One was the Sioux Indian, a deadly marksman, who knew how to penetrate enemy lines. They also took pride in several American-born Japanese who were members of an excellent intelligence-and-reconnaissance platoon.

Secrecy was the aim of the march on Myitkyina, but contact with the enemy seemed inevitable. A few Marauders congratulated themselves when, upon approaching a fork in the trail, they watched a Japanese scout pass by without seeing them. A little later, however, a Marauder accidentally fired a shot that alerted several Japanese cooking a meal and allowed them time to escape. The Americans wiped out a squad at a trail block, but were soon stopped by enemy machine-gun fire. Several skirmishes developed into such sizable fights that by May 10 the enemy was aware that Americans were in the Hpungin Valley.

May 11 was the hottest day the Marauders had known. The trail ran up and down inclines so steep that men were collapsing from weakness and exhaustion. At one point they had to leave mules and heavy weapons behind as they inched their way up an incline to attack a Japanese unit. Several attempts by the Americans and the Chinese failed to dislodge the enemy. The Marauders had been without food all day, and were running short of ammunition. Darkness made withdrawing difficult, especially while evacuating the wounded. Eight Americans had died; twenty-one had suffered wounds. The Chinese casualties were heavier.

These unsuccessful fights were probably not without some value; they held the enemy's attention well north of Myitkyina, and may even have fooled him into thinking this was the entire force of Northern Combat Area Command. The Japanese evidently did not know that while they were fighting M Force and K Force, Colonel Hunter's H Force was hurrying southward as secretly as possible. Across little-known trails a Kachin, trained by OSS, led them. Fifteen miles from Myitkyina a poisonous snake bit the guide; his foot puffed up and he became too ill to move. Without him the Americans would not be able to find their way in darkness across the intricate maze of paths. Two American officers slashed the spot where the fangs had penetrated and for two hours sucked blood from the incision. At two-thirty in the morning, the Kachin guide mounted Colonel Hunter's horse and continued leading H Force.

Early in the morning of May 16, when two natives saw the column moving down a trail, Colonel Hunter had them taken into custody and held so that they could not alert the enemy. After crossing a river and entering Namkwi, Hunter had the Kachin guerrillas round up all inhabitants of the village, many of doubtful loyalty, and hold them within H Force's perimeter until next morning.

In spite of all the skirmishes and fights up north, H Force reached the Myitkyina airstrip unknown to the enemy. A dozen Japanese worked on the runway, unaware that three Marauder scouts crouched in the grass a hundred yards away. The first estimate was that 350 Japanese held Myitkyina; later the figure was raised to 3,500, and then to 4,000. Nobody ever really knew for sure the enemy's strength.

The 150th Regiment of the 50th Chinese Division attacked the airstrip in midmorning of May 17, while Marauders captured the ferry landing down on the Irrawaddy. In less than an hour the message went to Stilwell, "In the ring," meaning the field was in friendly hands, and four hours later the general jumped with enthusiasm when the message "Merchant of Venice" came through, meaning that transport planes might now land.

"This will burn up the Limeys!" he said.

Mountbatten was burned up because he had not been informed of the attack on Myitkyina. Yet he was tactful in a message of congratulations to Stilwell, saying that crossing the Kumon Range and seizing Myitkyina airstrip were feats that would "live in military history."

Stilwell and Mountbatten were both too optimistic, for many dark days stretched ahead. The trouble started when Stilwell decided the Chinese should have the honor of capturing the town of Myitkyina. Two battalions, all green troops recently arrived by way of the Hump from China, were flown into the airstrip. In their attack on the town, each unit mistook the other for the enemy and inflicted heavy casualties on their own people. They were pulled back, and more-seasoned Chinese troops attacking the town also grew confused and killed each other. Trigger-happiness rather than poor leadership caused this; as Stilwell said, "The Chinese are jittery. They shoot at the crack of a twig."

Confusion gave the enemy time to bring up reinforcements. Within a few days, Maj. Gen. Genzu Mizukami moved five thousand troops into Myitkyina. Even though the British, operating in twenty-six columns of four hundred men each, were blocking the single railroad in north Burma, the Japanese could use the Irrawaddy for transport.

In the opening days at Myitkyina, General Merrill followed all action from the air. On May 19 he landed at the airstrip, departed late in the day, and, upon returning to Shaduzup, suffered another heart attack. On May 22 a colonel was named as commander at Myitkyina; within a few days he was replaced by a general. Changes of command up and down the line were frequent during those two and a half dark months at Myitkyina.

Of the 1,310 American Marauders to reach Myitkyina on May 17, about half were evacuated to rear hospitals within two weeks. Living in mud and water and fighting in a monsoon, many suffered ulcers, jungle rot, and infections that sometimes ate through to the bone. Dysentery and mite typhus caused more damage than the Japanese. And there was always the smell of fear that General Dorn once described as "strangely pungent, one that clings to sweat-stained uniforms."

The exhausted Myitkyina Task Force lacked the strength to deal with a strong enemy counterattack. If the Japanese recaptured the airfield, Chinese and Americans were doomed unless they fled by jungle trails over which they had suffered, and in doing that they might also be doomed, for they were very weak.

On May 22 things were so bad that Stilwell called it "Black Monday." He wrote, "This is one of those terrible worry days, when you wish you were dead."

When there were only two hundred of the original three

thousand Marauders left in the fighting, the medics were told to slow down the decline of troop strength. No one went to the hospital until he had a temperature of 102 degrees for at least three days. Some Marauders were ordered out of their hospital beds and flown back to Myitkyina before they were even remotely well. Medics objected, but that did little good. One frustrated doctor stopped a truck full of sick soldiers en route to Ledo airstrip, and sent them back to the hospital. Another group of recovering patients were declared unfit for combat as soon as they landed at Myitkyina, and were immediately flown back to India.

Troops untrained for combat began to arrive at Myitkyina. Cooks, truckdrivers, engineers, and clerks handled in an awkward way the weapons thrust upon them. Such untrained troops more than once broke and ran under Japanese attack.

Some Marauders had been fighting for more than three months across some of the meanest country in the world. Now a few went wild, creating such terror at Myitkyina that military police were afraid to arrest them. They destroyed things right and left, and threatened anyone who came along. Many had been rough fellows even before suffering the terrible agony of Burma.

The men who fought at Myitkyina will long remember a particular general who went out of his way to make himself repulsive. It was his custom to greet troops on incoming planes with the short speech, "Welcome to Myitkyina, men. You are here to die."

One day when things were going exceptionally badly, a chaplain stepped from a C-47. The general sneered in disgust, "A chaplain! For Christ's sake!"

The chaplain answered, "Yes, General, I hope it is for Christ's sake."

The story went around that one night the general came close to being shot by his own men. Just as they were about to spray his tent with a machine gun, two officers came to visit him. By the time the officers left, the hot anger of the would-be murderers had cooled enough so that they abandoned the plan.

Even through the discord of Myitkyina, Colonel Hunter remained a perfectionist. He lived by the book, and any departure

from Army regulations annoyed him. He so disliked the way
Stilwell often played things by ear that after the war he complained, "There was the Army's way and Stilwell's way."

Hunter also felt a certain unreality about Myitkyina. He later
said that when he was riding his pony through a Chinese battalion before an attack, he suddenly asked himself: "Is this Chuck
Hunter, of Oneida, New York, or General 'Chinese' Gordon?"

Colonel Hunter wanted to be a general, and had a right to feel
that way. He usually concealed his hurt, but not always. One
day several generals flew into Myitkyina, clean-shaven and crisp,
and called for Hunter who was nauseated, tired, dirty, and
disgusted. He had been campaigning for five months over some
of the worst terrain in the world.

A general said, "Colonel, we want to ask your advice about
something."

Hunter snapped, "When I start giving advice to generals, I'll
be wearing a star."

He turned and walked away.

Even when morale was at low ebb, the Marauders liked
General Merrill, but felt he got credit and publicity that should
have gone to Hunter. They did not hold it against the general,
for they knew he had not planned things that way; still, they
always saw Hunter as the workhorse who deserved more credit
than he got.

By the end of July the Japanese in Myitkyina were cut off from
supplies and reinforcements. The first of them to escape floated
rafts down the Irrawaddy. When they began retreating in great
numbers on August 1, Kachin guerrillas trapped many fleeing
south by river and those fleeing eastward toward China. Such
ambushes accounted for several hundred enemy dead.

On that crucial day, August 1, Maj. Gen. Genzu Mizukami,
commander of the Myitkyina garrison, sent the Emperor of
Japan an apology, and then, following the *bushido* code, committed ritual suicide. Immediately, 187 Japanese gave themselves
up, a remarkable turn of events, for prisoners had always been
hard to come by.

At Myitkyina the Americans lost 272 dead and 955 wounded,
plus 980 lost through severe illness. The Chinese counted 972

dead and 3,184 wounded. The Japanese had 790 dead and 1,180 wounded.

The Marauders got more publicity than any unit that size is apt to get. Perhaps this happened because Churchill made sure the Chindits were highly publicized, causing American correspondents to be exceptionally generous with newspaper space for their own troops.

A Distinguished Unit Citation awarded to the Marauders read, "After a series of successful engagements in the Hukawng and Mogaung Valleys of North Burma, in March and April 1944, the unit was called on to lead a march over jungle trails through extremely difficult mountain terrain against stubborn resistance in a surprise attack on Myitkyina. The unit proved equal to its task and after a brilliant operation on 17 May 1944 seized the airfield at Myitkyina, an objective of great tactical importance in the campaign, and assisted in the capture of the town of Myitkyina on 3 August 1944."

Later, Col. Charles Hunter called the Marauders "the most beat upon, most misunderstood, most mishandled, most written about, most heroic, and yet most unrewarded regimental-sized unit in World War II."

TEN

Although I traveled around Upper Burma, I still spent a good deal of time in the Buddhist monastery, the *ponjyi chaung*, as the monks called it. There I read unit reports so dull that the only way to bring them alive was through interviews with men who still felt the abrasions of war.

Although the reports were dull, life in the deserted monastery was not; interesting people kept dropping by. I remember with pleasure two charming correspondents, Martha Sawyers, doing portraits for *Collier's* covers, and her husband, Bill Reusswig, drawing pen-and-ink sketches for King Features Syndicate.

One night Martha Sawyers, Bill Reusswig, Lt. Jim McIver, the press censor, and I went to a movie in a jungle clearing high above the Irrawaddy. We sat on logs, amid noisy Chinese soldiers, watching Errol Flynn in a film set in wartime Burma.

Later, back in the monastery, Bill said, "Why do things look more glamorous on the screen than they do in reality? Even those scenes that showed GIs merely sitting around in the jungle talking! When we are a part of such scenes, why don't we see anything glamorous in them?"

"War does look more attractive in the movies and in four-color magazine ads," agreed Lieutenant McIver.

War also looks more glamorous in retrospect. It is like looking back on college days; we tend to recall mainly the sunny hours.

Martha Sawyers had come to Bhamo to do a portrait of Father James Stuart for *Collier's*. She knew that General Stilwell had said, "The biggest mistake the Japanese made was not taking Father Stuart prisoner," and that General Merrill had called Stuart "the bravest man I ever knew." It would have surprised none of us had we known that at war's end the shy little Irish priest from Derry would be appointed an officer of the Most Excellent Order of the British Empire for helping refugees, and would be awarded the Legion of Merit from the United States.

Shortly after meeting the missionary, Martha Sawyers wrote to her editor: "I had heard fabulous stories of Father Stuart for weeks at various points throughout India and Burma, until he became a huge, towering mythological giant shrouded in mystery. When I met him in Bhamo to draw his portrait I was bowled over by his personal appearance. Instead of the character that I had expected, here was a short stocky man with a handsome Irish face that was almost too good looking. His voice was quiet, well-modulated in tone, but he could hardly open his mouth without saying something clever, ridiculous, or just plain funny."

Just outside the monastery door, in a courtyard lined with statues of the Buddha, Martha Sawyers settled down to make a pastel portrait of Father Stuart. After a few minutes she said, "You are a man of few words."

"Yes, but I use them over and over."

"How did you happen to become a priest?"

"The police said that I could either go to jail or to the seminary."

In time he warmed up enough to tell the artist that Merrill's Marauders had taken up a collection to help finance his church in the Kachin Hills. "I'm an Irishman by birth, but I have gotten so much from Americans that I have become an American by 'extraction.'"

After completing the portrait, which included the dashing Aussie hat, Martha held it toward her subject for his inspection.

He studied it critically and mused, "No doubt I contributed to the beauty of it."

While Martha Sawyers was making a sketch of me, Father Stuart and Lieutenant McIver sat in the shadow of a Buddhist statue and spoke of Father Stuart's twenty-one fellow Columbans who had been held prisoners in a leper asylum in Mandalay until Saint Patrick's Day of 1945. The missionary said that he had recently visited them, and that one had been killed by a stray Japanese shell the day before release. Fragments struck Father Thomas Murphy, who was preparing to say mass in a room used as a chapel. Since no one in the asylum was skilled enough to perform the major surgery needed, one of the missionaries slipped out the back and waded through a canal to reach the British outpost. The officer there sent a radio message to headquarters for help; headquarters promised to fly Father Murphy to India within two hours.

Since the victim was in such critical condition, the missionaries who bore the stretcher decided not to take the back route, but to save time by going down the main road. The Japanese held their fire, and the group arrived safely at the outpost. A gun carrier was waiting to transport the victim a few miles to an ambulance, but before the ambulance could reach the field hospital, Father Murphy was dead.

Trucks could not come close to the leper colony because they would have been shelled by the Japanese. So the Columban missionaries and other internees, about 160 in all, slipped out the back way, sloshed through a canal, and moved along a remote road in an uneasy procession that included a nun with a broken leg, several patients so weakened by fever that they had to be carried, and a few priests hobbling along with pieces of shrapnel in their legs. On his back, Father Edmund McGovern carried a French bishop, eighty years of age. In spite of all the pain, they moved with spirit. Had it not been for Father Murphy's death, it would have been a glorious Saint Patrick's Day.

Just before leaving the monastery garden, Father Stuart told Martha Sawyers that I had volunteered to come to Burma to run mule trains through the jungle, but that instead I had been assigned to ride herd on fifty-five war correspondents on a trip to China. That story amused him so much that he told it to every visitor, and always ended by asking me, "Which would you rather ride herd on, mules or war correspondents?" and I always said, "Mules!"

Father Stuart took off down the bank of the Irrawaddy; where he was going I did not know. It was the last time I would see him.

Sitting there in the monastery garden, McIver told us a few anecdotes about Father Stuart. The Japanese, for instance, trying to trick him into admitting that he was an Englishman, even played "God Save the King," but the missionary stuck to his chair and his Irish neutrality.

"Surely he does not engage in combat," said Martha.

"No," said McIver, "but he has great influence with the Kachins. When the war started down in south Burma, all the natives seemed against the British and the Chinese. They even helped the Japanese. But up here they seem all for us. Father Stuart and those missionaries he was talking about, and Doc Seagrave and the Protestant missionaries, deserve credit. The Kachins think Stuart is great. Without the Kachins the OSS would not get very far; they form an intelligence network across upper Burma.

"You can't blame them for liking Stuart. Nothing is too much for him. He once walked 240 miles through Jap territory to reach the Kachin Rangers. He acted as interpreter between Kachins and Americans behind Jap lines."

Bill Reusswig said that Father Stuart's portrait was the best piece of work his wife had ever done. Of course, Bill and Martha were unhappy when McIver had to break the news to them that the censor at Theater Headquarters in New Delhi would not permit the portrait to be published. Nothing was to be published about the Irish priest, the censor said, because American Army authorities feared that if any indication were given that he had helped the Allies, the Japanese might kill every missionary in their prisoner-of-war camps.

This did not assuage Bill Reusswig's hurt feelings; I never knew a correspondent to accept a censor's unfavorable decision with grace. As Eric Sevareid, a correspondent in the CBI, wrote in *Not So Wild a Dream:* "The censors employed a thousand devious arguments to justify their deletions. Sometimes they said a paragraph would hurt the morale of the troops; sometimes they said it would hurt the morale of the 'home front'; sometimes they said it would impair a general's prestige with his troops and thus cripple their confidence and efficiency. Once in a while the censor was frank and simply said it would get him into trouble with his superiors—so out it went."

The picture of Father Stuart eventually appeared in the October 20, 1945, issue of *Collier's*. The article that ran with it carried the bylines of Lt. Col. Corey Ford and Maj. Alastair MacBain. It began with one of the anecdotes often told about the Irish missionary along the Ledo and Burma roads. It was about the time a P-40 pilot, hit by enemy ack-ack, crash-landed in elephant grass. When the pilot stepped free of the wreckage, he saw a face that to him looked Japanese, and so he turned and ran. Up and down hills and through mountain streams he ran. Each time he stumbled or looked back, he saw that face. When the pilot finally sprawled on the ground, too exhausted to go on, the Kachin handed him a note sent by Father Stuart: "Follow this guide. He will lead you to safety."

In the monastery at night we discussed everything from civilian occupations to our Army careers. I recall that Officer Candidate School was a typical topic. Somehow or other the question came up, "If you could return to the States for thirteen weeks, provided you spend them all in OCS, would you go?"

An unhesitant "NO!" came like a rehearsed chorus from Bert Parks, Finis Farr, and me—we had all been through OCS at Fort Benning. The training at the Infantry School was aptly described by *Time* as "the hardest thirteen weeks of a man's life." The physical and mental pressure that went into the making of an infantry officer was terrific. Everyone who weathered it was thankful for the experience, but swore he would never go through it again.

Despite the rigors of the Infantry School, it was the one organization in the Army that everyone admired who came in contact with it. I have heard men damn the Army from top to bottom, but stop short when TIS was mentioned; they always admitted that it was an organization that was really efficient.

Professors who had spent a lifetime studying teaching

methods were invited to Benning to give advice. They came, marveled, and said, "Don't change a thing."

Every college grad I talked with agreed that TIS had a system superior to anything found on any campus. The comparison, of course, was not fair; no university ever had the backing or the selection of manpower that Benning enjoyed.

The Infantry School's system was to select crack teachers and psychologists and to give them hundreds of excellent visual aids. Each lesson was approached the same way: explanation, demonstration, application, examination, and discussion. Officer candidates added three more: perspiration, exasperation, and exhaustion.

Usually five officer candidate classes started each week, with two hundred men to a class. The average number of failures was about fifty a class. Flunking out was not necessarily the result of low grades. Sometimes men with straight A's were dropped because they lacked what TIS called "leadership."

A tension was built up so that each candidate felt that any minute he might be dropped. His tactical officer, known as a "bird dog," graded him, his instructors graded him, and his fellow candidates graded him. Everything was noted, from the way he made his bed to the way he ate his lunch. He soon began to feel that eyes followed his every move.

Naturally, some men cracked. That's exactly what TIS expected. The school knew that no matter how hard it was on its men, the enemy would always contrive ways of being a little harder; so if anyone was crackable, it was best that he crack at Benning and not in combat, where the lives of others depended upon him.

A candidate committed suicide one morning in the barracks while the rest of us were walking to breakfast through the dark company area. Although his rifle was locked in a rack, he slipped a round into the chamber, held his head over the muzzle, and pulled the trigger.

Another candidate became unbalanced. We first noticed it when he began sitting on the edge of his bed after lights-out, holding stacks of field manuals in his arms. He said that if he sat that way for several hours each night, he would absorb the knowledge in the books. One day he jumped up in class, raced from the building to battalion headquarters, took off his shoes, and sat on the adjutant's desk. That was the day he left us.

Considering that we were playing dangerous games with dangerous toys, remarkably few officer candidates were lost through injury or death. A TIS demonstration, with all of its live ammunition and exploding shells, I feel sure, was safer than Loop traffic in Chicago. Even the paratroopers at Benning had few deaths, but they certainly had their share of broken legs.

One candidate was killed in our class. He was Charley Curtis, a bachelor from Atlantic City. It happened during the Hell-zapoppin' exercises in which two platoons, firing rifles and mortars as they went, moved in under machine-gun fire to attack a hill. Charges of planted dynamite were exploded among the advancing troops to simulate artillery fire. Curtis fell upon a charge just as it was detonated.

By the time we returned to the barracks, Curtis's belongings and his bunk, which had been next to mine, were gone. The bunk of Officer Candidate Buffington was now next to mine. Buffington sang the praises of his native Maryland morning, noon, and night. Fifteen years later, when I stopped at a military cemetery in Belgium, where white crosses stretched toward the horizon, the first cross I approached bore the name LIEUTENANT BUFFINGTON, MARYLAND.

One day while telling OCS anecdotes in Bhamo, Bert Parks said he'd flunked his spy test at Fort Benning.

I said, "I did, too. I blame it on the sun and how it hits the glaring clay in Georgia."

I told of how the company commander had sent for me on a hot, glaring morning. He nodded to a chair and slowly slid a piece of paper across his desk. It was full of instructions:

"Mail a report each Monday morning with the important information hidden in the innocent sentences of a personal letter. Use only one-cent stamps on the envelope. Start the second paragraph with a small letter instead of a capital." There were other unusual requirements to prevent the bad guys from sending a letter that looked as though it had been written by the good guys.

The letter was to be sent to a certain insurance company with a post-office box number. That was my "cover," as the super-spies say. What to write to the insurance company? I fretted over that all week. Just before the Monday deadline the commanding officer sent for me on another hot, glaring morning, and slid two pieces of paper across the desk. On each was printed the name of a classmate. He nodded as much as to say, "Do you understand?" I nodded and walked out into the glare of the company street.

Who were those two men? What about them? How to find out?

That night on a cross-country march I made a point of loitering near them during a ten-minute break on the bank of a drainage ditch. One spoke of his difficulty at assembling a machine gun while blindfolded; the other told of his favorite restaurants in Chicago. What kind of a spy report was that?

Soon both had unfortunate things happen to them, but not as a result of my Monday-morning reports. One was not allowed to graduate with his class; he was under suspicion because he had been an exchange student in Germany before the war. The one familiar with Chicago restaurants was given a trip to a penitentiary; as an undertaker in civilian life, he had buried people without the proper credentials.

"How did you learn about that?" asked Finis Farr.

"My informant was not a superspy," I said. "He was just a guy with the knack of picking up dirt."

"Maybe you were the object of someone's report," said Parks.

"I was, but didn't know it at the time. I should have been suspicious when Col. Lovick B. Pierce paid for the drinks. He said to me, 'After the war the United States should be . . .' Then he issued what sounded like *The Communist Manifesto*. He concluded with, 'Don't you think that is the way it should be?'

"I said no, and was surprised at how happy he was to be contradicted. At the time I credited the good cheer to the quality of the bourbon. A couple of days later I was cleared to handle top-secret documents."

"Ever figure out why you failed?" asked Farr.

"For one thing, I didn't want to find anything incriminating about anybody. If somebody had begun to reveal something, I might have changed the subject. For another thing, I felt silly playing the game. But I like to blame it on the glare of the company street. If on my first assignment I had walked out into the night in Vienna, with schmaltzy music in the background, and if the cobbled streets had glistened in the rain under the soft light of a gaslamp, maybe I would have played the game. But it takes a natural-born superspy to play the game when the sun hits the glaring red clay in Georgia."

Part of our recreation in Burma was playing basketball for a half hour each evening in the courtyard behind the Buddhist monastery. On both sides of the court sat rows of idols, ranging in size from three to twenty feet. No one ever played before less enthusiastic spectators.

One day Sergeant Boechlin, a combat photographer, started to sit down in a clump of weeds at the edge of the court.

"Not there," I said, "you'll sit on a cobra!"

He hesitated a moment, but, seeing that I was kidding, he continued his descent. Just then a cobra slithered from the weeds and continued along the length of the court.

Snakes were common. One evening a correspondent, who spoke with a central European accent difficult to understand, killed a snake in front of the monastery door. The correspondent came in holding the small, harmless-looking reptile, thinking it was of the garden variety, but it really was a krait, the most poisonous snake in Burma.

That correspondent was a strange fellow. One night, in order to get attention, he set his hair on fire. He was determined to make a parachute jump behind enemy lines, he said, and when his chance came he jumped with five OSS agents. He was never seen again. The rumor we heard was that he had been captured by the Japanese and imprisoned in the Lashio jail, where he was subjected to extreme torture. Three American planes happened to drop bombs on the jail, killing everyone inside.

One of the necessities of Upper Burma was the doughnut call, whenever the Red Cross truck came around. The Red Cross had several canteens spotted across north Burma with such names as Anopheles Gardens, Gurkha Grill, Atabrine Inn, Mango Manor, and Burma Vista. Such canteens were usually for enlisted men only, a policy I favored, but since Bhamo was near the front, the officers got in on the service.

174

I have come across veterans who speak unfavorably about the Red Cross. The biggest complaint is that the Red Cross charged for food overseas. That complaint is unfair, considering that the Army required that organization to make some charge for food, a fact I learned while digging into the history of the India-Burma Theater. The charges were nominal, and the pleasures that they bought seemed great at the time.

Sometimes when hungry for a change in diet, we would try to buy jungle eggs from natives, who laughed at our paper rupees. Silver rupees interested them because silver could be beaten into bracelets, but of what use was paper? Only trouble was we were never paid in silver. Col. Phil Cochran, head of the Air Commandos, said, "Three commodities could get you more in the Burma jungle than anything else—opium, one, salt, two, and kerosene, three."

Our pockets bulging with paper bills, we looked with longing at the eggs and realized how money can sometimes mock you. At such times a Red Cross truck bouncing along the Ledo Road looked mighty fine.

Besides the camaraderie and informality of Burma, we should have been able to enter on the asset side of the ledger the fact that the Chinese army provided us with houseboys. But we marked those houseboys down as deficits rather than assets. The Chinese Army sent us its bolos, and a bolo in the Chinese army was a new low in boloism. (A "bolo" in the U.S. Army was anyone who failed to qualify on the rifle range. And so anyone who made a habit of doing things wrong was called a bolo.)

We had Pong and Lo to take care of the tents and *bashas* occupied by the war correspondents, press censors, and public-relations staff.

The only English word they ever seemed to master was *tomorrow*. The answer was always "tomorrow" whenever we asked them to do something. It did no good to insist that they do the work today, because in that case they went ahead and did it in such a way that you wished you had kept your mouth shut. For instance, one day when I was getting ready to fly to India, I told Lo to clean my muddy boots today, not tomorrow. He put shoe polish on top of the mud.

Pong went off on binges for days on end. He always returned

looking like something that had crawled out from under a wet rock. The first morning back he would go around shaking hands with everyone, saying, *"Jo, pee jo, ting bu hao,"* meaning, "Beer and liquor, no good!"

When Pong became ill with what I thought was influenza, I sent him to the medics. He returned to the monastery with a box of pills that bore the instructions, "Take one three times daily." To explain those instructions I went into a performance that one of the correspondents referred to as "high drama." To get across the word *daily* I used my arms to bring up the sun in the east and lower it in the west. Then I pointed to the pills and pointed to my mouth three times.

Dr. Seagrave said, "Nursing Chinese patients is about as difficult a job as a nurse can possibly be asked to handle. They simply won't take their medicine."

So Pong probably did not take his, or maybe he took all the pills at once, just to get it over with, as Seagrave said sometimes happened.

Pong's breath was always so heavy with garlic that an hour after he had left the room the melody lingered on.

Pong and Lo, however, did have some value; they lifted our morale sometimes. None of us will ever forget the day Bert Parks made a recording of Pong and Lo singing. During the playback the two coolies were so beside themselves with glee that they fell down on the floor and rolled around. During the rest of the day they giggled and laughed almost incessantly.

Another time Pong amused us was when he tore pages from *Life* and pasted them together for pinups. His selection: a Three Feathers advertisement, a snowman wearing a top hat in an antifreeze ad, gamboling lambs and coy bunnies in a Clapp's baby-food ad, and a girl wearing a fur coat. He tucked the collection under his arm and took off for his barracks, beaming.

Americans felt that the biggest cross they had to bear in Burma was the presence of the Chinese soldiers. Were the Chinese really as incorrigible as we thought them, or did we use them as scapegoats on which to blame everything that went wrong?

Our major annoyance was with the Chinese soldier's penchant for stealing. If caught, his officers punished him, not for stealing but for getting caught. It was the getting caught that made him lose face. If he was caught stealing from an American he received little or no punishment, but if he was caught stealing from a Chinese the chances were that he would be shot. So naturally it was open season on Americans; they not only had more, but were also safer.

Practically every American had something stolen from him sooner or later. It was more than annoying when such things as fountain pens and wristwatches disappeared, items that, at the end of the longest supply line in the world, took on a value far above their intrinsic worth. Probably the theft GIs resented most was to have their pet dogs stolen for stew.

Another complaint against the Chinese concerned their conduct in the outdoor theater. They arrived an hour before showtime to get good seats, and once the movie was started they laughed and talked among themselves so that everyone found it difficult to understand what was being said on the screen.

After the show, each Chinese lighted his way home with a GI flashlight, while Americans stumbled over things. No one ever learned how Chinese soldiers got U.S.-made flashlights while they were usually on the "impossible" list for American soldiers.

The same thing had happened in regard to cigarettes at the opening of the Burma campaigns. At one time the Marauders took the situation into their own hands and lifted Luckies and Camels from the Chinese at riflepoint.

Every American had a long list of petty personal grievances against the Chinese. One of mine was the time I was walking along and a Chinese driver swerved his jeep all the way across the road to see how close he could shave me without actually knocking me down. Either his aim was excellent or luck was with me, because all I lost was the skin from the back of my hand.

Lieutenant Dodge's grievance had to do with the night he took the three wives of the Sawbwa of Hsenwi to the movies. During the show, Chinese soldiers hooted at the women and held flashlights in their faces. When the women were leaving, the Chinese stoned them. There was nothing Dodge could do except boil; the official American attitude was that the Chinese were always right.

The grievances weren't always personal; sometimes GIs had

complaints that were strictly upper-level. For instance, when Chiang presented Mountbatten with a medal for building the Ledo Road, Americans griped about it. They knew that Mountbatten was against the road, and that it had been Stilwell who had fought for it and Pick who had built it.

Racial annoyance was not wholly one-sided. According to reports from the U.S. Embassy in China, the "better class of people" looked down on Americans, noting their rowdy and boorish ways, and were especially shocked by the "unkempt and disreputable" appearance of the personnel in the 14th Air Force.

An annoyance that had nothing to do with the Chinese suddenly ran the full length of the Stilwell Road: U.S. newspapers announced that the Chrysler Corporation was setting up a program to send civilian mechanics to Burma at a salary of from $450 to $550 a month. The pay, according to the press release, would be "practically unencumbered as men on the jobs will be given military uniforms, eat Army food, and sleep in barracks." The program called for engineer-mechanic crews to man six stations along the road, with 248 employees at each station; eight stations would have 164 employees.

It did not take the old Burma hands long to figure out that each civilian would receive base pay equal to that of a brigadier general, six thousand dollars yearly.

It seemed more than somewhat incongruous to GIs to pay civilians $450 to $550 a month to come to Burma, plus Army maintenance, as compared with the pay of a private who got $60 a month, plus Army maintenance, and it might be added, Army discipline.

Nothing ever came of that program, as far as I know. It fell through, I suppose, because the Japanese surrendered before they were expected to.

From time to time, when going through the jungle, we would come upon the body of a Japanese soldier that had not been buried. It gave us pause to realize the penetrating stench that a decomposing human body gives off, an odor that sticks in the nostrils for hours after you have left the corpse behind.

After such an incident, we were more appreciative of the monastery, inconvenient though it was. When rain fell, for instance, we put steel helmets under each leak; the engineers tried time and again to repair the roof, but never succeeded. One night when a stream of water struck Bert Parks in the face, he complained, "Those engineers can build the Ledo Road, but they can't repair a roof!"

We slept under netting to ward off malaria-bearing mosquitoes and marauding rats. Bhamo rats had a bad reputation; Colonel Seagrave told us that their fleas had caused an outbreak of the plague. Certainly they were arrogant; whenever I threw a heavy GI shoe at one, it would duck to the side and just sit there glaring.

I had made quite a dent in the history when I received a message from General Merrill in mid-April telling me to tuck all I had written under my arm and hurry to Theater Headquarters at New Delhi. The message added that I would fly from there to Southeast Asia Command headquarters at Kandy, Ceylon, for a conference with Adm. Lord Louis Mountbatten.

On the way to New Delhi I had the unpleasant experience of spending two days at Chabua waiting for a plane. Chabua might well have been the most mismanaged installation in the U.S. Army. It was notorious for its inefficiency, even in the early days of the theater. Stilwell, hearing stories about the low morale and especially about the vileness of its mess halls, made a special trip there to see for himself. He found the stories true. After he dressed down a few people as only he could, things improved, at least for the time being.

My first experience with the base's inefficiency came when eight of us who had landed at Dinjan and had been trucked the fifteen miles to Chabua walked into Operations to get our names down on the manifest. The lieutenant in charge, instead of taking one at a time, grabbed orders from all eight of us. When he started filling out forms in duplicate, the accumulation of orders caused him to admit, "I'm so mixed up I don't know where to begin."

About that time someone asked him, "How many passengers did you say would be on 475?"

"Sixteen," he answered.

"Well it's ready to take off, and there is nobody on it, and no baggage."

179

The lieutenant merely shrugged his shoulders, and 475 took off empty.

Announcements over one of the public-address systems were made by a sergeant who considered himself a minor Bob Hope and used the instrument to direct wisecracks at his friends throughout the area. His more businesslike announcements went something like this:

"H-a-m-l-z-o-r-n, at least I guess that's how you spell it. That's the best I could get over the phone. Come on the run. Chop, chop! Your plane will leave soon. If you don't hurry you'll find two thousand miles a long way to walk. H-a-m-l-z-i-o-r-n. I guess that's how you spell it. Come on the run."

No Hamlziorn came on the run. Maybe a fellow with a name something like Hamilton spent the rest of the war waiting for an airlift out of Chabua.

The billeting area I was sent to was ten miles from Operations. The mess hall was three miles from Operations in the other direction. The tents had no bunks in them. The lister bags had no water in them. The light sockets in the tents had no bulbs in them. After begging a bulb, you learned that the wires had no juice in them. And so it went on, and on, and on.

The personnel at Chabua were like characters in a GI stage show who had taken it upon themselves to burlesque Army inefficiency. They made me recall the demonstrations at Fort Benning in which someone called "Murphy" always did everything the wrong way to impress upon the class what not to do. At Chabua was the greatest accumulation of Murphys ever gathered in one place. It was good to get away from there!

On the flight to New Delhi I was haunted by a certain nostalgia for the monastery in Bhamo.

ELEVEN

In New Delhi the first person I met was Col. John Mott, head of the India-Burma Theater Historical Section, a handsome, affable, cosmopolitan gentleman. He had spent his youth traveling with his famous father, John Mott, Sr., international secretary of the YMCA, who would win the Nobel Peace Prize in 1946.

Colonel Mott said, "During the First War, I served as a private in New York's Fighting 69th. I admired Father Duffy, the chaplain; he was especially kind to me because I was one of the few Protestants in the outfit. I was in the same squad as Joyce Kilmer. You remember him as a poet, but I remember him as a soldier who volunteered for more than his share of dangerous missions."

When John Mott volunteered for World War II, he was director of International House in New York. Before that he had lived in India for thirteen years as adviser for Tata, the country's top industry. That background made him a fine traveling companion on our flight to Ceylon. He pointed out big-game country, telling of the tiger shoots he had enjoyed there, and during a stop in Bangalore he took me to the palace of the Maharajah of Mysore.

As we soared over Hyderabad, Colonel Mott pointed to the palace of the Nizam of Hyderabad, the richest man in the world. Although his wealth was estimated at two billion dollars, he spent only five dollars a week of his own money, lived in a little house, and drove an ancient Ford. Meanwhile his twelve-million-dollar-a-year income gathered dust; the royal elephants grew restive; long, sleek cars rusted in the garage.

In our flight to Ceylon we became impressed with the efficiency and the hospitality of the Air Transport Command, an impression that grew with each trip in the India-Burma Theater. I often wondered how such a sharp outfit as ATC could put up with the inefficiency at Chabua.

The ATC passenger service was operated like a commercial airline seeking patronage. Some of ATC's personnel had been associated with commercial airlines before the war, and many others hoped to work for commercial lines after the war.

The flight attendants were especially courteous. Their way of doing things was what we later came to expect of commercial airlines. For instance, just before takeoff they would make such an announcement as, "Our next stop will be Agra. We will be there in forty-five minutes," and after takeoff they offered us chewing gum, coffee, and magazines; upon landing, they announced, "You are now in Agra. We will be here twenty-five minutes." For the military that was unexpected courtesy.

As the plane door opened, a group of Indian coolies would wheel a streamlined ramp up to it in a manner remarkably efficient for Indian coolies. At the end of the ramp a couple of smartly uniformed Anglo-Indian hostesses would ask, "Could we show you to the dining room? Or would you prefer just to go to the PX for a Coke?"

The Indian sun beat on the aluminum transports with such fierceness that after they sat on the ground a few hours, one flinched when entering them. All the ATC pilots I knew were thoughtful enough not to have us board until they were about to take off.

At the end of a trip, each passenger received a card on which to express opinions about the service and to make suggestions on how it could be improved. That wonderfully efficient Air Transport Command had not existed at the start of the war, and by war's end it covered the globe.

It was love at first sight when we landed in Ceylon. My feeling for the place grew as we traveled by train from Colombo to Peradeniya, in the interior. That emerald of an island, set in the Bay of Bengal just off the south coast of India, was a well-kept jungle, a tropical paradise. An old Icelandic map shows the biblical Paradise fitting snugly into the island of Ceylon. Arab traders called it Serendib, from which comes the word *serendipity*, an unexpected happy experience. When that comely country became a republic, in 1972, the name was changed to Sri Lanka, "the resplendent island."

It was refreshing to see that the humblest of Sinhalese had a dignity not found in the begging, cringing Indian coolie, or in the expressionless Chinese peasant. The villages were clean; the garbage of generations did not clutter up the place as in India and China, and the odors that blanket the Orient were not there.

Peradeniya and Kandy, practically side by side, are known for their Royal Botanical Gardens. Weather conditions are so ideal that plants and trees from all climes grow and thrive there. Tucked away in one section of the gardens were the offices of South East Asia Command, where British and American brass plotted strategy and lived the good life.

Colonel Mott and I settled into a bamboo *basha*, a glamorous Hollywood type, not the crude model usually found in Burma. A native servant stood by to care for our laundry and quarters.

The American officers' dining hall, a picturesque, low, rambling bamboo structure, stood in a clump of trees. Inside was what American soldiers dreamed of in the jungle: plenty of delicious food of great variety. The service was at the same level of excellence as the food—snowy tablecloths, napkins, glistening glassware, good silver, and even individual butter knives.

Adjoining the dining room was a bar that served practically every mixed drink found in Irvin S. Cobb's recipe book. Murals in the bar were in the Sinhalese motif, done as three panels: the first showed elephants and natives in dignified procession; the second featured a troop of jubilant townsfolk passing out drinks to elephants and natives; in the third, the elephants turned pink and along with the natives acted convivial.

I congratulated the warrant officer responsible for the excellent dining room. He was surprised to hear kind words, saying there were fewer complaints made in jungle messes than in Kandy. The latest complaint was that ice cream six times a week was too much.

I told him of conversations I had heard about ice cream in Burma. Grown men spent hours talking very seriously about ice cream, cold drinks, ice cubes, milk, and other things rich or cold. One night Bert Parks had burst into the Buddhist monastery with the exciting news that the engineers down the road had brought in an ice-cream maker. "It really works!" Parks exclaimed. "Let's try it!"

I called his attention to the monsoon bucketing down and observed that the side road to the engineers was a quagmire. Parks insisted. As we churned along in a jeep through the miserable night, he admitted that it was hard to believe that two men at age thirty, somewhat sophisticated, should make such a big deal about ice cream.

A cool, clear drink was something else we had dreamed of in Burma. Tepid water, doped with medicine, caused the scalp to crawl every time we took a swig. No one would have touched the stuff had not the instinct to survive been operating within us. We tried many ways to cool the water; one of the best was to keep it in an earthen jug and another was to dig a hole in the floor of the *basha* and put a water container in it, a system used until an officer reached for his jug and grabbed a snake that was enjoying the cool spot. I had all of this in mind while listening to the Kandy mess officer tell his troubles.

Mountbatten said that he wanted to have a luncheon conference with Colonel Mott and me, but that we were five days early. We were pleased to hear that, especially after Lord Louis offered us one of his cars and a chauffeur who knew the island well.

Mountbatten also suggested that Lt. Col. John L. Christian go along as our guide. The rotund, likable, middle-aged American was stationed at headquarters of South East Asia Command. For eight years he had been principal of Meiktila Technical School in

Burma. At the outbreak of the war he was assistant professor in the department of Oriental Studies at the University of Washington, Seattle. From that position he joined the Military Intelligence Division of the War Department, and was of great help to the OSS. Few other white men in Southeast Asia knew that part of the world better than Colonel Christian, the author of *Modern Burma, Burma and the Japanese Invaders*, and *Burma*, as well as nearly fifty articles and monographs on India, Burma, and Thailand written for American, British, and Oriental journals.

Our first trip was to Nuwaraeliya, a hill station 6,200 feet above sea level. We went past tea estates owned by Europeans and worked by Indians, and terraced rice fields owned by Sinhalese. I expected to find Nuwaraeliya one of the last outposts of civilization, and was jolted by a large billboard at the edge of town, advertising Bing Crosby in *Going My Way*. The swank hotel and beautiful golf course exemplified what we Westerners think of as civilization.

On our next trip we enjoyed several hours with yellow-robed monks in a Buddhist monastery, visited the Temple of the Tooth, where the Buddha's tooth is said to be kept, saw the massive footprint of the Buddha in another temple, and went to the ancient palace of the King of Kandy.

One morning I took off on my own to see Kandy by rickshaw, but conscience caught up with me as we approached a steep hill in the middle of the trip. I climbed out, paid the coolie, and walked. Forty years later, while reading Malcolm Muggeridge's autobiography, I learned that he did the same thing at the bottom of that very same hill.

It is not difficult to describe such freaks as the ironwood tree, whose wood is so dense that even a branch will sink in water, and the balsa tree, the logs of which are so light that a small boy can lift one; but try to describe the majesty of the king palm, which grows fifty years and flowers for two, and then dies at the height of its glory; the Japanese bougainvillaea of Formosa, and the amazingly tall, slender Cook pines of Australia. Try to do justice to the fragrance of the pink, waxlike flowers that grow on the cannonball tree, and the striking walks lined with large, rugged almond trees of Malaya. So much beauty all in one place makes the head swim.

The three of us sat on a garden bench through warm, soft nights, talking about the war. Colonel Mott and I were aware that we must get down on paper all of the anecdotes that were readily told but rarely written, and so we drew on Colonel Christian's rich experiences and good opinions.

I happened to mention the general in Burma who had said to arriving replacements, "Welcome to Myitkyina, men. You are here to die," and had almost got shot for it. This reminded Colonel Christian that Wingate had once told some Chindits, "Your bones will whiten in Burma, but your fame will live evermore." On another occasion he said to a soldier, "You are going to die in Burma."

Colonel Mott observed that when moods were darkened by months of despair, things happened in combat that would shock anyone not there. He recalled Stilwell saying, "Good job!" upon hearing that a Chinese general had shot a captain and a lieutenant for retreating without orders.

Christian repeated some amusing anecdotes that British officers told in Kandy about Wingate's egotism. For instance, at the Quebec conference, when Churchill, Roosevelt, and Mountbatten had Wingate come to a private meeting, the general gave a stellar performance. Churchill said, "Brigadier Wingate, we owe you our thanks. You have expounded a large and complex subject with exemplary lucidity." Wingate responded, "Such is my invariable practice, sir," and he did not smile as he said it.

Colonel Christian told us that British officers had told him that Wingate believed that any report going to higher headquarters should exaggerate the enemy's strength to get credit for achievements, but any report going to a lower level should minimize the enemy's strength to give encouragement to the troops.

I started the two colonels talking about Stilwell's recall by saying I had come across mixed feelings on the subject. A combat sergeant had said, "Some days we called him Uncle Joe. Some days we called him Vinegar Joe. It depended. But no matter how he was feeling, he got you believing that he knew what in the hell he was doing. Not everybody can do that!"

Colonel Mott believed that while most British and Chinese officers might feel pleased with Stilwell's recall, most Americans felt let down. Mott said they admired General Dan I. Sultan,

Stilwell's deputy who became commander of the India-Burma Theater, but admitted that "he does not capture the imagination like the skinny old man in the battered campaign hat."

Colonel Christian nodded his agreement and added, "Stilwell has scant patience with politics. He thinks as an old soldier thinks: You go out and do battle and win, and that's that! He thought everybody ought to stand aside and let him do what he felt in his bones he was meant to do."

On the eve of his dismissal, Stilwell had told Brooks Atkinson, of the *New York Times*, and Theodore White, of *Time*, why he and Chiang Kai-shek were always at odds: "This ignorant son of a bitch has never wanted to fight Japan. All he cares about is hoarding supplies so that when the Japanese are defeated he can fight against the Communists."

Both colonels agreed that after the recall everyone was able to look back and see that it was inevitable. As much as a year earlier, Chiang was pushing for it. Even Churchill had asked General Marshall to relieve Stilwell because "he can't get along." When talk of recall was first in the air, in the fall of 1943, Mountbatten and Madame Chiang said that they wanted the general kept on where he was. Strangely enough, had Madame Chiang been in her husband's position, the chances were that she and Vinegar Joe would have got things done. She gave Stilwell a sentence he often repeated: "What good will politics do us if we lose?" The American general and the Chinese lady saw to the heart of things.

Colonel Christian said, "Chiang's dislike for Stilwell grew by the month. And vice versa. Most of the bitterness centered in Lend-Lease, the Communists, and Y Force."

Lend-Lease was a touchy matter because the Generalissimo wanted to control it. Stilwell wrote to Marshall, "If CKS and Co. are allowed to control supplies you know who will get them. You also know who will not get them. Somehow we must get arms to the Communists who will fight."

Colonel Christian thought that Stilwell's promotion of the Communists might have disturbed Chiang more than anything else. The general promoted the idea that the 18th Group Army, a Communist unit, be supplied with U.S. weapons so that they might fight against the Japanese.

Yoke Force also caused arguments. Stilwell wanted those troops to cross the Salween and fight westward until they had trapped the Japanese between themselves and the Americans and Chinese fighting eastward from India. Chiang said that Yoke Force might be needed against the Japanese in China, or even against the Communists, should they start to move southward.

Colonel Mott recalled that Yoke Force had shown real promise on May 11, 1944, when some 32,000 troops crossed the Salween to catch the Japanese by surprise. In the next two days, eighty thousand more crossed on rubber boats and bamboo rafts. They won the Battle of the Clouds, fought on an eleven-thousand-foot-high snow and ice field, the highest land battle in World War II, but when the Chinese met some fresh Japanese reinforcements, it all came to a sudden halt.

I told the two colonels that I'd failed to realize what an anticlimax I was witnessing the morning I took the war correspondents to see the Y Force and the Ramgarh Chinese meet near the Burma Road. The Japanese slipped out from between them, allowing the two forces to clash and fight each other with a zest that was hard to subdue.

As late as September 19, 1944, just a month before the recall, Roosevelt sent a message to Chiang, berating him for his do-nothing attitude. Stilwell was instructed to deliver it, and did so with delight. A few days later a Japanese broadcast said that Stilwell was planning to oust Chiang and make himself Czar of China.

Chiang Kai-shek sent a message to President Roosevelt through Ambassador Patrick J. Hurley, who had been sent to China with the impossible task of making peace between two incompatible men. The message was very hard-nosed: "So long as I am Head of State and Supreme Commander of China it seems to me that there can be no question as to my right to require the recall of an officer in whom I can no longer repose confidence."

Hurley added a message of his own, saying he felt that Roosevelt ought to choose Chiang over Stilwell. By now Roosevelt was completely fed up with all the discontent; he had once complained to Marshall about the CBI, "Everything seems to go wrong there!"

He partly solved the problem on October 18, 1944, when he ordered Stilwell's recall. The general heard of it in a radio message from General Marshall on October 19. He also learned that the CBI Theater was about to be split, with Maj. Gen. Albert C. Wedemeyer in command of the U.S. troops in the China Theater, and Lt. Gen. Daniel I. Sultan in command of the U.S. troops in the India-Burma Theater.

Stilwell said good-bye to the CBI when he left from Karachi on the morning of October 27. His feelings were summed up in a single sentence: "I tried to stand on my feet instead of on my knees."

The three of us sitting in the botanical garden that night in Kandy did not know that the U.S. Army was unsure of what to do with Stilwell when he reached the States. Although he wanted a combat unit, he was assigned to command the Army ground forces in Washington. When the war was coming to a close, he took command of the Tenth Army in Okinawa, and after the Japanese had surrendered he became commander of the Sixth Army, with headquarters in San Francisco.

An hour before our luncheon with Mountbatten, Colonel Mott and I strolled with Colonel Christian along avenues of his selection, where the drone of insects and the scent of jasmine hung heavy in the air. I gave a rambling conversation some direction with the question, "Did Mountbatten and Stilwell get along?"

Colonel Christian weighed his sentences. "Certainly, they did at first. Eventually there was friction—Mountbatten wanted to attack from the sea and Stilwell wanted to cut through the jungle. In time, Mountbatten wanted him recalled. Both respected each other. Each was a man of action. They ended, I think, with a love-hate attitude."

Through the years, when reading things written by Mountbatten and things written by Stilwell and much written about the two of them, I always recalled that morning under the trees in Ceylon, when Colonel Christian had summed it all up in a few sentences.

Stilwell wrote in his diary on October 7, 1943, "Louis is a good egg . . . full of enthusiasm and also of disgust for inertia and conservatism."

189

Edward Fischer

That is a remarkable statement considering that Stilwell's favorite passage from Shakespeare was Henry IV, Part One, act 1, scene 3, in which Hotspur speaks of a "popinjay," a lord "neat, and trimly dressed,/Fresh as a bridegroom" who talked with battle-weary soldiers and demanded their prisoners. It made Hotspur mad to see someone who smelled so sweet talking "so like a waiting gentlewoman/Of guns and drums and wounds."

From the very beginning, Mountbatten eased much of the distrust between the Chinese and the British. The first thing he did upon arrival in Southeast Asia was to fly the Hump to Chungking to pay his respects to the Generalissimo. According to Eric Sevareid, in China at the time, Lord Louis captivated Chiang by beginning, "Sir, I have come directly to see you. I have not even paused in Delhi to collect my staff. I realize you have been fighting this enemy much longer than any of us, and I know how heavily I shall have to rely upon your counsel."

Sevareid reported that the Generalissimo was almost speechless. No other Englishman had ever spoken to him with such respect.

In *Not So Wild a Dream*, Sevareid said that Mountbatten shook up the British more than he did the Chinese: "He blew a blast of fresh air into the stale British military hierarchy in New Delhi, packing many torpid pukka sahibs off to England at once. He refused to allow the traditional summer pilgrimage to Simla to escape the heat, refused to believe that 'nothing can be done' in the monsoon season, and called special meteorologists, psychologists, and medical experts from England to find a scientific answer to the problems of fighting in wetness and jungle heat."

The "pukka sahibs" did not accept this with good grace. They called Mountbatten an amateur saltwater sailor who did not understand the Far East. Mountbatten really did understand the Far East, however, and, as Sevareid wrote, "his methods were long overdue."

When Mountbatten made that first trip to China, on October 16, 1943, he learned that Chiang had asked Roosevelt to recall Stilwell. Lord Louis did not want to lose a general who had worked so hard getting troops ready to recapture Burma, and so he asked Chiang to withdraw his request.

190

Within a month, however, Stilwell was beginning to grow suspicious of Mountbatten. On November 10, 1943, he wrote in his diary that Mountbatten "is after my scalp." He believed that Brigadier General—later Major General—Patrick J. Hurley had warned Mountbatten that if he got rid of Stilwell he would be in plenty of trouble in the United States, for Americans considered Vinegar Joe the "Savior of China."

Stilwell's lack of tact must have made Mountbatten uneasy. For instance, one day the general said, "Admiral, I like working with you! You are the only Limey I have met who wants to fight!"

General Marshall, though an admirer of Vinegar Joe, admonished him upon hearing that when dining with the British, Stilwell not only did not sing "God Save the King," but did not even stand.

By mid-January of 1944 the general, becoming disillusioned with the way Mountbatten worked, wrote in his diary, "He doesn't wear well and I begin to wonder if he knows his stuff."

And yet on March 9, when Mountbatten flew into Walabum to speak with the victorious Marauders, Stilwell wrote to his wife, "Louis and I get along famously even if he does have curly eyelashes." He voiced a less optimistic opinion in a letter he wrote her in early July: "I have been thinking of Mountbatten as a sophomore but I have demoted him to freshman."

When Mountbatten flew to London, Stilwell believed the admiral was going there to get him fired. While filling in for Mountbatten in Ceylon, he heard a BBC newscast reporting that he had been promoted to full general, a rank he shared at the time only with Eisenhower, Marshall, MacArthur, and Arnold.

Upon Mountbatten's return to Ceylon, Stilwell was waiting at the airport. Vinegar Joe felt that Lord Louis seemed ill at ease for having failed to get him fired, and wrote, "Maybe the fourth star threw a monkey wrench into the machinery."

Despite the friction, both men showed a touch of class when Stilwell was finally recalled. Upon leaving India, the general sent Lord Louis a note that included the sentiment, "I offer my best wishes for great success in your forthcoming operations. When news of that success reaches me I shall be one of the first to throw my hat in the air." Mountbatten replied with equal grace, "I always had the greatest admiration for your fighting qualities."

As Colonel Mott and I were leaving for the luncheon, Colonel Christian summed up his love-hate theme: "The remarkable thing is that they got along at all. They are so different. Mountbatten is a gifted director of public relations; he makes sure the British get more than their share of the praise. That annoys Stilwell, when, win or lose, all announcements are filled with self-esteem. I believe Stilwell felt sure that Lord Louis was itching for action but was taking his cue to stall from Churchill. Mountbatten admires Stilwell as a fighter, but he is glad to have him at some distance. He knows that Stilwell will never be able to accept the Oriental way of doing things."

At one o'clock, Mountbatten sent his long, glistening Cadillac for Colonel Mott and me to bring us to the King of England's Ceylon palace. In peacetime the governor of the island used the palace; with Mountbatten living there, it was a matter of keeping the place in the family, for he was cousin of the King of England. This relationship came through his mother, the great-granddaughter of Queen Victoria. His father, German-born Prince Louis of Battenberg, became a British subject and First Sea Lord of the Admiralty; he anglicized his name to Mountbatten in 1917, when anti-German feeling ran high in Britain. Lord Louis's uncle and godfather was Czar Nicholas of Russia. Lord Louis, soon to be an earl, was a part-time guardian of Philip Mountbatten, the son of his sister and brother-in-law, Princess Alice and Prince Andrew of Greece; he looked after the boy while the couple was in exile. Philip later married Princess Elizabeth, who became Queen Elizabeth II.

At the door of the palace, one of Mountbatten's aides, a very smooth article, met us. Hardly were we inside when servants descended upon us with cocktails, cigarettes, and cigars.

The woodwork was massive and hand-carved, the walls a rich ivory. Much of the wall space was covered with oil paintings, about twelve feet high, of various kings and queens of England. A horse walking across the rugs would have sunk in up to his fetlocks. Brass glistened all over the place. Staircases started at each side of the hall and met high above the center of the room, with each tread about the size of a double bed.

Handsome Mountbatten breezed in with sixteen ribbons on his chest and more knickknacks on his shoulders than are sold at Woolworth's. However, they were not armchair decorations. Early in the war he had commanded the destroyer HMS *Kelly* and made German subs fear it in two oceans. Four times his ships were bombed or blown up under him. Later, when part of his job was to serve as chief of commandos, he planned and carried out landings at Dieppe, St.-Nazaire, and North Africa. Surely Stilwell must have admired that.

At lunch, Mountbatten explained that he wanted me to do a story on the Chinese and American combat achievements in Burma so that he could incorporate it in the report—"despatch" he called it—of SEAC.

He said the report must tell the truth even though it might hurt and embarrass, for he did not believe history should be all sugar and honey, and that any mistakes made should be recorded. As an example he told of an incident that he thought would probably not appear in history, but should:

At Brest, the RAF made the blunder of bombing ships in the British fleet. Mountbatten gave the order that any plane attacking the fleet should be shot down. He was asked to revoke the order, but refused. He reasoned that a ship cost much more than a plane, and so it was foolish for a ship to sit and take it while a plane made mistakes.

While on the subject of mistakes, Mountbatten went on to give some examples of bungling in high places:

At the Cairo Conference, Mountbatten had proposed that the problems of his command be discussed by both American and British Joint Chiefs of Staff, that their decisions be forwarded to the Combined Chiefs of Staff, and that the final decisions be placed before Roosevelt, Churchill, and Chiang. This procedure, however, was thrown into reverse. As one British officer said at the time, "The trouble is that all the admirals are on land and all the generals are at sea."

When the problems of Mountbatten's command were tossed before the Big Three, without previous discussion on lower levels, the Generalissimo balked. He said he would not start his Yoke Force in Yunnan moving west toward Burma unless the Allies made an amphibious landing in southern Burma. Without a moment's hesitation, Churchill and Roosevelt agreed to Chiang's demands. They soothed him with assurances that Mountbatten already had an amphibious force at his disposal and that he could expect even more equipment and personnel.

However, at Teheran, Joe Stalin voiced a loud "No!" to this proposal, and Churchill and Roosevelt had to backtrack. Stalin was unbending in his demands that the European Theater come first. To assuage Stalin, Churchill and Roosevelt told Mountbatten they would have to take away part of his amphibious forces.

"This would not have been too disastrous to our plan," said Mountbatten, "had I been allowed to talk with the Generalissimo. I am sure that I could have convinced him that although the amphibious operation would not be on a grand scale as was previously planned, it would be sufficiently large to make it worthwhile for the Yunnan armies to start for Burma.

"Roosevelt, however, sent a message to the Generalissimo saying that half of the amphibious force had been taken away for Europe.

"The Generalissimo then said, 'I shall not move my Yunnan armies.'

"And so the Allies decided that even the smaller-scale amphibious landing was not necessary; so they took the rest of our amphibious equipment for the French invasion."

Mountbatten gave another example of how bungling had cost him equipment: South East Asia Command asked for a shipment of tanks. Someone in an armchair in Washington said, "There must be a mistake in that order. Tanks can't be used over there. This must be for Europe." So the tanks went to Europe.

"Eisenhower had many headaches," Mountbatten said, "but priorities was not one of them. He was always on top of the priority list; South East Asia Command was always on the bottom. Eisenhower got not only the things for which he asked, but his needs were even anticipated, and he was asked what more he needed."

Encouraged by Lord Louis's apparent love of truth in history, I asked, "How about our troubles with the Chinese troops?"

He hesitated, thought a moment, and said that the report would not need to go into American problems with Chinese troops because it might cause the Chinese to lose face. "After all," Mountbatten said, "Chinese officers aren't even asked questions in Staff School, because if they do not know the answers they lose face."

Over coffee, Lord Louis explained his ideas of how history should be written. He said he thought it should be horizontal, not vertical, and explained:

"When we went to school, we studied the history of England, the history of France, the history of Germany, and so on. It was all vertical history; we never saw how the pieces fit together. History should be written so that the student sees the relationships between the different elements all the time. That's horizontal."

Colonels Mott and Christian and I flew from Colombo to New Delhi together. On the way I outlined a work schedule. When I had asked Mountbatten for a deadline, he had set September 1, four months away. I decided to go back to the monastery in Bhamo and spend three months completing the history for the war department and then give the fourth month to condensing it for Mountbatten's "despatch." I did not know that Chiang Kai-shek would change those plans.

Colonel Christian left us at the Delhi airport to continue on to join British troops who were planning an assault from the sea at Rangoon. Although the landing was practically an excursion, John Christian died when the barge in which he rode struck a mine.

TWELVE

ack in Bhamo, I settled down to writing the history. In the early days of May 1945, the monsoon struck with such force that I had to shift the manuscripts around the room daily to avoid new leaks spurting through the roof.

A message from General Sultan, on May 20, said to pack all manuscripts and come immediately to New Delhi. General Merrill had sent the message directing me to report to Mountbatten, but here was one from the Theater Commander—what kind of assignment would this be?

Only generals rate a number-one air priority, I had been told, but now I was traveling on one. Lieutenant McIver, the press censor, left Bhamo on the same plane, with a number-three priority that got him to New Delhi twenty-four hours behind me.

I reported to the Historical Section in Theater Headquarters, and within minutes I was hurrying along the corridor to the office of General Sultan. The general, a calm and quiet man, said that Chiang Kai-shek wanted a report similar to the one I was writing for Mountbatten. Had Vinegar Joe still been sitting behind that very desk, he might have growled, "When those damn Chinese hear about somebody getting something for nothing, they want to get in on it, too!"

Colonel Mott said that if Lt. Paul Geren worked with me on the projects, we should be able to make both deadlines by September 1. I knew of Paul Geren from Dr. Seagrave's *Burma Surgeon*, a book dedicated to him. Seagrave, in praising the work of the young American, said that the Burmese nurses always got their ideas of God and Paul Geren mixed up.

As I mentioned earlier, Geren received his doctorate in economics from Harvard before coming to Burma as a member of the American Baptist Foreign Mission to teach at Judson College, in Rangoon.

From Paul I learned the dramatic story of the start of the Baptist mission in Burma, in 1813, when Dr. and Mrs. Adoniram Judson arrived in Rangoon from the United States. The Burmese decided these intruders were evil, and threw them into a dungeon. The Karens, however, had a legend predicting that a white-haired man would come bearing a powerful book. Since Dr. Judson was white-haired and carried a Bible, they were interested in the new religion and even smuggled the Bible into the Karen hills.

This so annoyed the Burmese that they took Dr. and Mrs. Judson to the court of King Thiebaw in Mandalay; here they were strung up by their feet and lashed with whips. Since they would not deny their faith, the king was impressed and allowed them to go to Upper Burma to start a school near Bhamo. Soon large numbers of Karens and Kachins became converts; a century later their descendants joined Dr. Seagrave in his work as a medical missionary.

When the Japanese struck Lower Burma, in late 1941, Paul hurried to join Seagrave's medical unit, which eventually joined Stilwell for the walkout. In recalling those days, Paul said, "My outstanding memories are of General Stilwell. He marched at the head of the column, setting the pace. Often when going down a mountainside, I'd look ahead and see the general with that slouch hat on his head and a tommy gun over his shoulder. Every night he cleaned the tommy gun."

The glorious sight of the first food drop made a lasting impression on Paul's mind. The food situation was bad when a British bomber finally flew over and dropped some supplies. Instead of landing on the bank, the bundles landed on a sandbar far out in the river. Acting like a bunch of elated children going to a circus, Stilwell and his party waded to the sandbar and returned to the bank hugging sacks of food.

Paul never told me about it, but an American officer who had been on the walkout said that if there had been no Paul Geren, there would never have been a military unit called Merrill's Marauders. The unit might have had a different name, because it was only through the gentle care of Paul Geren that Merrill survived the heart attack he had suffered on the walkout.

Upon arriving in Imphal, Geren stayed with the Seagrave group to help handle thousands of Indian refugees. "It was pretty bad," he said. "They died so fast we didn't have time to bury them deep enough. The jackals would dig up the bodies at night."

The Seagrave unit eventually moved to Ramgarh when Stilwell set up a training school there for the Chinese. At that time, Paul, still a civilian, joined the faculty of Forman Christian College, in Lahore. He could have had an officer's commission, but he was suffering from a tropical fever and wanted to get away from the jungles to see if he could recover.

Upon recovering, in the fall of 1943, he went to New Delhi and joined the United States Army as a private. He was immediately sent to north Burma to rejoin the Seagrave unit, which was beginning to tramp through the jungles, caring for sick and wounded Chinese soldiers starting the reconquest.

Geren served with two Chinese divisions early in the campaign, and later went on two missions with Merrill's Marauders. At Myitkyina he worked in a lean-to operating room where the Seagrave unit carried on surgery through two and a half months of monsoon and artillery fire. Just before the fall of the town, Paul was flown back to India, worn thin from fatigue and disease.

He was assigned to the Historical Section of the India-Burma Theater, where, after five months as a corporal, he was commissioned a second lieutenant. Three months later, in a special ceremony held in Theater Headquarters, he received the Bronze Star for the work he had done in Burma.

I knew I was fortunate to be working with Paul Geren on the Mountbatten and Chiang Kai-shek projects. He could speak from personal experience on almost any aspect of the work.

In the Mountbatten report we tried to give the British a little more credit than they were due; Geren thought we were giving them too much. We must have applied just the right amount of ointment, because the high brass passed it along to Mountbatten without a flutter.

The Chinese story was a different matter. We knew that General Sultan would not want the Chinese to appear in an unfavorable light, and so we went out of our way to be kind to them. When Sultan read the first draft he said, "It looks as though you leaned over backward to make the Chinese look bad." That took our breath away, but it should not have, because Sultan, now sitting in Stilwell's chair, knew that it was a conflict with Chiang that had got Vinegar Joe recalled.

General Sultan handed the first draft to General Merrill, asking that he do some thorough editing. It was easy to like the big, affable Merrill, even when he was turning your manuscript into a public-relations piece. A soldier in the Marauders had captured the spirit of the general's kindness when he said, "Merrill used to come around and shoot the breeze with us. If, while talking to him, you dropped a package of cigarettes, he would stoop down real quick, pick them up, and hand them back to you."

Merrill was so adept at applying soothing ointment that soon the report had everything the Oriental mind and heart could desire. For instance, the Chinese and the British disagreed over the capture of Mogaung, each claiming the victory. In the report to Chiang, General Merrill said that the Chinese had captured it. In our report to Mountbatten we allowed the British to capture it. From our research, Paul Geren and I felt sure that the British had taken over the mangy little town. The Chinese had been assigned to do it, but they dawdled, as usual, and arrived just as the Japanese were beginning to retreat.

In the report to Chiang Kai-shek we omitted anything unfavorable about the Hump flights. For instance, the smuggling ring. Smugglers made several million dollars before the U.S. Army Criminal Investigation Department of the Theater Corps of Military Police finally clamped down.

I saw a list of U.S. Army officers who had made a fortune in the operation. Beside each name was quoted the amount of the take; several had cleared a million dollars or more. Smugglers were also members of the American Volunteer Group, better known as the Flying Tigers, China National Airways personnel, Red Cross members, technical representatives of U.S. aircraft manufacturers, and British, Indian, and Chinese civilians. Many of the Americans drew sentences at Leavenworth.

The list of smuggled items flown across the Himalayas and disposed of in China included weapons, ammunition, clothing, all types of military supplies and equipment, drugs, foreign currency, gems, and sundry PX supplies, with emphasis on cigarettes.

One USAAF pilot admitted he had parachuted from his plane after tossing overboard gold bullion and drugs. He collected ten thousand dollars for the cargo and reported that it was lost when the plane crashed.

One Hump flight that had nothing to do with smuggling became a legend: A brass hat in the U.S. Army was sending a piano to Chiang Kai-shek via the Hump. Everyone on the flight resented risking his neck to take a piano to the G-mo when so many other things were needed in China. The plane took off from Calcutta with the instrument on board, but landed in Kunming without it. The crew reported that it had run into bad weather over the Hump and had found it necessary to lighten the plane. All other Hump reports that day showed perfect flying conditions, but the crew stuck to the story and no one doubted their word—officially, that is. Need it be added that the brass hat who sent the piano was not Stilwell?

Another Hump story that was not passed along in the report to Chiang concerned the souring of morale of Air Transport Command pilots. Tonnages dropped to a new low as pilots sought an excuse for not flying. Morale broke down for several reasons: the lack of a rotation policy; the belief that Chinese generals and warlords did not use equipment flown across the Hump to fight the war, but stored it in warehouses for personal gain; anger that new planes were sent to the CBI without being properly tested for the rigorous demands of Hump flights, so that crashes came with disturbing regularity; and a feeling that food, recreation facilities, living quarters, health conditions, and the monsoons were very bad.

No one could change the monsoons, but morale improved with the start of a new system of rotation and the improvement of food, living quarters, and recreation facilities.

Of all the high-ranking officers I came to know while working on the history in New Delhi, the one I most respected was Brig. Gen. John P. Willey, a handsome forty-two-year-old cavalryman from Hampton, Virginia, and San Antonio, Texas. He resembled the movie version of a fighting general, and was soft-spoken, kind, and unbelievably honest.

When he was checking the history I had written about Mars Brigade, the unit he had commanded, we sat at desks side by side. If I happened to be busy writing at the time he wanted to make a point, he hesitated to disturb me. Noticing such hesitation out of the corner of my eye, I would toss down the pencil and lean back in the chair, acting as though I had completed a phase of work. He would then bring up the point he wished to make. It is hard to believe that there ever was a general who hesitated to disturb a lieutenant.

I was startled by his honesty when he told me that the Theater Commander had ordered him to cut the Burma Road, but that he had refused to do so.

"I wanted to cut it here," he said, pointing to a spot on the map. "Had I been given permission, I would have done it, because I could approach the road without exposing my men too much. But General Sultan said to cut it here"—he pointed to another spot—"and I didn't do it because I would have lost too many men crossing the wide-open approaches to the road."

Even though he had been chief of staff during the battle for Myitkyina, General Willey wanted to admit the truth about that sad event. "We must put down Myitkyina just the way it was," he said. "It is not a pleasant story. It's embarrassing. But we must write it the way it was. Maybe others will read it and not make the same mistake. The biggest lesson we learned at Myit-kyina is that you can't use green troops and get by with it."

General Willey had read proof sheets of *Merrill's Marauders*, a booklet published June 4, 1945, by the Military Intelligence Division of the War Department. While reading it, one gets the feeling that people in high places were ashamed of what had happened at Myitkyina. The 113 pages follow the Marauders from September 1, 1943, when the War Department began recruiting for "a hazardous mission," until the capture of the airstrip on May 17, 1944. Although the Marauders were not disbanded until after the fall of Myitkyina, on August 3, 1944, only a few sentences are given to the long fight for the town.

General Willey was disgusted with the Chinese, and was not afraid to say so for the record. He did not hold with the theater policy that the Chinese were always right, no matter what. I recall one of the anecdotes he gave me for inclusion in the history, but it was almost surely deleted:

A Chinese pack train was supposed to pick up a supply of blood plasma at an airdrop and deliver it to the medics of Mars Brigade. The need for the plasma was great. When the medics did not receive it, they radioed Services of Supply and asked what had happened. The answer came back that the plasma had been dropped at the time and place directed. The situation was so serious that General Willey, himself, began to check. He finally located the commander of the pack train and learned that the Chinese had given the plasma to their packhorses.

"Why did you do that?" General Willey asked.

"We wanted to make the horses strong," said the pack-train commander.

"Were the horses weak?"

"No, but it never hurts to make them a little stronger."

General Willey doubted that the unpleasant attitudes of some Chinese commanders would be told in the official history. Their greed, he said, showed in many ways; for instance, some soldiers being shipped from China to India were ordered by their commander to take off their clothes at the Kunming airport because the Americans would provide them with new ones. During the flight across the Hump, several died from the cold.

Time and again the Chinese shocked the Americans at high

202

levels. Gen. Frank Dorn, for example, jokingly told General Tu that the day he left the States his niece had asked him to send her a pair of Japanese ears. The next day one of Tu's aides presented Dorn with a bulky, newspaper-wrapped bundle, saying, "For your little niece." Dorn unwrapped the newspaper to find a Japanese head.

I said that on the drill fields at Bhamo I had seen Chinese officers slap and kick soldiers. General Willey remarked that officers sometimes beat to death soldiers guilty of minor offenses, and were puzzled that General Patton should be reprimanded for slapping an American soldier he believed to be a malingerer.

Neither General Willey nor anyone else around Theater Headquarters ever mentioned the plan to assassinate Chiang Kai-shek. Perhaps no one there knew about it. Certainly, I didn't hear of it until 1970, when Gen. Frank Dorn wrote *Walkout*, the story of his experiences with Stilwell. In his book, Dorn tells of how he had been asked to prepare such a plan.

When Stilwell returned from the Cairo Conference, in late 1943, he visited Dorn, then chief of staff for Yoke Force. In a manner uncharacteristic of him, Stilwell approached the subject with wariness. He said he had been told to plan the assassination but not to execute it until an order came "from the very top."

When Dorn wanted to know whose idea this was, Stilwell refused to say, but gave him a hint: "I doubt very much if anything ever comes of this. The Big Boy's fed up with Chiang and his tantrums, and said so. In fact he told me in that Olympian manner of his, 'If you can't get along with Chiang and can't replace him, get rid of him once and for all. You know what I mean.' "

For a week, Dorn tried in vain to plan an assassination and finally spoke of his problem with two trusted officers. "They sat back in shocked silence," Dorn wrote. The three spoke of shooting, bombing, poisoning, but none seemed right for this job.

Finally, one of the officers had the idea that Chiang should be talked into inspecting the Chinese troops training in India. The plan was that during the flight over the Hump the pilot would announce that the plane was about to crash. Everyone would jump and all parachutes would function properly, except the one worn by the Generalissimo.

Perhaps the officer who made that suggestion got the idea from Chiang himself. Once, while flying the Hump, the Generalissimo became so interested in his parachute that he undid the pack to study how it fit together. An American officer watched with horror, realizing that if the plane started to crash, some member of the crew would lack a parachute.

One day, in summing up the problems of the war in the Far East, General Willey said: "The British think Americans talk too much. Brag. Oversell. Too willing to say we can do something without really giving it enough consideration.

"The Americans think the British do too much planning. They are great ones for planning staffs. Meeting. Everything is weighed, measured, pondered, discussed. Things move from planning staff to planning staff.

"The Americans think the Chinese are too dilatory. They lack all sense of time. We want things to move along with machinelike precision. Stilwell knew how to earn the admiration of the Chinese; they often fought well for him for fear of losing 'face.' Stilwell saw possibilities, not in officers, but in the common soldier, who had the endurance of the peasants."

I recalled that statement about the peasant soldier, in 1964, when Gen. William H. Tunner's book, *Over the Hump*, was published. The general summed up the Chinese virtues in a few definite sentences:

"Though the individual Chinese are usually thin from malnutrition and hardly impressive as physical specimens, there are so many of them that they accomplish wonders by sheer numbers. I remember well flying over an airfield being constructed in a big bend of the Yangtze, and remarking each trip how the construction was coming along. The field seemed to grow beneath my eyes. And yet that field was built entirely by Chinese using little hammers to break large rocks into gravel, then carrying the gravel to the runway in little baskets. The baskets didn't hold much, but they didn't have to, for there were over one hundred thousand Chinese men, women, and children carrying them."

I said to General Willey, "I suppose it is admirable the way

Americans in high places go out of their way to be kind to Allies, even when the Allies are being annoying."

"I suppose so," admitted the general. "The Chinese are especially touchy. Even when they are getting combat troops, weapons, and supplies, they still complain. Our high command is trying hard not to hurt feelings in small ways and in great ones."

The general and I then returned to the report, making sure it would hurt no feelings in small ways or great ones. We were moving into the part that Willey knew especially well, the six months of combat from the fall of Myitkyina to the recapture of the Burma Road. First he had to train some new American troops, and while he was doing that, all hell broke loose in China.

As soon as Myitkyina fell, the Japanese in China began showing what could happen whenever there were not enough ground troops present. In September the 14th Air Force base at Lingling fell to the Japanese, and on November 10 the beautiful city of Kweilin fell. The Japanese hurried on to take Chennault's base at Liuchow and four bases around Nanning.

The enemy seemed back in stride, determined to capture Chungking and Kunming. In December, however, they overextended their supply lines and stopped three hundred miles short of Kunming. And, of course, they were aware that Chinese, American, and British forces in Burma were starting once more to move eastward toward them.

Fortunately, after Myitkyina was captured in August, the Air Transport Command was able to fly a shorter route at lower altitudes without fear of Japanese fighter planes. The Hump was "flattened" to the extent that deliveries to China jumped from eighteen thousand tons a month in June to forty thousand tons a month by the end of 1944. Since that was more tonnage than the road would carry, Stilwell's enemies said this proved the road unnecessary, failing to admit that without the ground victories the Hump would not have become a shorter and less dangerous route.

On August 10, 1944, a few days after the fall of Myitkyina town, the 5307th Composite Unit, popularly called Merrill's Marauders, was reorganized as the 475th Infantry Regiment, which became a part of the newly organized 5332nd Brigade, called the Mars Task Force, which also included a cavalry regiment.

Many of the men in this brigade, under General Willey's command, had arrived in the theater during the siege of Myitkyina. Some had been taken from ships at Bombay, hurried to waiting transport planes, and flown into the thick of the fight. They replaced those untrained for combat who had relieved the exhausted Marauders—truckdrivers, mechanics, cooks, bridge builders, and clerks. Although these newly arrived troops were not battle-wise, they at least had been trained in the use of weapons. After the fall of Myitkyina, the men of Mars trained for three months at Camp Landis, at the edge of the town.

While the Americans were in training, veteran Chinese and British troops started a new operation on October 16. The Chinese moved southeast toward Bhamo, and on the right flank, in the railway corridor, the British moved toward Pinwe. Both found the Japanese showing their former spirit and were soon engaged in heavy fighting.

The Chinese had Bhamo surrounded by November 15. Heavy dive-bombing by American pilots softened the Japanese defenses, and yet each time the Chinese made an attack they were thrown back. Waves of American planes continued diving, dropping bombs scarcely a hundred yards in front of the Chinese. One report said, "Jap arms and legs mingled in the air with heavy debris." The Chinese, however, failed to capitalize on the softening process, and aside from capturing a few bunkers, they made no headway.

Down in the railway corridor, the British 36th Division threw a frontal assault at Pinwe. They felt a close-knit resistance while crossing the Gyobin Chaung, but continued a frontal assault, hemmed in by dense jungles on the east and west. On November 29 the British moved into the town, which had been hastily vacated by the enemy.

General Festing's 36th British Division, now under command of General Sultan, continued on through Naba and Naba Junction to move unimpeded into Indaw, four miles to the west. One company occupied Indaw while patrols scouted the important river town of Katha, fifteen miles east of the junction.

The thrust down the corridor was a good example of Allied teamwork; at last everyone was learning to work together. A united effort by Americans, Chinese, British, and Indians made the push possible. The British 36th spearheaded the drive; their success was shared by Chinese commanded by General Pan, who protected the British flank and rear. A Chinese artillery group under command of an American, Lt. Col. Trevor Dupuy, gave such effective support that Dupuy received the DSC from the hands of Lt. Gen. Sir Oliver Leese, Commanding General Allied Land Forces in Southeast Asia. With great efficiency, Indian sappers repaired roads and built bridges to keep supplies and artillery pieces rolling; from time to time they even fought Japanese who had infiltrated the lines. Americans planned and directed the advance, transported supplies, gave medical care, evacuated the wounded, and furnished the close-in air support of the Tenth USAAF. So that the advance of the British need not be delayed, American cargo planes dropped a steady stream of supplies and American ambulance planes landed on temporary fields, many so soft that ruts eighteen inches deep were usual; from such inadequate fields they flew out the British sick and wounded to hospitals. American medical units followed close behind the leading elements all down the corridor.

For security reasons the 50th Division, part of the Chinese Sixth Army, moved for several weeks under a blanket of secrecy. The blanket was not lifted until after the British had taken Katha on December 11. The Chinese were protecting the British flanks and rear so that the 36th might focus attention on a narrow zone of action without fear of either flanking counterattacks or of being cut off from the rear, a favorite Japanese maneuver.

Three prongs had been driving toward the heart of Burma for a month when a fourth was added. The Chinese First Army was battering Bhamo; the Chinese Sixth Army was well past Shwegu, and the British 36th Division was moving in on Katha, when the fourth prong, an American regiment, marched south from Myitkyina.

The 475th Infantry Regiment, of Mars Task Force, had trained for three months at Camp Landis before starting on its combat mission in mid-November. The Second Battalion of the

475th, with the 31st Quartermaster Pack Troop attached, left Camp Landis on November 16; the Second Battalion followed the next morning. A day later the 612th Field Artillery took to the road, and on the fourth day the First Battalion and Headquarters of the 475th started. By this time the Portable Surgical Hospital had been attached to the Third Battalion. The rest of the brigade, the American 124th Cavalry, a federalized Texas National Guard Regiment, continued training.

The 475th Regiment, joined by Kachin Rangers, split at Tali, just north of Bhamo. The First Battalion moved southwest toward Shwegu to arrive there December 7, while the rest of the unit marched south to Tonkwa. Near Tonkwa, on December 8, the I-and-R platoon of the Second Battalion, with elements of the Sixth Chinese Army, fought off a Japanese attack. Two days later the First Battalion had its first taste of combat when a patrol contacted a Japanese platoon, killing thirty of the enemy and routing the rest.

At this point in the story, General Willey spoke in some detail about the first American casualty of Mars Task Force. During an ambush between Man How and Mo-Hlaing, Pvt. Walter C. Mink saw a friend of his sprawled wounded in the trail. When Mink crawled out to help his friend he was caught in crossing machine-gun fire. Almost immediately several Mars men, aided by a few Chinese, killed two Japanese officers and twenty-six men, and captured two.

This was followed by another brief encounter at Nga-O, on the Shweli River, in which thirty Japanese were killed at the cost of one American wounded.

At Tonkwa the fighting was bitter. Americans and Chinese fought side by side, often sharing the same foxholes. For two days the enemy threatened to encircle them, but they threw off every attack. Americans were credited with killing forty, the Chinese with eighty-six. Losses among the Allies were light.

Mars artillery, which packed its big guns on Missouri mules, went into action as the first completely American artillery unit in Burma. At Mo-Hlaing it bore the brunt of a Japanese attack. Here Maj. John Lattin killed a Japanese grenadier who had wounded a battalion commander. During a bayonet charge an American was stabbed in the abdomen; he jumped up, ran down the Japanese who had bayoneted him, and killed him with bare hands. The American lived.

At this point in the story, General Willey spoke with amusement of a nosy American officer. "He was wounded," said the general, "while trying to find a redheaded Japanese reported to be among the dead."

By Christmas day, advance elements of the men from Mars had walked two hundred miles, fighting the enemy all the way over terrible terrain.

All this time, the Chinese First Army was pounding at Bhamo. The suicidal defenders of the town were compressed, by December 13, into an area two thousand yards square. Various Chinese units advancing from different directions were beginning to meet and form together like pieces of a giant jigsaw puzzle.

What made it hard on the Chinese was that the Bhamo area was one of the best natural defensive positions in Burma. The town was tucked away in an elbow formed by the junction of two rivers and the ground was pitted with small lakes and swamps. This forced attacking troops to be channeled into narrow causeways. Each causeway was defended by machine guns protected by pillboxes and bunkers; those under five feet of crisscrossed logs and earth defied destruction except when pounded by direct hits of 155-mm shells.

The Chinese were under orders to take Bhamo, but not to waste casualties, and so they moved slowly and carefully to allow artillery and the Tenth Air Force bombers to pulverize each segment.

Bhamo was captured December 15, after twenty-eight days of resistance. On the night of December 14 the Japanese tried to break through the encirclement at the south end of the city. Many died and some managed to escape to the wilderness, with combat patrols in pursuit.

Bhamo's value was great. It was the terminus of the navigable portion of the Irrawaddy River, and a key road hub. The road from Bhamo to Namhkam could now be tied to the Myitkyina-Bhamo road as part of the ever-growing Ledo Road. It also made available an old caravan route, branching northeast from Bhamo through the mountains to China, the route used by Marco Polo centuries earlier. The capture of the town also cleared the important east-west river line from Katha to Bhamo, a good route of communication and a natural defense line.

While the 38th Division of the Chinese First Army was pounding at Bhamo, its sister unit, the 30th Division, commanded by Gen. Shou Chih, cut through rough jungle country to the southwest. So when Bhamo fell, the 30th was already thirty-five miles nearer Namhkam, which then lay only thirty-six miles ahead of them.

Secrecy about the Kachin Rangers was lifted at this time. The world press was now free to give them recognition for their remarkable performance in the drama of north Burma.

General Willey said, "Without those Kachins the OSS would have been nothing. They were superior jungle fighters. They killed three thousand Japanese while losing only twenty-five Rangers. Some may have exaggerated the damage they inflicted, but others were too conservative. For instance, a Kachin crawled up to a trench held by several Japs and lobbed in eight grenades. He reported that there must be several wounded, but he reported no dead simply because he had not been able to count the bodies. While killing Japanese and playing havoc with communications, the Kachins blew up bridges and railroad tracks and rescued more than two hundred airmen who had crashed or bailed out."

While the Chinese were crossing the high hills and starting down into the Shweli valley toward Namhkam, another prong was added to those already prodding the Japanese. The American 124th Cavalry and the 613th Field Artillery marched from Camp Landis, at Myitkyina, and hurried southwest to help in the battle that would eventually take the Burma Road.

Because of the victories of Mars Task Force, the Ledo Road not only reached the Burma Road, but the pipeline and the telephone line soon stretched from India to China. The Ledo Road had opened to great fanfare in February 1945, but the opening of the pipeline and telephone line got little attention in April.

Since it took a ton of gasoline to deliver a ton of cargo to China, the planners at the Quebec Conference decided that a pipeline was needed. American engineers used Indian and

Chinese labor to lay four-inch and six-inch pipe from sea level at
Calcutta to elevations as high as nine thousand feet crossing
Burma. At each of the many remote pumping stations, accurate
gauges indicated leaks and other troubles. Sometimes the pipeline engineers had to pick up weapons to fight the Japanese.
Weather, terrain, and disease always seemed on the side of the
enemy. Pipe Dream is what the builders named their assignment.

The Signal Corps followed the Ledo Road to link India to
China by telephone for the first time in history. Like the Ledo
Road and the pipeline, it could move forward only at the pace set
by combat troops. The Americans set more than sixty thousand
poles across the 1,750 miles from Calcutta to Kunming, the
distance from New York to Denver, and tied all of this into the
British lines throughout India.

In a radio address on February 9, 1945, General Sultan said to
the troops: "We have licked the Japs in north Burma."

To the south, though, the British still had to face six months of
combat as they fought with effectiveness over the same ground they
had fled in shame three years earlier. Maneuvering brilliantly,
General Slim moved forward with little loss of life. Through
trickery his 14th Army forced the Japanese to flee Burma.

A new Japanese commander, General Kimura, replaced
General Kawabe in the Burma Army area. His plan was to
withdraw to the east bank of the Irrawaddy and wait until the
British attempted to cross. General Slim knew that to cross a
river under fire was a costly action, and he preferred to have the
14th Army's 33rd Corps finesse the Japanese out of position. He
set up a fake headquarters with active radio communication of
fake messages near Mandalay; soldiers acted as though they were
preparing a river crossing. Meanwhile, the Fourth Corps, with
radio silence, made an unopposed river crossing well below
Mandalay and moved up behind the Japanese.

Kimura was so fooled that he had withdrawn some troops who
were fighting Mars Brigade in the north so that they might attack
the 33rd Corps at its faked river crossing. When he realized that
the Fourth Corps was behind him, he began fighting his way out
of the trap. The 33rd Corps rushed down upon him from the
north, meeting slight resistance along the way.

At Mandalay, however, the British ran into some well-entrenched Japanese. It took days of heavy fighting before Slim's highly professional troops took what had once been a lovely town, on March 20, 1945.

Should Slim continue on toward Rangoon, three hundred miles to the south? The 14th Army would need to be in possession of that port before the monsoon started in four weeks, or else have its supply lines stretched dangerously thin, so that marauding bands of Japanese could cut them at will.

Mountbatten helped Slim by having the 15th Corps make an amphibious landing at Rangoon. The troops of the 15th Corps had made a series of landings to seize air bases along Burma's west coast after having been successful in the Arakan region early in January.

Slim was still forty miles from Rangoon when the monsoon brought him practically to a standstill. Amphibious and airborne landings, however, went right ahead with great success. Paratroopers of the 50th Indian Brigade and troops of the 15th Corps came ashore from boats on May 1, 2, and 3. On May 3 they entered the town to find that the Japanese had hurried off toward Thailand, leaving little damage behind them.

The Burmese people were helpful in the quick recapture of Rangoon. The Burmese Independent Army, trained by the Japanese, had learned through the years that the invading Japanese were more difficult to endure than the British Raj had ever been, and so that renegade army and other native units were soon taking orders from General Slim, all the while providing information and harassing small enemy units. Villagers who had been violent toward the British and the Chinese in that terrible spring of 1942 were now equally violent toward the Japanese.

The war in Burma came full circle as it neared the end. When the Japanese had invaded Burma from Thailand in 1942, they had killed thousands of British troops at the Sittang River, and now, three years later, the British trapped them at the Sittang as they were trying to flee back to Thailand.

The end would have come sooner had it not been for the monsoon; it slowed everyone down. Slim moved with caution south from Mandalay, for he did not want to lose anyone in the last days. The troops who had landed at Rangoon moved northward toward him, trapping the enemy in the valley. The Japanese fought fiercely, but Slim was determined that none escape.

Later he wrote, "They were surprised as they launched their rafts, they were shot as they swam and drifted across on logs, or they were swept away by the rapid current to drown."

When the Japanese 28th Army tried to cross from the west to the east bank, the 17th Indian Division was waiting. Of the seventeen thousand enemy troops attempting the crossing, only about one-third succeeded. In that action only ninety-five British soldiers lost their lives. When 740 Japanese allowed themselves to be taken prisoners, the British realized that their morale was low.

On August 6, two days after the Battle of the Breakout ended, Americans dropped an atom bomb at Hiroshima, and two days later they did the same at Nagasaki. On August 10, Mountbatten was in London, meeting with Clement Attlee, the new Prime Minister, when word arrived that the Japanese government was prepared to discuss terms for the surrender of the Japanese Empire. On August 14, Japan surrendered unconditionally.

Back in Kandy, on August 15, Mountbatten issued orders for suspension of all combat in Southeast Asia. Small Japanese units in remote places continued to fight, for they had not received orders to stop. The last shot was fired in Burma at the end of August.

Paul Geren and I completed the reports for Mountbatten and Chiang Kai-shek by September 1. All in all, things had gone well during the writing; for instance, when General Willey checked my 25,000-word story on the siege of Myitkyina, he deleted one paragraph and added about fifty words. When he got around to reading about the action that followed Myitkyina, I bragged in a letter home: "Considering that he was the Commanding General of Mars Brigade, I felt a little uneasy when General Willey began to check the chapter which deals with his unit. When he finished he said, 'You have far more here than I had ever expected to find. And it's all right. I wish more military histories were written that would be a pleasure to read instead of a chore.' In the fifty-page story of Mars, he made no deletions and added a scant thirty words."

I stayed in New Delhi long enough to get the final draft of the Burma campaign typed. My instructions were to go back to Burma, get the manuscript approved, and then return to work on various aspects of the history of the India-Burma Theater.

In Bhamo I found the headquarters of Northern Combat Area Command ready to fold up and go home. Its job was finished. Everybody was so happy at the prospect of getting back to the United States that all of life looked good, including my history. It was a hundred thousand words for the archives, and that was all that NCAC really cared about. Col. Joseph Stilwell, Jr., seemed especially pleased with it. The few remaining brass hats gave me their blessings and assured me a captaincy, which they made sure that I got when they returned to Theater Headquarters.

THIRTEEN

As soon as the Japanese surrendered, in August of 1945, many military units began folding. Since our work at the Historical Section was to make sure nothing got lost that ought to be filed in the archives, we stayed behind and waved good-bye to others.

We were so anxious to quit India that it clouded our good sense. We acted as though a theater of operations, like a circus, could fold and move almost overnight. In Calcutta, GIs held meetings to protest their being kept overseas, and from Karachi to Assam they counted service points to determine when they would be released from the military.

Many of the natives seemed anxious to see us go. Scrawled on walls all over the country were two words: "Quit India!" A British soldier pointed to the admonition and said, "I wish to God I could!"

All of us sensed that night was descending on the empire "on which the sun never sets." We felt we were seeing the last of colonial polo, tennis at the club, gin slings at the bar, and tiger shoots in the jungle. We told each other that the British would depart and that civil war would begin, but we had no idea how fast all this would happen, and how severe would be the conflict.

In the Red Fort, at Delhi, soon after the end of the war, I attended the trials of the Indian National Army. The British had brought three Indian officers to court on charges of treason, murder, and abetment of murder.

The trial had its roots back in early 1942, when, at the fall of Singapore, British officers surrendered their Indian troops to the Japanese. Many of those prisoners of war formed an Indian National Army to side with the enemy and to fight for the freedom of India.

I attended the trials with Paul Fung, correspondent for the China Central News Agency. From the time we approached the massive, red outer wall of the fort until we reached the trial chambers deep inside the grounds, we were stopped by guards and made to show our press passes time and time again.

The courtroom was small; everything in it looked worn and unkempt. Across the front sat eight British judges. On their right were prosecutors; on their left, defense counsel. In front of the judges sat three Indian officers with a cocky attitude unbecoming men on trial for their lives.

The first four rows were given over to desks for the press. Next came the onlookers, mostly well-saried Indian girls who had brought their knitting with them.

Bhulabhai Desai, one of the greatest attorneys in India, was chief counsel for the defense. Somebody described the likable old fellow as "a suntanned William Jennings Bryan," and an apt description it was.

In the defense he made so well, Desai lacked substantial arguments. The officers were as guilty as they could be, and they and everyone else knew it. In any other country they might have drawn the death penalty, but all of us felt sure that the British, at this time, would not impose such a stiff sentence.

Protest riots were breaking out all over India; people were serving notice of what would happen should the verdict be unfavorable. In Calcutta, rioters killed a black American soldier. His death was ironic because he had written verses telling of his dismay over India's bondage and hoping for India's freedom.

When the three officers were let off scot-free, everyone felt

216

that the Empire was really on the run. Friends whisked them away into Delhi, where a parade formed and the officers, with garlands of marigolds about their necks, began living like celebrities and heroes.

Perhaps only the Anglo-Indian girls hated to see the Americans leave. Romance ran wild between them and the U.S. soldiers. The years of American occupation may be remembered as the golden era in the annals of the Anglos.

The offspring of an English parent and an Indian parent lacked social standing with both British and Indians, and so they formed a community of their own, one not shunned by Americans. The average Anglo-Indian is usually handsome. Pick a hundred Anglo-Indian girls at random, and their beauty may surpass that of a hundred girls picked at random from any other nationality. Many none-too-handsome Americans had dates with women far more beautiful than they would rate in the States.

Free-spending Americans entertained Anglo-Indians as they had never been entertained before. In some cases, true romance bloomed. Under Stilwell, however, no American soldier could marry an Asiatic, so that stopped some blooming romances from flowering into weddings. After Stilwell's recall the rules were somewhat relaxed, but there was no great rush to the altar. For every happy Anglo-Indian bride there were hundreds of broken hearts. Usually the American left for home with the promise of sending for his exotic sweetheart, but few ever did.

The day the war ended, I saw an Anglo-Indian girl sobbing in Theater Headquarters. She said that she was crying because the Americans would soon be gone. Some of her friends had attempted suicide, but most sought solace in the Urdu proverb, "What does unhappiness matter when we are all unhappy together?"

Paul Geren knew India and the Indians, and loved both at a time when Americans did not seem to have a kind word for either. Those uneasy months after the war became memorable for me because Paul decided that he and I should explore various aspects of the strange land: remote villages where life was as it had been before the coming of the British; towns where the Raj was most evident; and even the elegant, unreal world of princely India.

Edward Fischer

We experienced princely India when Paul received an invitation for the two of us to spend a weekend as guests of the Maharajah of Jaipur.

At the maharajah's guest house, a white, massive-pillared place, Col. Kaseri Singh greeted us and introduced himself as the maharajah's chief huntsman. He explained that he and the prime minister of Jaipur, Sir Mirza Ismail, would be our hosts in the absence of His Highness.

Colonel Singh was a handsome man, in his early sixties, his coloring a deep tan. His lean, clean-cut features, steel gray hair, thin mustache, and piercing eyes gave him a look of distinction. His suntan uniform of the Indian Army was tailored, starched, and pressed to perfection.

What a wonderful raconteur he was! At dinner the talk inevitably turned to big-game hunting. The colonel hypnotized us with his tiger lore, speaking of wild animals as though they were human beings. He told of what they thought and of what they said to each other; it was as though he had gone into the jungle each morning to get the latest gossip from the beasts.

In the drawing room we listened to the colonel tell of cobras that avenged the deaths of their mates, charms that cured scorpion bites, and ghosts that were uncomfortable to have around. He became especially excited while telling of ghosts. With facial gestures and changes in tones of voice he told the story of a young man who had committed suicide and then come back to haunt his village.

The colonel spoke of conjurers he had known. "Those men perform remarkable feats because they have a contract with the devil," he said. "A conjurer can do things for others, but he is powerless to do things for himself. For instance, if one were in this room and you happened to say, 'I left a photograph in New Delhi that I had meant to bring along,' he might say to you, 'Go over to that table and you will find the photograph.' And sure enough you would, if it were of no advantage to him that you find it."

The colonel spoke of "a wondrous bull, a truly remarkable bull," an animal with extrasensory perception: "If his master should say to him, 'Oh, bull, tell me who in this crowd has a Japanese coin in his pocket, the bull would go up to someone,

218

muzzle him, and, lo, there would be a man with a Japanese coin in his pocket."

Paul Geren and I were so stimulated by weird tales that before retiring we had to walk around the palace grounds to clear the goblins from our heads.

After breakfast the colonel took us by Jaguar to visit two rogue elephants. Upon entering the great stone pits that held the beasts, he oriented us as to which exits to dash through or what stairways to race up, should one of the rogues break the heavy chains that bound his legs.

The number-one rogue had snapped his bonds a few days earlier, when the colonel was escorting E. M. Forster, author of *A Passage to India*. Forster scampered up the stone stairway to take refuge on a high platform.

The beast put on a good show when we invaded his pit, trumpeting, thrashing the air with his trunk, and leaning into his chains. For a second we thought he was going to repeat his chain-breaking performance.

The number-two rogue had lost much of his old fire; we could approach close enough to allow him to snatch bran cakes from our trembling hands with his trunk.

Why keep such vicious elephants? The colonel said that on festive days the rogues were brought together to do battle for the pleasure of the populace.

"Doesn't one elephant usually kill the other?"

"No," said the colonel, "elephants do not usually fight to the death. When one sees he is beaten, he will quit."

For the rest of the day we rode elephants. Three beasts, richly caparisoned in red and gold trappings, knelt at command of their mahouts. By small ladders we mounted to a padded howdah, enclosed by railings. We found that the slow, cushioned, side-to-side motion of an elephant was more pleasant than the jerky to-and-fro motion of a camel.

We spent the day visiting palaces and deserted cities, and even took a short ride into tiger country. Col. Kaseri Singh readily answered all of our questions and explained the things we saw in every instance except one: the dark, frowning fort that dominated a hill at one side of Jaipur. The old place intrigued us, and we wanted to go inside. Two or three times the subject came up, and each time the colonel showed an annoyance out of character with his natural suave manner.

Months later we heard the story that explained the colonel's attitude. The fort, called Nahargarh, or Tiger Fort, has a great treasure locked somewhere within its depths. An ancestor of the maharajah, returning from the war hundreds of years ago, brought a hoard of jewels from Afghanistan that he hid in grim Tiger Fort.

Once in a lifetime, and only once, each ruler of Jaipur might enter the vault and select one jewel for himself. No maharajah ever learned the exact location of the vault, because as soon as he reached Nahargarh he was blindfolded and led by a confusing route to the hidden hoard.

The treasure was guarded by a criminal tribe called the Thugs. Although the tribesmen have lived by pillage and murder for centuries, they have always been faithful to the trust put in them by a maharajah long ago.

On the next trip we experienced an India that outlasted power, and time, and change. The luxurious weekend in Jaipur loomed in sharp contrast to our visits to Kari Jat and Aligarh, especially Kari Jat. A student Paul had come to know well while in Lahore, Hari Singh, made arrangements for us to visit that village.

By jeep we started out to find the hidden place, accompanied by Lt. Joseph Mitchell, a military historian, and Col. Harry Mayfield, who had become Theater Historian when Colonel Mott returned to the States. Kari Jat was so distant from the beaten track that its people felt safe from trespassers. We could never have found the place, had not Hari Singh set up a system of runners. Each young man declined our invitation to ride in the jeep, but ran ahead quite fast until he dropped to the ground where another runner was waiting. We lurched along behind the runners, across rough country, right up to the mud walls of the village.

Almost everyone in Kari Jat was at the main gate to meet us. Hari Singh stood out from the crowd; in his white cotton suit and pith helmet, he alone was in Western garb. He climbed into the vehicle to direct us through the narrow, twisting village streets.

The village's mud houses, white and glaring in the intense sunlight, were two stories high, with flat roofs. From rooftops, women with veils across their faces looked down upon us until we looked back, and then they turned aside. A commotion of cows, goats, dogs, and children moved along the streets ahead of us, while in the courtyards bullocks and camels chewed their cuds. There was something biblical about it. The jeep and those of us who rode in it were anachronisms.

At Hari Singh's house he led us into an upper chamber, a long, low room that might well be used by an artist as a setting for a painting of the Last Supper. Into the room crowded big men of the village and of the Rota district—the headman, the moneylender, the champion wrestler, the policeman, the champion plowman, and a dozen other local celebrities. Hari Singh was the only one in the room who spoke both English and Hindustani, and so all conversation passed through him.

From the upper room we adjourned to a great field. Atop a low hill had been set a long table and a dozen chairs covered with gaudy tapestry. We were led there and told to seat ourselves and enjoy the entertainment.

The men of the village crouched on the ground to form a circle about 150 feet in diameter. The ancients sat next to us on both sides, and then came the middle-aged men, followed by youths, and at the far side crouched toddlers just learning to walk.

The women had remained in the village, except three little girls of about ten. When the headman saw them he sent them, with much scowling, growling, and waving of arms, scurrying back to the village to join the women on the rooftops, from where they could watch the entertainment.

"He said to them," Hari Singh told us, " 'Go back to the village, you slaves! That is where you belong. You are not fit for anything better.' "

Paul said later that he thought Hari exaggerated the translation just a bit. The young student, Paul explained, was so anxious to have the village adopt modern attitudes that it suited his purpose to make the old ways seem worse than they really were.

The entertainment began when the champion plowman of the district drove out a matched pair of white bullocks, caparisoned in red and white cotton sheets, and hitched to a wooden-tongued

221

plow. He got the beasts into a lope, plowed a circle, and bisected it with remarkable accuracy.

The champion wrestler of the Rota district, a massive fellow a little on the fat side, issued a challenge to all comers. No one accepted.

A number of lesser lights wrestled and were followed on the program by a rough and tumble game called kubbity-kubbity. In this game a runner races for a goal line while holding his breath. A tackler tries to stop him. He is not declared stopped until he takes a breath. So that the referee can determine when the breath was taken, the runner must continue to repeat the words "kubbity-kubbity" very fast.

During the entertainment, Hari Singh said, "The champion plowman thinks he should have *baksheesh*."

As we were handing Hari the *baksheesh*, he added, "The champion wrestler is sulking. He thinks he too should have *baksheesh*."

"But he didn't wrestle," said Paul.

"Just the same," said Hari, "he must live. He must eat to stay strong."

We decided at this point to give Hari a lump sum so that he might throw a *baksheesh* party for all who had entertained us.

We visited the cramped section of the caste of untouchables just before leaving Kari Jat. The quarters were unusually clean, but, like all such places, were dark and cheerless and filled with the acrid smoke of burning cow dung. The pariahs, with eyes of frightened deer, went slinking through the narrow passageways.

Hari told us that the untouchables did not draw water from the village well lest they pollute it. Custom demanded that they stand at a distance and beg the villagers to fill their water jugs for them. The untouchables, of course, had the lowliest job in the village: each morning at dawn they had to go through the streets picking up the night soil.

Shortly after our return to New Delhi, Hari Singh wrote us a letter to tell us what his people thought of our visit. He said that many of the women had cried because they felt sure we had come to determine the exact location of the village so that we might return to destroy it. We had noticed anguish in their eyes, but we had not guessed the reason for it. Hari also informed us that many of the women, who had never before seen a white man, had asked what we ate to make us white.

Paul and I went to another exceedingly remote village, one we reached in darkness after much hardship along the way. There we came upon three couples, all missionaries from England, who worked out their destinies in that hidden place.

The women wore evening gowns and the men were in tuxedos. I thought they had dressed because Paul and I were their guests, until one man explained that they dressed this way each evening because "it helps separate us from the day."

Variety was a characteristic of Paul's pursuit of culture in India. He made sure we visited the Taj Mahal, attended a performance of Tara Chaudhri, billed as the Pavlova of India, and sat through several interminable Indian films.

We had glimpses of Indian home life while visiting and dining with several families who admired Paul as much as we did. He would invite those families to his moonlight sings, held on the night of each full moon in the crumbling ruins of the old fort of Delhi. I recall a British army sergeant playing a violin to accompany the singing of four Indian girls, four Indian men, and six American Army officers. Most of the songs were such old favorites as "There's a Long, Long Trail A-winding," "Let Me Call You Sweetheart," and "My Old Kentucky Home."

As another way to keep those of us in the Historical Section from feeling too depressed, Paul Geren arranged for us to study the history of India while sampling the cultures of Colonials and Indians in and around Delhi. We appreciated this, but none of us, at the time, realized how much we would feel indebted to him through the years to come.

Paul asked his friend G. T. J. Thaddaeus, general secretary of India's million Boy Scouts, to teach us history. The general secretary, an Indian, had a biblical name because he had been born a Christian.

We delighted in his contradictions. For instance, when he returned from a trip he told us that while walking along the platform of a south India railroad station he had come across a native policeman beating a boy. The boy was not a licensed coolie at that station, and so had no right to be around the train.

Mr. Thaddaeus rushed forward to comfort the whimpering youngster, and gave the lad a rupee.

He turned to the policeman and cried, "You could have killed that boy! And if you had, I would have been glad to see you hang!" The policeman began to cry. So Mr. Thaddaeus felt the need to comfort him, and before it was over he had given the fellow *four* rupees.

Three nights a week at Central Vista, the American officers' housing, or in his home, Mr. Thaddaeus told us about the Mogul kings who had ruled India from 1526 to 1857. The next morning at daybreak, as I rode through the deserted fort of ancient Delhi on a chestnut polo pony named Magpie, I would feel I was disturbing their ghosts. The only signs of life that I might see in the ruins would be a peacock atop a tomb or a lizard slithering into a crack of a crumbling wall. At sunrise there was a feeling of timelessness amid the ruins, one I have never known anyplace else, before or since.

While Mr. Thaddaeus told us of the distant past, another of Paul Geren's friends, the Reverend E. D. Lucas, helped us understand the India of 1945. The American missionary had served on the faculty of Forman Christian College, in Lahore, for thirty-seven years, and during that time he had come to know all of the leading figures in the Indian National Movement.

Although he favored independence, Reverend Lucas began a talk to the American military, at their rest camp in Khanspur, in the Murree Hills, with this opinion: "Whatever criticism of the British government one shall make, at the same time one should fully recognize that they have done better in India than any other foreign government would have done. Probably much better. Amongst British officials in India there has always been a very liberal and creative group. I say that as a liberal socialist."

This reminded me of something Colonel Christian had said in Ceylon. He had predicted that after the British departure the new India would be a place of conflict and confusion and would be a less pleasant place to live for many years to come.

Reverend Lucas continued, in his talk to the Americans, "The national state is the dominant form of human organization in today's world. This has been true since the end of the Religious Wars, about 1690. Wars between nations are now rooted in trade and expansion. The terms *national* and *nationality*, however, are wholly un-Indian concepts. The Indian idea of political power in the past has been based not upon the concept of common citizenship governed by common laws and subject to common duties, enjoying common rights, but . . . upon Hindu and Moslem religious considerations."

The professor from Forman Christian College made us realize we had better begin studying Hinduism and Islam if we wanted some understanding of what was happening.

European materialism and a political way of looking at life reached India when British rule commenced after the Battle of Plassey in 1757. When Clive's forces defeated the Mogul army, the province of Bengal, the richest in India, fell into British hands. Clive, a mercenary hired by the East India Company, fought for neither king nor country, but for the money that was in it.

As the Mogul Empire declined, the trading companies— British, French, Portuguese, and Dutch—all called East India Companies, grabbed territory for more than a hundred years. In 1902, Cecil Rhodes wrote, in *Last Will and Testament:* "The world is nearly all parceled out, and what there is left of it is being divided up, conquered and colonized."

The Indian Mutiny failed, but a mutiny of mind and heart was in the making. An educational system introduced by missionaries planted the seed for Indian nationalism. Alexander Duff, a pioneering educator, established a new type of school in Calcutta, in 1830, an exact duplicate of high schools found in Edinburgh, Glasgow, and Manchester. Thousands of Indian students then became familiar with the speeches of Burke, the essays of John Stuart Mill, the American War of Independence, the facts of the French Revolution and the Napoleonic Wars, and the vibrant speeches of the elder Pitt and the younger Chatham.

Education helped Indians communicate with each other, and kept them in touch with things happening in the world.

For instance, they were much impressed when a white Italian army suffered a defeat in Abyssinia and when a small Asiatic nation defeated a colossus in the Russo-Japanese War.

As European-style education spread, India's creative life began to thrive. At the turn of the twentieth century, literature, painting, music, architecture, drama, and dancing awakened to new life. This, of course, encouraged the rising spirit of Indian nationalism. Reverend Lucas said that the British should have taken pride in the growing maturity and should have encouraged Indians to grow toward independence; instead the British clamped down.

The First World War gave impetus to the Indian National Movement. Indian troops fought in France and in Flanders and later defeated the Turkish army. According to the slogans, the war was fought for "democracy and freedom." Such propaganda made an impression throughout India.

The time was right for Gandhi to make his entrance. The great British Empire would, in time, lose its greatest colony because a little man in a loincloth came onstage. Gandhi was born on April 2, 1869; ten years before, Queen Victoria had bragged that by reigning over India she ruled one-fifth of humanity.

The Mahatma (whose name meant "great-souled") was an extraordinary "ordinary man." Einstein said of him, "Generations to come will find it hard to believe that a man like that ever existed on this earth."

He was five feet tall and weighed 114 pounds, a curious, bent little man, a visual caricature, called everything from rogue to saint. He set out to teach 300 million people civil disobedience through passive resistance.

Although the Mahatma promoted nonviolence and noncooperation, there was plenty of violence through the years. For instance, in May of 1930 some sixty thousand of his followers landed in jail, as police increased repression and brutality. The cycles of riots and terrorist attacks increased. Gandhi became so accustomed to confinement that he said, "I am always prepared to return to jail." He spent a total of six years in prison.

Near the end of World War II, Indians gathered with Viceroy Wavell, in Simla, in June 1945; those of us working in Delhi followed the proceedings with interest. Churchill had said that he had not become Prime Minister to destroy the Empire, and the British government suggested that India accept dominion status. Gandhi responded, "That would be like accepting a blank check from an insolvent bank." The war was scarcely over when Clement Attlee defeated Winston Churchill, a step forward for the India National Movement, but none of us realized at the time what a long step it was.

Through Mr. Thaddaeus, Paul and I were invited to a concert in the Viceroy's Palace. The invitation read: "Their Excellencies the Viceroy and Viscountess Wavell have arranged that a concert be held in the Ball Room of this House on Thursday, 25th October 1945, at 9:30 p.m. The concert will be given by Miss Phyllis Sellick and Mr. Cyril Smith, the well-known Concert Pianists who specialize in piano recitals on two pianos." The invitation came through the Earl of Euston.

The earl, a blond, handsome young fellow, was sent to India as social secretary to Wavell to get him far away from England because Princess Elizabeth had fallen in love with him. That this would not be a propitious match was the decision of whatever powers decided such things in England. So the earl later married a commoner, and Elizabeth married Philip Mountbatten.

At the concert, the vicerine, motherly Lady Wavell, entered on the arm of His Excellency, Field Marshal the Right Honorable Viscount Wavell of Cyrenaica and Winchester. They mixed freely with the guests. This was something new that the Wavells brought to the Viceregal Palace; hitherto each Viceroy had surrounded himself with a buffer of pomp and aloofness.

The viceregal couple seemed to enjoy the concert. However, short, thickset Wavell with his broad, plain, furrowed face and squinting left eye, looked more like the tough desert fighter and pigsticker that he was than a lover of classical music. But behind that rough façade was a sensitive soul; it showed through in his poetry anthology, *Other Men's Flowers*, and in the biography he wrote of his hero, *Allenby: A Study in Greatness*.

Wavell was in Palestine in 1917 as a member of the staff of General Allenby, master of desert warfare and conqueror of the Turks. The enemy nicknamed Wavell "the desert fox" and "the greatest bloodhound."

Twenty years later, Wavell returned to the Near East as commander-in-chief in Palestine and the Transjordan. In 1939 he assumed command of the British forces in Egypt. World War

II swelled his Egyptian garrison into the Imperial Army of the Nile. With that army he drove the Italians out of Cyrenaica. He gave up soldiering in 1943 to become Viceroy of India.

At the end of the war he did more than any other person to force Britain into keeping her promise to India. When he broached the subject to Prime Minister Churchill, he received the testy reply, "Why trouble me about this business now? Can't you wait?"

Wavell said no, he couldn't wait, because Britain had pledged her word that India should have self-government when the war ended. Britain must keep her word.

In fact, Wavell said he would not return to India until he had something definite to tell the Indian people. He sat tight for two months in London, waiting for something definite. At the time of the concert he had just returned from London with a plan that was a seed from which the freedom of India eventually grew.

During a half-hour intermission, refreshments were served buffet-style. Paul, Leela Thaddaeus, and I spent most of that time gawking around the palace. It was grandeur congealed in marble: the highly polished marble throne room, the panels of mirrors and the crystal chandeliers of the ballroom, the long, long impressive hallways flanked by strong arches, and the massive portraits of royalty.

Leela Thaddaeus was such a bashful thing that she never said a word until it was pried from her. To draw her out of herself and to make her feel a part of our trio, Paul said, "Well, Leela, what do you think about it?"

With great hesitancy she said, a little above a whisper, "I think everyone should have a home like this."

Each day, as the temper of India grew worse, even Paul Geren began to feel ill at ease. We both felt some relief the day we flew from New Delhi to Dum Dum, an airport near Calcutta, and continued by truck the twenty-five miles to Kanchrapara, a staging area. There we settled down to wait for a place on a transport. For ten days we lived in a cluster of tents known as Jackal Heights, because every evening at sundown the jackals came howling in and circled us the rest of the night.

The Red Cross conducted tours in neighboring Calcutta. Paul and I noticed that the Red Cross girls who served as guides had learned to lord it over the natives as much as any British *mem-sahib*.

I recalled the opening pages of the novel *A Passage to India*, in which three Muslims discuss whether or not an Indian can really be a friend of the British, whether he can deal with a Britisher on equal footing. They conclude that he cannot, because no matter how good the intentions of an Englishman when he comes out, all Englishmen are alike in their treatment of the natives after two years—and all Englishwomen are alike after only six months.

This attitude of the Red Cross girls did not surprise us; we had often seen Americans slip into it with all the ease of their British brothers, whom they criticized. An Occidental seemed to develop a superiority complex in the presence of Orientals.

I felt uncomfortable once when Mr. Thaddaeus complimented several of us on our relationships with our bearers. He said he noticed that Americans treated Indian servants like members of the family and did not, like the British, shout, "Bearah!" with the challenge of the Empire ringing in their voices. I felt uncomfortable because I believe Americans did not deserve to be compared too favorably with the British in this respect; I had often heard the demanding shout of "Bearer!" ring across the verandas at Central Vista.

The Red Cross girls in Calcutta did a wonderful job of conducting tours. They were filled with facts and figures and had a ready answer for all questions.

One of the most interesting tours was of the Kali Temple. According to legend, Kali, the Hindu goddess of love and wife of Siva, killed herself when she heard her father berating her husband. Siva threw the limp body across his shoulder and went mourning through the universe. To relieve Siva of this burden, Vishnu cut Kali's body into bits and tossed them toward the earth. The pieces fell into fifty-two spots in different parts of India. A temple was built at each spot to mark the place as holy for Hindu worshipers. Hindu mythology says that a toe of Kali's right foot fell in Calcutta, where the temple was built three centuries ago.

Those of us on the tour agreed that the Kali Temple was one of the most filthy and sordid places we had seen in India. Part of the ceremony in the temple was the beheading of young goats—this must be done with a single stroke—and the smearing of the blood all over the place. The guide said that women often got down on hands and knees and licked the blood as it trickled through the dust.

Women who wished to bear sons bathed in the nearby Hoogly River, considered sacred because it is a tributary of the Ganges. While bathing, they picked a pebble from the bottom of the river and twisted a piece of their hair around it. They returned to the temple grounds and tied the pebble to a branch of a certain sacred tree. The tree was so filled with pebbles we wondered how it was possible to tie another one on it. If a pebble didn't fall, it was considered a sign that a woman would have a son. Judging from the age of the old crones we saw bathing, those poor pebbles were put on the spot.

A burning ghat, a large courtyard where Hindus cremate the dead, was located near the temple. Although the place had been used for centuries, it gave the appearance of a temporary expedient. It consisted of nothing but a few trenches about eighteen inches deep and six feet long, spotted here and there in a large yard.

The body of an old man was brought in while we were there. He had been dead but two hours. One of the relatives said that he had died of black fever. We didn't know what black fever was, but the sound of it made us step back a few feet.

In cremations, a part of the body was saved. This was rolled into a ball of mud and tossed into the river a few yards away. Relatives of the deceased bathed at the spot where the ball sank.

Outside the burning ghat were several naked Saddhus, holy people in Hinduism, clothed "only by the four directions" because they never wanted to have any more earthly possessions than they had at the moment of birth.

Wherever we went, we saw students waving green-and-gold Indian Congress banners. They screamed at us, "*Inquulab zindabad!*" "Freedom forever!"

After ten days of waiting we got the good word, but were warned that our truck might be attacked on the way to the port. We made the trip without incident, but the day our transport, the *General Ballou*, churned the eighty miles of the Hoogly River from Calcutta to the Bay of Bengal, a riot broke out in Calcutta. Nineteen GIs suffered minor injuries when angry natives stoned the convoy that followed ours to the port of embarkation.

A lieutenant gazed at the receding shoreline of India and said, "I don't think I left anything back there. If I did, I'll never go back after it."

His feeling was typical. All the magazine articles that explained how overseas experience would make the boys One World–conscious didn't quite ring true in the CBI. Most Americans, upon leaving the Orient, agreed with Kipling that East is East and West is West and never the twain shall meet. They thanked God that there was a whole world between the East and the West, and hoped it would stay that way. Maybe other theaters made Americans One World–conscious, but the CBI—no. Only a few exceptional people, like Paul Geren, felt the way the magazines said all Americans would feel. But the exceptions felt that way even before the war.

We passed the Gulf of Martaban, south of Burma, and slipped through the Strait of Malacca, which separated Sumatra from the Malay States. After the lights of Singapore winked at us off the port beam, we plowed northward through a hilly South China Sea to the Philippines. We passed Bataan and Corregidor and went into Manila Bay, where skeletons of hundreds of ships stuck up from the water. After refueling at Manila we rounded the north end of the islands and cut east across the North Pacific for San Francisco.

I was in charge of a compartment of 250 GIs, most of whom were seasick for the full twenty-eight days. The compartment was located well forward, so that when the ship lurched like a bronco, we got the full benefit of the rise and fall. The sensation, like that of an elevator's starting and stopping too fast, was too much for most of the men.

A seasick case is a sad sight to behold. The ashen complexion, the eyes that don't focus, the mouth that is not under control, the limp hair, and the sagging body lines make you wonder if the victim can possibly live. And to hear one vomit! Especially after he is all vomited out, but still keeps trying. It is a sound that

231

makes the soul shudder. You think he is tearing himself up by the roots from the inside. I thanked God often that I turned out to be a good sailor.

The passengers, of course, were happy to be on the way home. However, there was no New Year's Eve effervescence in their spirits, as might be expected. They were restless to the point of being jittery; the calm resignation so evident on the way over was gone.

On the transport going over, almost everyone lived in the past and in the future. But on the way home, living was confined pretty much to the present. There was some talk of the immediate past, with such names as Kirmatola, Myitkyina, and Kweilin slipping into the conversation. But there was not much of the talk of prewar days that had been so much a part of the conversation on the way out.

And talk of how wonderful life would be when we were all civilians once more, a prospect that used to brace our morale, was now little heard. We were too near the future. We feared disappointment, and wondered if perhaps the magazine writers were correct when they said we had changed. Would there be an unpleasant period of readjustment? We were so sure a few months ago that that was all bunk, and wrote home saying so. But now we were wondering.

On the last night out, I stood on the superstructure talking with an officer who was more articulate than most, and more willing to express his doubts and fears. The wind was blowing hard into our faces, so that I had to listen close to get his questions. But it did not make any difference whether or not I heard them; he wasn't expecting answers. He knew that neither I nor anyone else aboard knew the answers.

"I wonder how it will seem to get back to civilian routine?" he mused. "I wonder if I can be happy behind a desk again." He had spent the past year and a half piloting a C-47 around the Orient.

"I wonder if Springfield will seem dull after Calcutta, Rangoon, Singapore, and Chungking? I didn't enjoy those places when I was there. I hated the noise, the smells, and the dirt. But maybe I'll miss them anyway. Right now I don't think I'll ever go back. But I wonder if I'll change my mind? Wonder if I'll find out that I don't fit into the old pattern anymore? Wonder if . . ."

He paused, touched my arm, and pointed toward the horizon. The lights of the Golden Gate Bridge were winking up ahead.

POSTSCRIPT

When the Emperor of Japan announced over Tokyo radio, at noon on August 15, 1945, that the Japanese were surrendering, Maj. Donald Born, of the Harvard history faculty, and I began expressing our opinions about life after the war, many of which turned out wrong. In discussing the GI Bill, for instance, we decided that of the twelve million Americans who had served in the war, those who would take advantage of the offer for a free education would have a hard time settling down in the classroom. We asked each other how those fellows who had built the Ledo Road, flown the Hump, and fought in the jungle could sit listening to some chalk-streaked professor.

We were wrong!

Never has a generation of students done better. Maybe this happened all over the world; George Macaulay Trevelyan wrote of the period, "Never had Cambridge been so full of strong and splendid life."

When I began teaching at Notre Dame, such "strong and splendid life" filled the classroom. Chronologically, students were three or four years older than those before or after them, and psychologically they were about ten years older. Discipline had been thrust upon them. They had known troubles not of their own making, a maturing experience; it is trouble of one's own making that is destructive.

The experience of teaching those veterans made me realize that war, with its horrors, waste, and sadness, does also have some good points. I once remarked to Frank O'Malley, a distinguished professor at Notre Dame, that I was a better human being during the war than ever before or since, and he said, "Ignatius of Loyola said that four hundred years ago."

Anyone who served in the war was changed by the experience. For one thing, he could never say that he had lived his entire life "in quiet desperation." He might not have enjoyed the jolting experience, but he would forever recall it as a high point.

A veteran spoke some truth in a zany way. "I was whistlin' 'Chattanooga Choo-Choo' when I got a letter that started, 'Greetings!' Soon I was makin' twenty-one dollars a month. Pearl Harbor! I missed out on blue stamps for canned goods and red stamps for meat that civilians got back home. I had greatness thrust upon me!"

During the war we became aware of our mortality, a maturing experience. Such awareness deepened through the years as we came upon obituaries of men who had seemed larger than life and beyond destruction.

For instance, I was back in the States the day General Stilwell died, October 12, 1946. I had followed his career since his recall two years earlier, and had found that period of his life anticlimactic, but I still was not prepared for his death notice.

He had wanted to command in combat, and was sent to Okinawa to get the Tenth Army ready for an invasion of Japan. The war soon ended and he returned home.

While Paul Geren and I were writing reports for Mountbatten and Chiang Kai-shek, Stilwell wrote his own seven-hundred-page report. When it was completed, in the summer of 1945, he would like to have seen it published, but to get it into print officially, he would have to delete his sharp criticism of the Chinese and the British. He refused.

Stilwell wanted to return to China for a visit after the war, but Chiang Kai-shek said he would not be welcome. The Generalissimo had offered him the Order of the Blue Sky and White Sun, the highest Chinese decoration awarded a foreigner, but Stilwell had refused it. Chiang remembered the insult.

While in command at the Presidio in San Francisco, General Stilwell took ill. On October 3, 1946, at Letterman General Hospital, he underwent surgery that revealed cancer of the stomach and liver. Nine days later he died.

Those of us from the CBI were shocked when the peaceful Gandhi died a violent death on January 30, 1948. A deranged Hindu approached, bowed low, said, "I honor the light within you," and shot the Mahatma because he had not stopped the partition of India.

India was then a land of despair. The monsoon of September 1947 had been especially severe; it drowned thousands of refugees when eleven million were on the move, trying to reach their proper countries: India, where Jawaharlal Nehru was prime minister, or Pakistan, where Mohammed Ali Jinnah was governor-general.

When Calcutta, the most fanatical city in India, was in a stage of siege, Mountbatten, whose assignment it was to give India back to the Indians, had sent for his "poor little sparrow" asking for help. Gandhi lowered the pressure in Calcutta, but then severe fighting broke out in Bombay. In the first four months of freedom—August to December 1947—Muslims and Hindus murdered each other until the count of the dead reached 500,000.

On February 28, 1948, a month after Gandhi's assassination, the last British soldier boarded a ship at Bombay. Soldiers on the ship and Indians on shore sang "Auld Lang Syne" together. With that, the British presence came to an end.

Another shock came one day many years later, when I was packing for a trip to Ireland. A bulletin came across the radio announcing that Lord Mountbatten had died at eleven o'clock that morning, August 27, 1979. As his twenty-nine-foot fishing boat, *Shadow V*, cleared the harbor at Mullaghmore, Mountbatten raced the engine and a bomb exploded. The IRA had detonated it by remote control.

How ironic that these fanatics should kill a man who was all in favor of having the English clear out of Ireland. After all, he was the one who had helped India reach what is considered freedom. He had turned over the Jewel in the Imperial Crown to Nehru and Jinnah at midnight on August 15, 1947.

When given the assignment, much to his surprise, in February of 1947, he may have recalled an old Burma saying: There are five major disasters—floods, famine, fire, disease, and government. To these he probably would have added religion. He found it easier to free India than to unite Moslems and Hindus. His main problem was Jinnah, the Moslem leader. Mountbatten called him "a man with a difficulty for every solution." India was also a mosaic of nations; each minority feared all others, and no one was willing to compromise. As soon as independence was at hand, thousands began to kill and get killed. Gandhi once more began a fast; he had fasted often to get his way with the British, and now he would try it on his own people.

Now Mountbatten, a man who could trace his family all the way back to Charlemagne, was dead. All the Irish I met on that trip, in 1979, were shocked and angry. The IRA had done a terrible thing, they said.

I was in Ireland working in the archives of the Columban Missionary Fathers in Killiney, on the Irish sea, when I came across a photograph that sent my memory back thirty years to the officers' mess hall in Bhamo, Burma. In early May of 1945, I saw a tall, thin man pause in the doorway and glance about; he had "the look of eagles." I saw him for only a few seconds, but the memory stuck. Thirty years later, in the archives in Ireland, in a manila folder full of photographs, I came across the remarkable face. It was that of Patrick Usher.

When Col. William R. Peers, commander of Detachment 101, OSS, wrote *Behind the Burma Road*, he included a letter from Usher:

9 May 1945

Dear Colonel Peers:
    It is my pleasant duty to write on behalf of twenty-two missionary priests acknowledging a great debt we owe to you and your organization. During the Japanese occupation we were interned at the St. John's Leper Hospital, Mandalay. Your

237

planes kept away most carefully from that area, so
that not a single bomb fell within the enclosure.

I have been informed by Father Stuart that
this was due to the special orders issued to the Air
Corps. We have the best reasons for appreciating
very much your kindly action.

Monsignor Patrick Usher
Catholic Bishop of Bhamo

In the manila folder with the picture of Patrick Usher was a
photo of a young priest riding a mule across a stream in Burma.
The animal had the fine, compact conformation of an Army
mule from Missouri, and there was something familiar about
him. When a drunken major had told me, on Christmas Eve
1944, that I was not needed, my mules were still on a ship miles
out at sea; through the years I had wondered what had been their
final fate.

To find out, I went to see Father James Devine, an old Burma
hand, now retired in Ireland. He said, "Ah, yes, I would say that
was one of your mules. I heard that a sergeant was trying to find
a good home for them, and so I sent a catechist on a three-day
journey through the jungle. The sergeant said he could have all
forty of the redundant ones, but the catechist said that ten would
do."

The ten mules soon became missionaries when Father Devine
distributed them to his colleagues in the Kachin hills. The priests
marveled at how well-mannered those animals were. Native
ponies, said Father Devine, let their eyes roll white and their
nostrils flare red at any sudden sound, but the mules were
nonchalant. I explained how such manners were instilled in the
mules after they had arrived at the Cavalry School, green and
mean. So that they would not take off at the sound of an
exploding shell, we gave them a noisy schooling. Inside a stone
corral, some of us sat atop the mules while others threw metal
helmets and firecrackers at them. Paroxysms of wild-eyed fear
gave way, little by little, to resigned passivity.

Father Devine told me that Father James Stuart was dead.

"The hardships of war and the jungle took their toll," said the
old priest. "Even when he made a trip to the United States in

1947, and then went on to visit his home in Ireland, it did not help much. Upon his return to Burma, his old vitality was gone. He came back to Ireland in 1955 on sick leave, knowing he would never go back to Burma. He died suddenly, on August 11, 1955. He is buried in the cemetery at the Columban Fathers' seminary in County Meath."

At war's end, Father Stuart was appointed an officer of the Most Excellent Order of the British Empire for his help to refugees. Later the United States awarded him the Legion of Merit. During his visit to the States he was much interviewed by newspapermen who had wanted to write about him during the war, but had been stopped by military censors.

A reporter asked, "Who in this country would you most like to meet?"

"Ginger Rogers," the priest replied.

The story went out over the press service wires, and after having read it, Miss Rogers sent the missionary a note saying that when he came to California she would be honored to meet him.

On the plane to Los Angeles, a stewardess asked Father Stuart, who had a way of looking lost, what was his final destination. He showed her an address and asked which bus he might take to get there.

"Don't take the bus," said the stewardess. "Take a taxi."

"And where might I find a taxicab?" he asked meekly.

"When you get outside the terminal, turn right."

When the plane rolled to a stop, a high school band struck up "When Irish Eyes Are Smiling." There stood Pat O'Brien, the actor, who had entertained troops in Burma, and John Ford, the film director, a great admirer of the OSS. And Ginger Rogers.

In the midst of the commotion the stewardess worked her way into the crowd until she was close enough to hiss in Father Stuart's ear, "You and your taxicabs!"

I went out to County Meath and stood at the grave. According to the dates on the stone, he was forty-six when he died. The miracle was that he lived that long. I recalled stories of the day he threw himself onto the floor of a bamboo hut just as bullets tore through the back of the cane chair on which he had been sitting.

239

And the time he flattened himself against a tree as machine-gun slugs chewed away the bark on each side.

Were the situation reversed, and he stood at my grave, I know what he would have said. Whenever he spoke of someone's death, he always said, "Ah, yes, he has gone to where the comfort is."

Paul Geren and I kept in touch for a few years after the war. He brought his wife, Elizabeth, and their infant daughter, Natasha, to visit us in South Bend in September of 1947. In the eighteen months since leaving India he had married a Louisiana girl, had been defeated in a run for the United States Congress in his district in Arkansas, had taught courses in economics at Berea College in Berea, Kentucky, and had written two books about Burma.

Shortly after that visit, Paul joined the United States Department of Foreign Service and was, in time, stationed in Bombay, Damascus, and Amman. Late in 1955 he settled in Washington to serve on the Middle East Desk of the State Department.

After a few years Paul resigned to become executive vice-president of Baylor University. Two years later he was elected executive director of the Dallas Council on World Affairs.

When the Peace Corps was founded, Paul was its deputy director. He left that position in September 1967 to become president of Stetson University at De Land, Florida.

On a Sunday night in July of 1969 he was driving through a storm near Lexington, Kentucky, when his car collided with another. He died at age fifty-five and was survived by his widow and three daughters.

When I read in the paper that Theodore White had died, I recalled what a problem he had been on the first convoy across the Ledo Road from India into Burma and on up into China. He was always complaining, and darkening the day with a look of annoyance on his face.

By the time I came upon his obituary, however, I had some idea why he had acted that way. He wrote in his book *In Search of History*, in 1978, that by late 1944—when we met in Myit-kyina—the Chinese Communists, the Kuomintang, and the American government no longer trusted him: "But I was confident, even arrogant, knowing that I wrote for *Time*, for *Life*, and was Harry Luce's man in Chungking. And then Luce, too, repudiated me."

White said that when he sent anti-Chiang stories to *Time*, they would appear in print as pro-Chiang stories that misled American opinion, "something which it was Luce's duty, and mine, to guard against."

I have often wondered what happened to some who played leading roles in the CBI and then dropped out of the news. Gen. Sun Li-jen, for instance, a man much admired by soldiers of several nationalities. I did not hear until after the war that he had proposed that Chinese officers send a petition to Roosevelt asking that Stilwell be returned. What was his fate?

Fragments of information about him reached me through the years. A Chinese artist who came to Notre Dame said that General Sun had started a military school for boys soon after the war. He went to Taiwan when Chiang fled there. The Generalissimo, for some reason, always thought that Sun was plotting against him.

Gen. Frank Dorn wrote in 1970: "When an American general visited him in 1958 the once forceful and intelligent Sun Li-jen had been reduced to such a condition that he was without memory of World War II events and unable to make much sense in either English or Chinese." The American general believed that Sun had suffered much physical and mental abuse.

Gen. Sun Li-jen died on November 19, 1990, at age ninety-one.

So many of those I wrote about, all filled with vitality in time of war, have since appeared in obituaries:

> Lt. Gen. Daniel I. Sultan (1885–1947)
> Maj. Gen. Frank Merrill (1903–1955)
> Maj. Gen. Lewis Pick (1890–1956)
> Maj. Gen. Claire Chennault (1890–1958)
> Maj. Gen. William Donovan (1883–1959)
> Dr. Gordon Seagrave (1897–1965)
> Col. Joseph W. Stilwell, Jr. (1912–1967)
> Field Marshal Sir William Slim (1891–1970)
> Generalissimo Chiang Kai-shek (1886–1975)
> Col. Philip C. Cochran (1910–1979)

Brig. Gen. Frank Dorn (1901–1981)
Col. William R. Peers (1914–1984)

Through the years I have followed the careers of Bert Parks, Finis Farr, and Fred Friendly.

Parks and I were having breakfast at Central Vista, in New Delhi, when Noor Mohammed handed me an envelope, "Letter for *sahib*. Not from *memsahib*."

It was from the University of Notre Dame, asking if I would join the faculty. Without comment I showed it to Parks, who was about to leave India for home.

Ten years later, when Bert Parks had a network game show, one of the contestants was Jim Kelleher. When Kelleher identified himself as a student at Notre Dame, Parks asked, "Did Ed Fischer ever join the faculty?"

"I'm taking a course from him this semester," said Kelleher.

A year later I dropped by the studio and talked with Parks before one of his shows. That has been the only personal contact between us.

Finis Farr has been easy to follow through his writing. He did biographies of Frank Lloyd Wright, Jack Johnson, Margaret Mitchell, Franklin D. Roosevelt, John O'Hara, and Westbrook Pegler. He also wrote a spy novel, a history of Chicago, and scripts for radio and television.

Fred Friendly has also been easy to track, through his documentaries produced with Edward R. Murrow and later through his teaching at Columbia.

Memories of the war return in many ways, some of them amusing. For instance, a dean at Notre Dame gave a talk saying that education ought to make better use of the various hidden abilities among its teachers. Soon afterward, the Army football team's mascot, a mule, was unloaded at the Notre Dame stadium, just across the road from my office. I heard later it was quite a battle between the mule and the cheerleaders who tried to get him off the truck. There I sat, perhaps the only university professor in the history of American education with a diploma, bearing gold seal and yellow ribbons, from the Cavalry School, saying I was a master muleskinner. But nobody sought my advice. The dean is right, education should make better use of various hidden abilities.

Whenever a story about Army mules appears, friends send me the clipping; for instance, a long article in the *Wall Street Journal*, April 28, 1988, carried the headline, "Did American Mules Persuade the Soviets to Quit Afghanistan?" It told of how useful six hundred mules had been during the past six months. At first the rebels had struggled along with their own sorry mules, and the Turks had sold them equally inept animals. The Egyptians were quickly drained of their supply. The Chinese charged outlandish rates, $2,500 a mule. Those from Tennessee sold for between $600 and $1,300.

The writer admitted that certain geopolitical conditions played a role in the Soviet withdrawal, but he stressed that the U.S. mules had carried tons of equipment, food, and medical supplies across the mountains from Pakistan to Afghanistan, and continued, "They have also carried munitions into battle and continued the mule's long tradition of serving as a vital military operative. Since the mule shipments began, the guerrillas have gotten more supplies, and the Soviet Union has decided to remove its army."

Military jargon also reminds me of the war years when I was writing training books for the Infantry School at Fort Benning, Georgia. A strange coincidence occurred in 1952, when an agency in Chicago asked me to write training manuals that would clarify the old ones. It had a contract with the Navy to make military prose more readable. The agency did not know that I had tried in vain to do that during the war; all the editor knew was that I preached simplicity and clarity in the classroom. He offered me a salary far higher than that which I made as a lieutenant while writing jargon during the war. I did not, however, accept the opportunity to bring clarity to military prose.

The memory of Gen. Sun Li-jen's aide returns from time to time. My class in film production, for instance, made a film called *Shake Down the Thunder*, in 1953, about how "The Notre Dame Victory March" was composed by a couple of students on an old piano in the basement of Sorin Hall, and, from that humble beginning, went on around the world. The film shows how the song surfaced in strange places during the war—in a marketplace in Tientsin, China, where old craftsmen played it on violins they had carved, and in a prisoner-of-war camp in Poland, where British inmates played it on a phonograph, using it as a theme song for their daily concerts.

We also dramatized the incident of General Sun's aide sitting on a log singing "Cheer, cheer for old Notre Dame," not missing a note or a word. On an island in the Notre Dame lake, covered with dense, junglelike growth, a young Chinese engineering professor and I, dressed in combat fatigues, reenacted the incident, which had happened near the Burma Road.

Thirty years after its production, that sequence appeared on national television. When NFL Productions made a documentary about the history of football at Notre Dame, the director spliced in a few frames of the Burma incident.

Forty years after I had written about the Japanese enemy in Burma, I was on a ten-hour flight from San Francisco to Tokyo, sitting next to a Japanese man about my age. He was poised and elegant in a gray suit and a dark blue shirt, his black shoes highly polished. To use an old-fashioned expression, he seemed a "gentleman of breeding."

In the war he had probably served the Emperor of Japan. Maybe, like me, he was in Burma. What if we had met in the Kachin Hills?

Fortunately for him, a language barrier separated us, or I might have bothered him with questions during the long flight across the Pacific. One thing we would have agreed on was that I was visiting his country on a mission that would have seemed improbable four decades earlier, and that I would arrive at conclusions that no one along the Ledo Road would have found acceptable.

A few days later, in Fujisawa, I told a priest from Ireland about the Japanese man on the plane, and said I was surprised that I hadn't felt any resentment toward him. I felt the way Gen. Chuck Yeager did when he spoke of going on hunting trips with pilots who, as German aces, had flown planes against him. When someone asked how he could bring himself to accept them, the American ace said, "They were doing their job the same as we were doing our job."

I said to the Irish priest, "I wonder if the experience of war links men. Even former enemies. They have shared an experience that was special. Horrible but special."

The Irish priest said, "That old man on the plane did not hold any resentment against you, either. But the older folks do. The parents of the soldiers hate the Americans. Their hate is such that they sometimes make it a matter of confession."

On that trip I wrote a book, *Japan Journey*. Vibrating through it is a theme I would not have used forty years earlier: The Japanese are an admirable people.

The personal discipline of the Japanese is the thing that struck me most favorably. Courtesy, a mark of personal discipline, shows in the quality of service, which is not offered in expectation of a better tip, for tipping is not done in Japan. Discipline is also implied in the literacy of the people; about ninety-eight percent of the population is literate. The belief that knowledge is more important than money begins in the home. From parents and children, the attitude goes out to teachers and to society as a whole. Personal discipline is also reflected in a low crime rate. There are 1.4 murders per 100,000 people as against 10.2 per 100,000 in the United States; the incidence of robbery is 1.9 compared with 234.5 in the United States.

The Japanese are not slobs.

During the war I was a journalist turned historian. That is not such an extreme change as it sounds; the difference between the two is a matter of verb tense. Carl Becker defined history as "knowledge of things said and done." Journalism is knowledge of things *being* said and done.

I am now aware that the past continues to live in us; we are not inclined to let bygones be bygones. The war, now nearly half a century in the past, is still a part of those who lived through it. Many of the details have faded, of course; had I not written hundreds of letters and made notes galore, I could never have recalled all the anecdotes in these pages, and my story would have been less accurate. In rereading the contents of that attic trunk, I find that my attitude has softened somewhat.

Until recently, I never let World War II enter my classroom; there was no reason to speak of it while teaching writing, film, or design. In the past three years, however, I have been asked to give guest lectures in a course in Chinese history; when Professor Dian Murray teaches the war, she has me speak to her class out of personal experience. On the day of the lecture I am aware of how fleeting memories can be. When I was growing up on a farm in Kentucky, for instance, I knew men who had fought in the Civil War, but now there is not a person in the world who was alive during Civil War days. So, when I stand before that class in Chinese history, I know that when those freshmen reach the age I am now, no one will be left in the world with memories of World War II. Our war generation is fading fast; time is running out for anyone who wants to write a memoir such as this.

A student asked me how I felt about having served in the war, looking back across nearly a half-century. I said that I felt about it the way I feel about life: I am thankful for having had the experience, but would not want to go through it again.

INDEX

247

Index

Index

Singh, Kaseri, 218–219
Slim, William J., 100–101, 104, 133,
    143–144, 146–147, 211, 212
Smith, Cyril, 227
Soong Mei-ling, 91
    See also Chiang Kai-shek, Madame
Squeeze, 62
Stalin, Joseph, 194
Stilwell, Joseph Jr., 45, 88
Stilwell, Joseph W., 1, 28, 31, 35, 38,
    48, 50, 62, 78, 85, 86, 93–96,
    99–123, 104, 133, 140, 142–144,
    146–149, 154, 161, 178, 214,
    235–236
Stilwell Road, 74
Stilwell, Winifred, 95
Stimson, Henry, 96
Stuart, James, 33–37, 89, 129,
    167–170, 238–240
Sultan, Daniel I., 48, 57, 124, 186, 189,
    196, 199, 206, 211
Sungshan, 64
Sun Li-jen, 50–51, 103, 241, 243
Sun Yat-sen, 91

Taipha Ga, 143
Tanaka, Lieutenant General, 140
Taunggyi, 102
Teheran Conference, 120
Temple of Confucius, 66, 67
Temple of the Tooth, 185
Thaddaeus, G. T. J., 223–224, 227
Thaddaeus, Leela, 228
Three Men on a Flying Trapeze, 78
Thugs, 220
Tiger Fort, 220
Tilly, James, 149–150
Tjung, Eddie, 76

Tokyo Rose, 58, 66
Trevelyan, George Macaulay, 234
Triangle, 42–43
Trident Conference, 118–119
Tu, General, 203
Tunner, William H., 204
Tu Yu-ming, 102, 104
T. V. Soong, 59, 79, 92

Usher, Patrick, 237–238

Valley of Death, 104
Von Richthofen, Manfred, 78

Walabum, 145–146, 149, 191
Walkout (Dorn), 203
Wallace, Henry A., 148
Wavell, Archibald Percival, 28, 99, 100,
    114, 131, 227–228
Wedemeyer, Albert C., 189
Wei Li-haung, 67
Weller, George, 90–91, 93, 97
White, Theodore, 45, 46, 57, 187,
    240–241
Wild, Hugh, 83
Wilkes, Jack, 45, 56
Willey, John P., 201–209
Willkie, Wendell, 117–118
Wingate, Orde, 77, 131–139, 142
Woomer, Lieutenant, 155

X Force, 122

Yamamoto, Isoroku, 94, 95
Yenanyaung, 104
Yoke Force, 120, 121, 148, 149, 193
Yu Fei-p'eng, 62, 102
Yunnani, 69

250